To Alana —
Thank you for [having me?]
here at your shop. The weather
may have been a bit unpleasant,
but the spirit & friendly folk
left a warm glow that will
last and last. Enjoy the read!

Iyola Collins

Island of Color

Where Juneteenth Started

By

Izola Ethel Fedford Collins
Edited by Cheryl Collins Crayton

authorHOUSE

1663 LIBERTY DRIVE, SUITE 200
BLOOMINGTON, INDIANA 47403
(800) 839-8640
www.authorhouse.com

© 2004 Izola Ethel Fedford Collins.
All Rights Reserved.

No part of this book may be reproduced, stored in a retrieval system, or transmitted by any means without the written permission of the author.

First published by AuthorHouse 06/06/05

ISBN: 1-4184-6976-9 (e)
ISBN: 1-4184-6974-2 (sc)
ISBN: 1-4184-6975-0 (dj)

Library of Congress Control Number: 2004094442

Printed in the United States of America
Bloomington, Indiana

This book is printed on acid-free paper.

DEDICATION

Respectfully, I dedicate this book to all those who have shown love and kindness, devotion and service to God's people of every color, creed, gender, age or station in life.

Particularly do I dedicate this written record to the members of my family and friends who have gone on to another plane: Papa, Mother, Daddy, Roy, Jewel, Juanita, Annie Pearl, Natalye Ruth, Mother Lois, Mother Ethel, Godmother, Aunt Corinne, Sorors Jessie MacGuire Dent and Barbara Jordan, and so many others who have touched my life in a special way before moving on to another life.

To my twin, although not kin: Dr. Florence Crim Robinson, who shares my birthday – same year, same field, same so much.

To my best friend – you know what you mean to me – Che.

To my future: my children and their children. (When I started this, I had no grandchildren. Now I have eight.)

Children – To June, my firstborn and right hand, who is following my musical path;

Roy III, computer whiz, lawyer and minister, and my only son; Cheryl, my journalist-teacher and youngest, and Anita Donatto, who is my godchild, who have done most of the work of putting this together.

Grandchildren – Jessica, Shakira, Roy IV, Mikael, Janae, Jasmine, Samuel and Daniel.

May God bless you with the greatest of virtues – love.

ACKNOWLEDGEMENTS

The very first "thank you" must go to my Creator. Motivation, desire, ability, endurance, tolerance and interaction with so many wonderful people all came directly from God.

From my grandfather, with his vision and wish for a better future, I received a historical account including his earliest memories and his knowledge of everything in Galveston that had to do with African Americans and their surroundings. Having this in his own handwriting was an added blessing.

Next must come my own father and mother. Having had two parents for all of my growing-up years is one of my richest blessings, as I now know. Having had my mother as my best friend will always be my stabilizer, and inspiration to be all that I can be.

I have laughed much with my sister over the fact that people continue to mix us up, although she and I are five and a half years apart. We each learned long ago to answer to the other's name. We retired the same year from teaching, both of our only husbands are now deceased, and we have three children each, so we have a bit in common. The only sibling I ever had, she was my main companion through my early life, and she remains my confidante today. I am very grateful that God has let us both live to this point.

Next I want to thank the friend who served as incentive for this work, Sister Jelaine "Jill" Jaeb, an Ursuline nun. After reading one of my letters, she told me that I should write a book, praising my style as colorful, with the ability to capture her attention, and keep her laughing or crying. We met in a musical setting, with common points including our master degrees in music. She and I have shared much fun, as well as much spiritual thinking.

Through all this time, another friend has been a loyal constant – advising, consoling, just listening, sharing her own life experiences, and giving me care and concern. Her name is Valencia Victoria Huff Arceneaux. She is a creative genius in her own right as well.

Also, much credit for direct literary assistance goes to the personnel at Minuteman Printing & Graphics – Gail Peterson, Michelle Johnson, and Mary Enriquez.

And to author Sandy Sheehy for constant support, and especially to Dorothy Karr, who directed me to Thomas Hargroves, who guided me to these publishers.

I should list all of the wonderful people who have advised me, encouraged me, given me interviews, asked to receive one of the first copies of my book, or lifted my spirits when I was low. I am afraid I might omit a very valuable name. Writers are very caring, special people, and I have yet to meet anyone whose work is already published who refused to give me any help. God bless them all.

Galveston, I love you. Wherever I travel, I don't find any place I would rather live. You certainly have faults. That's OK. I glory in the fact that here I get smiles and waves from all kinds of people.

PREFACE

This book will endeavor to document or note the many ways in which African Americans entered the American scene via Galveston, and played roles on the stage of life that changed history. Leaving out these players in historical accounts is akin to trying to chew food without one's back teeth – swallowing anything, and wondering why the food won't digest.

It should be known and appreciated that in Galveston, African Americans established their first schools, churches and businesses in this part of the country; played in their first organized sports clubs; attended the first medical school in the Southwest; produced leading post-Civil War politicians and the first African American world boxing champion; played orchestral instruments, and helped originate jazz music at the same time it was becoming known in New Orleans, maintaining this musical leadership in the Gulf Coast region through the blues explosion. Texas' first daily newspaper, the Galveston Daily News, used information and data from an African-American institution of higher learning, now known as Prairie View University.

I take this opportunity to state that the capitalization of racial terminology is purposely inconsistent throughout the book. I have capitalized all proper names, with occasional exception of the word *Negro* in quotations, and capitalization of the words *white* and *black* varies, according to the context as well as time periods in which they are used.

This book is a communication – through me -- between you, the reader, and a segment of our world, in its past, present and future. My best form of expression is music. That being the case, this book automatically took on musical designations. (As anyone close to me would expect.)

My first musical element, then, is the Prelude. Just as any prelude, it prepares the listener for what is to come.

The book also includes intermissions as the story unfolds, which I called Interludes. Outside of the story's flow, they are meant to refresh as they give the flavor and color of the people in the time periods described. These are not titled "Interludes" they are not fiction-they are very real, and very representative.

The Postlude is like a recessional. The story is as complete as it can be, because life is ongoing. The Postlude just ushers you out the door for the time being.

And punctuation, grammar and even vocabulary may not always follow strict rules of composition. At times, within the parameters allowed, I may improvise – or jam, if you will.

Realizing that additional editions of this book will probably be necessary, this is a passionate attempt to bridge a gaping void as much as is possible at this time. It is with great excitement that I entreat you to read on.

PRELUDE

Rev. Ralph Albert Scull's Description of 19th-Century Galveston Island "Gail Borden came to Galveston about 1850 and with him was a colored woman, Helen Rowe. She says they landed at Avenue H and 20th Street. At that time there seems to have been a channel across the Island at that point. In 1866, to my recollection there was a slew or waterway clear out 21st from Broadway to the South Beach; later sand piled up and closed the Gulf end, but the inner body of water still remained.

Up to 1873 there was a large pond of water at 21st and 22nd and M. The Gulf of Randle, another cut, ran in at about twenty seventh Street. There seemed to be several places where the water partly cut across the island.

In the Storm of 1875, the Gulf and Bay waters met first on 25th Street. This storm also opened a channel on Sixth Street which led from the Gulf to the bay. It was called the Rosenberg Channel ... closed at Gulf by the wave motion and the sand. Crabs were caught on Broadway from the ditches from Seventeenth Street back to twenty first, and from there nearly to the Gulf on the South.

At the foot of Broadway were many small deep ponds, where fish of two or three pounds were found. Late in the Seventies [1870s], Mayor C. W. Hurley engineered the filling of Broadway from the high sand hills on the beach. Before that time the mule cars on Broadway ran on trussels [trestles] in some places three to four feet from the ground.

On the bay front water washed up to the Strand. The sail boats brought wood to town and came in three feet of water, then the[y] would drive out to the boats, load up and deliver it to the buyers. At this time no boats or ships drawing over twelve feet of water could come into Galveston over bar at the Gulf end of the channels.

There were two channels of the Gulf going into the bays, the Galveston and the Bolivar channels. Sometime after the building of the two jetties, the Galveston side filled up and left only one channel and the depth now over the bar is kept at about thirty-two feet.

Much cotton and goods had to be litered and loaded in the Gulf outside the bar, but the jetties and the one channel have overcome that. The waters of East Bay and West Bay rush through one channel over the bar and keep deep water.

The early wharves were built on piling extending out to the edge of the channel, but later on many piles were driven down, fastened together, and formed a bulkhead near the channel and back along the sides to shore high land. In behind these the mud was pumped, forming solid ground, and the side dug out for more landing space for vessels. These are called slips.

Nearly two blocks of land was gained this way – almost the entire bayfrount. Where the water dashed Strand, it is now held back to Water Street, which makes another street north of A, beyond which is the wharves and boat landing slips.

After the forming of the North and South jetties, the ponds and bayous between South jetty and the Gulf gradually filled up and the land made out until at this time [1931] the Gulf shore line at the jetties is more than a mile further South and there are many acres of land on East Beach that was not there in the 70s.

While the land in the East has made – the waves have continued to cut off the land from Twentieth Street westward on the Gulf side. In Seventy [1870] a hotel called the Ocean House stood on a hill fully two blocks further than where waves now lap the shore.

About 1885, there was built what was called the Little Susie Railroad, a narrow gauge road that ran about twenty miles down the island to the westward. This road hauled a great deal of sand and sodding with which Galveston homeowners filled up low areas and the city generally was elevated and grade from the material brought from the West End by this train.

There were several pleasure resorts built up along the route where the citizens enjoyed an outing from time to time.

Midlakers Place about twelve miles down was a noted resort for picnickers.

Lafitte's Grove, about twenty miles down the island, was another place of amusement. These places were much used while the filling was being hauled, but as businesses dulled, and rolling stock ran down, it slacked; then came the storm of 1900 that destroyed much of the road, as well as the amusement places [and] the road was finally abandoned."

Scull-Fedford Family Home

This account is so beautiful to a Galvestonian who has seen much change, and wished for a way to record it. To have something I never saw described to me in full by my grandfather is almost like experiencing it. I have to express my gratitude to my grandfather for having the patience to write in his tablet night after night, as I watched him, until he was too old to remember. Or too tired to do it – he remained active long after he wrote this, caning his chairs and caring for his gardens in Dickinson, Texas City and La Marque. God bless you, Papa, thank you!

Because five generations of my family have lived on the island of Galveston, a calling to write down as much as I can learn and recall, of a history that has an impact beyond the lives of African Americans, has impressed itself on me more and more.

Scull Family

My grandfather recorded his memoirs with detailed information on African Americans dating to 1865, when his father brought him to this island at the age of five. He was also able to learn of much that happened here before they arrived, especially in regard to the founding of our church, Reedy Chapel African Methodist Episcopal Church.

As an international port in the latter 19th century -- surpassed only by New York City in volume, and merely rivaled by New Orleans in volume and "color", if you will -- Galveston was the initiator, the source, the parent of much of civilization as it became known in the South. An island smaller in area than New York, and not as geographically advantaged as New Orleans, Galveston was still well on her way to world prominence when the Great Storm of 1900 changed the plan.

The very fact that Galveston did survive, and continues to, is testimony to her tenacity and permanence. Her most devastating physical setbacks included the Fire of 1883 and the Storms of 1900 and 1915. Much of the city burned to the ground in 1883, and the whole city was rebuilt after the Great Storm of 1900, the nation's worst natural disaster to this day.

After the 1900 Storm, the city literally raised itself from sea level, like a lady of that era lifting her skirts to step over a big mud puddle. The entire city was put on stilts, house by house, building by building. This was called grade-raising, and the 18-foot-high seawall was started, to be amended several times to its present length of 10.4 miles, as of 1962.

From the Battle of Galveston during the Civil War, to World Wars I and II, Galveston has faced the direct threat of invasion by sea and air.

Economically speaking, we survived rationing during the World Wars; the loss of our youth, who participated in the armed forces; and the most disastrous of all, the deepening of the Houston part of Galveston Bay into the Houston Ship Channel. This last event negatively impacted our city the most, emotionally as well as economically, diverting our wharf business 50 miles down the road to what was then a little country town named after Sam Houston. Galveston's African Americans faced the loss of jobs on the wharf and at sea with the Merchant Marines with great serenity.

The work ethic of our people fit in with Galveston's economic recovery, which was also aided by the end to legal segregation in the Civil Rights movement of the 1960s. Paying for two sets of everything -- such as two complete school systems, even two sets of restrooms everywhere – cost a lot more money than Southern whites would like to admit.

With the City of Houston's ongoing expansion, and the Space Center between Houston and Galveston continuing to boost the area's economy, Galveston began to look forward and upward.

TABLE OF CONTENTS

CHAPTER ONE
    CROSSING GALVESTON BAY 1

CHAPTER TWO
    POLITICS: EMANCIPATION TO OWNERSHIP 9

CHAPTER THREE
    POLITICS: OUR VOICE 23

CHAPTER FOUR
    EDUCATION: OUR JOURNEY 37

CONVERSATION WITH CHARLES MCCULLOUGH OF RADIO STATION KGBC 66

CHAPTER FIVE
    EDUCATION: OUR LANDMARKS 75

CHAPTER SIX
    OUR CHURCHES 117

CHAPTER SEVEN
    MUSIC: ART, RECREATION & WORSHIP 166

CHAPTER EIGHT
    MUSIC: THE JAZZ GENERATION 208

LADIES IN THEIR 80s 234

CHAPTER NINE
    MEDICINE & HEALTH CARE 242

CHAPTER TEN
    THE 1900 STORM 269

CHAPTER ELEVEN
    EMPLOYMENT AND BUSINESS: The Recovery Years 286

CHAPTER TWELVE
> EMPLOYMENT AND BUSINESS: Prosperity 297

CHAPTER THIRTEEN
> LIFE IN THE DEPRESSION 309

CHAPTER FOURTEEN
> WORLD WAR II AND SOCIAL CHANGE 322

CHAPTER FIFTEEN
> EMPLOYMENT AND BUSINESS: AFTER WORLD WAR II ... 357

CHAPTER SIXTEEN
> TEXAS CITY EXPLOSION & MAINLAND GROWTH 390

CHAPTER SEVENTEEN
> CIVIL RIGHTS MOVEMENT 406

CHAPTER EIGHTEEN
> MODERN TIMES 420

CHAPTER ONE
CROSSING GALVESTON BAY

As the ferry pulled away from the dock, its recorded message started, and I decided to get out of the car, lean on the rail, and soak up the sights and sunshine. Staring across the glistening water, feeling the gentle rise and fall of the ferry deck, I saw past the freighters parked in the channel, past the old cement hulk of a long abandoned ship, now a key fishing spot.

I reluctantly thought of my mission. As president of the Board of Trustees of the Galveston Independent School District, I was invited to the Bolivar Elementary School for a school function. I liked the folk over there, most of whom remembered me as their kids' successful choir director of a decade or so ago.

But I was pretty tired, and longed for time to sail away on one of these passing boats to some exotic location, and just doze under some palm trees.

Unexpectedly, I got a vision of a small boat going in the opposite direction, a long, long time ago. Instead of seeing the speeding motorboat headed away from us, bow up out of the water, leaving behind a wake of blossoming froth, I saw an antiquated sailboat. Or maybe it was only a sturdy raft, logs bound together.

On this vessel were my great-grandfather, Horace Scull, his wife Emily, and their young family of expectant children. I could almost feel their excitement, see their faces, straining to see the promised land of freedom -- Galveston Island. The year was 1865, and my grandfather's composition book reads:

Horace Scull

"Horace Scull lived on Bolivar Point during the Civil War and at the close of the war moved his family to Galveston...."

My grandfather, Ralph Albert Scull, was 5 years old in 1865.

Ralph Albert Scull

I could imagine, in this spring of 1995, that 130 years ago, Horace Scull was full of apprehension and fear, which he suppressed with that faith he had learned to have. I could imagine Emily and Horace holding their arms around the youngest ones, dreaming that these precious offspring of theirs would have a chance. They must have had some special dreams of their children learning to read, write, maybe even how to earn a successful living for themselves.

Could they have believed then that Ralph Albert and Clara would learn so well, that they would be able to attend college in Ohio and Indiana and then come back to teach other African American children to read and write?

Well, it was 1865, the awful war was over, and word had come across the water to Port Bolivar of FREEDOM! President Lincoln had sent the order down! These slave owners might not like it, but they had to obey it. Our folk were free! Free to earn their own living. Free to go wherever they could. Free to join forces with old friends and family.

And over there in Galveston, you could find work. You could find things going on. Ships came in with imports from all over the world, and things from all over Texas and neighboring states were exported to places like Paris.

Galveston was full of excitement. In spite of the nightmare of shelling and invasion during the war, Galveston had resisted decay. Galveston was a haven, an oasis from grief, and Black people of differing nationalities walked the streets.

Some of these were free Blacks who spoke Spanish, who had been freed years ago by the Mexican government. Some were dark-skinned people from India, with wavy long hair and a language unlike the others'. But most were abducted Africans, brought to America to do the hard work that the whites either couldn't or wouldn't do.

They had retained no names of their own, had taken on their captors' surnames and values. But their hearts remembered their faraway heritage and beat to the pulse of the drums of their past culture.

And all of this I felt as I neared the Port Bolivar ferry landing. I would have to come back to 1995, check my appearance in the car mirror, freshen up and prepare to meet the almost all-white faculty and student body as their educational leader.

But my mind summarized quickly.

Could Horace have possibly dreamed that his son Ralph would have two boys and a girl to survive to adulthood? (Horace had already lost six children in their infancy.) And that Ralph's girl, Viola, would be the one to follow in her father's footsteps, teaching all of her life too – right here in Galveston, the Promised Land?

That Viola's daughters, Florence and Izola would end up as teachers too, themselves raising families in Galveston? That some of their children would also teach, and that Florence's husband, Theasel Henderson, would be elected as the first African American member of the school district's Board of Trustees? That after his resignation after 18 years, Izola, in retirement, would be the third and last African American to be elected at large – by the whole city of Galveston – three times to a position on the board?

So, 130 years later, the Scull boat that strained toward freedom and education came back to Bolivar as a ferry boat, with a Galveston school board president with Scull blood pulsing through her veins. God be praised! Ride on, King Jesus!

But I sobered up, as I drove off that ferry, and felt the heavy garment of responsibility drop on my shoulders. Tired or not, I had better get cracking and start getting more facts, and write up our history.

Putting Color Back Into Earliest Galveston

Most of the pictures taken in the early days of color photography have deteriorated with time. With the color that was once there now faded, the image that remains is a false one.

Some historians have omitted the information about Galveston's people of color that they lacked. But a crime has been committed by those who knew the stories and purposely left the heroes of color out.

As a port of foreign trade, Galveston's exposure to the wider world gave its residents some natural tolerance for and understanding of varied cultures; people of every race and creed walked the streets. Although others have tried to say otherwise, there has been limited racial conflict here in Galveston since its birth.

Estevanico preceded white Spanish explorer Cabeza de Vaca off the boat in 1528, more as partner than slave, and black slaves in Galveston received legal rights long before the Civil War due to the lobbying of the city's German settlers. In its earliest years, there were slaves, indentured servants of color, and already freed Black people living quietly here. And information is slowly emerging that free people of color enjoyed some measure of citizenship. They built homes, supported this island, and made lasting contributions to Galveston's welfare.

An early African American businessman, Major Cary, who opened the first livery stable in Galveston in 1838, was noted for heroic conduct in the Battle of San Jacinto. Captured runaway Negroes helped build a formidable battery on Pelican Spit. African American women founded a charitable society called the Daughters of Zion right after slavery officially ended in 1866. Short references like these bear out the fact that Black men and women were very active in the life of Galveston. They just are not given equal coverage for what they did, and the identification of these persons is very poor at best.

The exclusion of our history from record, allowing the inference that no one cared to note it, is criminal. Local African American newspapers in the 19th century reported on Black community activities and participants. And although memorabilia such as printed programs from those events have often been misplaced over the years, I am certain that more records of our culture from this time exist.

My grandfather had done his part, writing nightly before he went to bed. He started recording his information in 1931, a couple of years after I was born. I remember passing his bedroom late evenings, and seeing Papa (as we girls called him, since this is what my mother called her father) sitting at his little desk, writing in the green composition tablet. He'd write what he remembered, then kneel down on his aged knees and pray. I'd peek around the hall corner and see this every night. He'd close the door just to change into his nightclothes and retire for the night.

Many of his valuable memories reflected our family's long history in education. Papa began teaching in the Galveston public school system in 1883, and I left the school board in 1995 – a span of 112 years in service by our family to schools in Galveston. And some of our children have continued to teach the children of Texas in other communities.

At one time, the only professions open to educated African Americans were preaching and teaching. African American teachers did not often leave their posts for reasons other than retirement or death in those days; that is why so many of us remember the same teachers.

Although Papa taught for 52 consecutive years, and Mother taught for 52 years, excluding the five years after I was born, I retired once I qualified for a pension, determined not to teach until I could no longer do anything else. As our children came through public schools, opportunities emerged in other fields of endeavor. Education in formerly all-white colleges was possible in Texas, and they chose other careers.

Crossing Galveston Bay

When Galveston faced more and more economic hard times, our children sought livings elsewhere – in businesses of their own, or with respected firms.

In the generation known as Baby Boomers, and the generation since, African Americans have found that the world waits with open arms for their expanded knowledge. But few have been able to return to Galveston, to survive its economic drought.

So what is happening to the threads of our community? Do they know from whence they came? Should they care? Is it worth the trouble to dig deep – find their roots?

We must inform our children of the opportunities that call to them from outside Galveston. But let us also undertake the work of informing them for their journey -- of the history they share in, from the place they call home.

CHAPTER TWO
POLITICS: EMANCIPATION TO OWNERSHIP

Galveston's racial climate has long been more amicable than elsewhere in the South. My opinion that this includes the post-Civil War era is echoed by Charles Hayes' *Galveston,* which was recorded at that time by a native Galvestonian and serves as the best source of information about the people of color here. Hayes said that Reconstruction was accomplished "with less difficulty, less vexation, and more harmoniously in Galveston, in Texas than any other state that had seceded."

Ironically, the abolition of slavery, fought by most whites of Galveston, encouraged wholesale migration to Galveston, because there was a published demand for white laborers. Yet on Valentine's Day in 1866, *Flake's Bulletin* reported that business was prosperous all over town, but the city was a real mess. It struggled with murder, theft, and health problems. The streets were nasty and the wharves were in dangerous condition. With the military and civic authority in a power struggle, nothing was being done about it.

Women organized clubs and demanded the sanitation of milk, meat and streets. Black women worked tirelessly at these endeavors, but separately; white women did not join efforts with them.

The standards of cleanliness and health were raised with repairing, rebuilding, painting and whitewashing, and filling in of water holes. As more manufacturers came into Galveston and new steamship lines were

Politics: Emancipation to Ownership

established, churches were also reopened, and schools were organized for both White and Black students.

Although Abraham Lincoln signed the Emancipation Proclamation on January 1, 1863, it took a long, unbelievable stretch of months for the news to arrive in the port of Galveston. To be sure, there was no computer Internet, or information highway, or TV news such as CNN in those days. But the news did eventually reach the shores of Galveston on June 17, 1865, as it is recorded in the Wharves Seaport Museum in Galveston. And it revolutionized the development of a city.

Proclamation of Our Freedom

At the end of the Civil War, over 500,000 slaves had made it to freedom behind Union army lines. About 200,000 Black soldiers and sailors, primarily former slaves, served in the North forces. And Galveston had the distinct honor of being the port that received the word of President Abraham Lincoln's declaration of a new era for all of the South.

When General Granger and crew arrived in Galveston for that purpose, on June 17, 1865, the African American labor team on the wharf found out the reason for this ship's arrival and started rejoicing. Granger announced the proclamation to the African American community on June 19th at Ashton Villa, when he addressed the Confederate soldiers with their general orders.

In recent years, historians have asserted that the first official announcement of the proclamation was made to the community on Jan. 1, 1866, at the Galveston County Courthouse -- at 20th to 21st streets and Avenue I (Sealy) -- and followed by a ceremonial march to an African American church at 2013 Broadway, later known as Reedy Chapel A.M.E. Church.

Island of Color

Whatever the location for the announcement, June 19th is when most of the African American community received the news, and it has therefore celebrated that date from then on. Now an official state holiday, it has also come to be celebrated in faraway places as Texas African Americans have settled all over the world.

Many younger adults have asked: What is the big deal about Juneteeth? And why don't African Americans just celebrate July Fourth like everybody else in America?

Hayes said the first persons in Galveston to celebrate July 4th as a day of freedom were the newly freed African Americans! Confederate-loyal white Galvestonians were not at all happy about the Northern conquering regime taking control of their lives – giving them orders, taking away their slaves, etc. They therefore did not want to celebrate the new Union holidays. July 4, 1776, was a date to which they felt little allegiance. On the other hand, the Galveston African Americans, thrilled with their new status and new opportunities, wanted to show their appreciation and support for this new government. Hayes states, "So, the African Americans paraded up and down the main streets of Galveston, and may have been the first African Americans in the whole South to have an organized parade for July 4th."

Dr. Elizabeth Turner in her research states, "The only parades held on Independence Day in 1905 were provided by the African American Loyal Knights of Progress and the Hawley Guards. On that day Blacks eulogized the contribution of Crispus Attucks, who was slain in the Boston Massacre of 1770. One must wonder what it meant to Black Galvestonians when they alone celebrated the nation's independence?"

Politics: Emancipation to Ownership

Today's Galveston African Americans must also wonder why these people chose to celebrate the freedom of a nation from oppression, when they themselves were still oppressed, mistreated, endangered. But the reason is clear when you realize the freed slaves were celebrating the freedom they had obtained -- due to the shift of power to the Northerners from Southern whites in Galveston, who had fought to lead separate lives, and who were not going to embrace any celebration of a Union that removed their slaves from their control. This Union had ushered in a new life for African Americans, even if it wasn't all worked out yet.

As many of our great leaders and speakers have said, what should freedom represent for us today? Freedom from what, now that our bodies can no longer be enslaved by others legally? We know, thanks to spirituals, that our forefathers were probably freer in spirit than we are today, that they felt themselves destined to be free, in fact, in another world. They did not feel hopeless about the next life, even if their present held no hope for them. We bear the responsibility of passing on that spirit of freedom as legacy for today's youth.

Property Ownership In Deed

Mrs. V.C. Scull-Fedford with her first car

Politics: Emancipation to Ownership

"Politics" can be considered either a dirty word or the way we all survive.

I view it from the perspective of survival, in which politics is simply the process of deciding who will determine how we live. When defined by those seeking to dominate others' lives, or profit from someone else's hard work or misery, politics is a dirty word.

Both versions are correct. One is an optimistic view, the other is a pessimistic one. If one takes the pessimistic viewpoint, someone is always trying to "get over" on you; the evil usually win over the good; and there is no point in trying to have a moral life. From such pessimists come remarks on the futility of the African American's condition: "Ah, they ain't never gonna let you have nothing. I don't care who it is. They white -- they gonna always stick together."

Are pessimists deluded? Not really. The environment in which they were raised has had to be one of caution, disbelief, even disillusionment. Trickery is the name of the game that the white people in their experience have always played, putting much in the way of any African American trying to get ahead. This came to be expected, not denied.

It has been so even from the days of the Freedmen's Bureau, when even the federal agents of the Reconstruction era -- those who were supposed to be our protectors when we had little other recourse -- were often the ones to do us the most harm. Thanks to some determined good folk, some good did come out of these efforts to help the Black man survive. To be sure, beatings, torture and even killings were tolerated, but at least the offenses could be reported.

Skeptics question the account that since even post-Civil War times, residents here have simply got along, but in Galveston both races have had common enemies -- the elements of nature and economic hard times. And friendships did occur. After the war, there were some well-meaning white people who harbored no resentment toward their colored servants, and some even had real affection for the people who had nourished their very souls in hard times.

The post-Civil War Southerners' politics caused us to get property we would not have had, often used for churches. Rather than give up their property to the winning team -- the North – some Southerners gave it to their ex-slaves, with whom they had a friendlier relationship, in spite of the injustices.

But we did face considerable obstacles to becoming land owners. I quote from my grandfather's writing, who described his family's move after the Civil War to Galveston:

His father "lived on Tremont between H and I till 1866...Our next home was Ave. K and 16 Street ... Late in 1867 he built a house as a home on 816 Winnie Street, where we lived till 1872 when he moved his house to 1119 Ave. J ... not being permitted to buy a lot there, he moved the house to 1105 H where he was offered a lot to buy for a home, but after remaining there from 1873 to 1879, the owner changed his mind or refused to sell the land.

He then arranged to purchase a home at 915 Ave. J 1880 ... In the early days of freedom H. Scull carpentered and built many houses for the ex slaves, nearly all on leased ground."

Other accounts reinforce his, that property not only was difficult to buy for African Americans, but next to impossible to hold onto after purchase.

Politics: Emancipation to Ownership

For this reason, it was hard to hold my temper when a misguided man challenged our effort in the late 1990s to name a city park, Menard Park, for its original owner, Robert "Bob" McGuire -- an African American who owned much of the property in the park area.

McGuire-Dent Recreation Center

It was on that property that Galveston's Black community finally had a bathhouse that they could comfortably attend. According to city directories of that period, the land was later taken from them and used for a city park after storm-related grade raising.

McGuire owned and managed a hack stand in downtown Galveston, with a horse and buggy used to transport people across the city for a fee as taxicabs do now. He earned enough money to build the bathhouse, which operated for at least a generation. All of the older residents I interviewed spoke of having such good times in his bathhouse and the hall below in the late 19th century and early 20th century.

The bathhouse area, where he had his businesses and homes, was known by people who did not live in Galveston as "The Beachfront." In the days of segregation, many African Americans, both residents and visitors, thought it was the only other place they were allowed to use the Gulf of Mexico, other than at the end of the seawall at 61st Street, where one could drive down a ramp onto the sand. Since McGuire's time, the businesses on the Seawall from 27th to 29th streets have continued to be owned or at least managed by African Americans.

I undertook an effort to have 27th Street renamed as McGuire Boulevard, and to also rename Menard Park for McGuire, whose property evidently was taken from him by the law of eminent domain for the city park. The city paid him only $11,000 for the several properties that he owned.

In response, the Parks and Recreation Board supported retaining the name Menard Park, but did recommend renaming the park's Recreation Center as the Robert McGuire-Jessie McGuire Dent Center. The 1999 City Council accepted the recommendation, and also voted to erect a plaque on the property to list other African American families whose homes were once on the property.

One way or another, present residents need to know that the area does not belong to a few roustabouts who seem to have claimed it as a place to hang out. And that historically, this is the only area behind the seawall that welcomed African Americans.

White owners of businesses on the sand did not want their patrons to be turned off by the presence of former slaves in the water with them.

Politics: Emancipation to Ownership

Such owners, and sometimes even police, told them to move on, that they were not allowed to swim in those areas. People do not often go where they are not wanted, though some of our people knew all along that no one could legally keep them out. More than a mile of water into the Gulf, and all of the sand beaches, belong to the state, and everyone may use the property.

I remember going to the beach every evening in the summer between 8th and 10th streets, right in the area where we lived, and on occasion going far down East Beach for all-day outings. I suppose my mother knew there was no real prohibition, and also didn't look very threatening with the children she always had in tow. But I do remember my mother telling us that we didn't really want the snack food that was for sale, when people built vendor stands on the sand near where we always bathed. Similarly, she discouraged us from using the playground equipment that was sometimes placed down there. Our parents tried to protect us from the ugly truth as much as they could, and we thought ourselves privileged rather than deprived because of the several things we had that neighbor children of other races didn't have, like the playhouse our father built for my sister and me.

At any rate, such racial exclusion is why people today should know what happened in McGuire's day – about his success in such times.

The opponent of the effort to rename the park had challenged in meetings of the Parks Board and City Council: "What did this man ever do for Galveston? Mr. Menard owned a lot more property there, and was the founder of the city!" I countered that the very fact that Mr. McGuire held onto his property as long as he did -- and managed to send a daughter to college who returned as an educator to help make a better life for those still here -- was itself worthy of our praise. He also created a climate for our people to follow in his footsteps. He gave the African American community a place of its own, and kept a lot of folk from despair by his very example of courage.

Property ownership in Galveston was very elusive in those early days of the 20th century, and so African Americans placed more importance on it than many do now. Ownership is more important to those who have difficulty accomplishing it.

From one book about the back-alley houses and businesses of Galveston, by Ellen Beasley, one might get the mistaken notion that most African Americans lived in Galveston's alleys. Not so. Although a lot of our people lived in those houses, many who were domestic servants for the people in the front houses, a lot more owned their own homes, many on the front streets of Galveston. Although I contributed to Beasley's book myself, detailing the businesses that some of our folk had in rear houses, and I recognize the veracity of the reports she obtained from other residents, her book was not about property ownership by all of our people. As any Galvestonian who is over 60 years old can tell you, African Americans owned quite a bit of land in Galveston, and much of it has been lost as they moved away or passed on without heirs to continue the upkeep and pay taxes.

The huge growth in residential property on the mainland in Galveston County is the result of much economic change. Residents in that area have no idea how isolated that land was only a few years ago, before the Space Age and the introduction of NASA to the area. My grandfather bought land very cheaply on the mainland in his day, and grew many crops on the almost barren land that is now Texas City. He also gave away a

Politics: Emancipation to Ownership

good bit of acreage to family members and other people so they could grow their own, in a little place that was named after just a mark on the map: La Marque.

After the Texas City explosion, when many who could not afford to buy property here went over there and settled down, there were more African Americans than any others who settled in nice homes. Property ownership became the thing to do on the mainland, with cheaper property, lower property taxes, and even cheaper insurance. The buyers were more or less displaced or disgruntled Galvestonians.

Statements about Galveston's past vary greatly among the people interviewed. But each one tells the truth; it is simply that the truth seen with the eyes of a person who has lived with hope and faith is quite different from the truth of one who has known hard times, suffering and deceit.

It was politics that brought post-war conditions in the South to the government's attention, that brought carpetbaggers to attempt to correct those conditions, despised as they were by whites who already lived here – and the Blacks that they misinformed. The effort in those times to get Black people on juries, to get men and women to come South to teach the students who were eager to learn -- none of that happened by any method other than politics. How, then, can a Black person speak disparagingly about politics?

In some cases, politics prevented the two races from getting along when they wanted to, as when segregation was introduced to a tolerant Galveston. But, as we all know, the advent of stronger political forces in the African American's behalf -- the court cases argued by Thurgood Marshall, as an example -- created a new and better world for the next generations of African Americans.

With such dramatic changes, one would expect these freed and more empowered people to cherish their new right to vote, hold office, etc. How disappointing when that doesn't happen. To this day, the problems for most of Galveston's African Americans are much like the problems felt all over the nation by our people. We are taught to divide, to distrust each other. This prevents us from ever gaining any real control over our own lives. We don't always help each other understand what is transpiring in local or national politics, for fear that someone else might beat us to opportunities we desperately want for ourselves and our loved ones.

Our churches have been a political force, and certainly could also point the way to moral, charitable leadership, but how many of our religious leaders really seek that? My grandfather and father were very worthy and dedicated ministers, and my son has followed a sincere calling to become ordained as a minister as well. But truth be told, there are those who use the pulpit to further their own political and economic interests, and are not helping their people to become the best they can be.

All else being equal, if African Americans would work toward becoming their level best, and sticking together, they could solve many problems through the political process. This requires that they vote their convictions, and not just simply complain about the problems inherent in our society. Many capable African Americans still won't run for office when something is really at stake, looking at politics as something negative. And those who do run are often not trained for the job they seek, leaving others of their race with inadequate reason to vote for them. These are not problems limited to our race, of course.

As one who hesitated to run for office myself, questioning fully whether it was advisable, I know that one must have a pressing need to

Politics: Emancipation to Ownership

participate in the political process, as well as some degree of assurance that participation can make a difference for the better. One also has to have the time to participate.

In Galveston, to be a member of the City Council, the Galveston Independent School District Board of Trustees, or several other boards of large scope requires an independent source of income and a great deal of free time. Many people seem to think that the politically active are paid a salary to serve, and they certainly are not. Such volunteer service deserves a lot more appreciation than it gets from the general public. There are communities that can afford to pay people in similar positions and do, in states that allow this compensation.

Galveston is currently giving a lot of grief to its elected officials, demanding they account for every expense as though they were being paid to serve. Although these positions demand integrity, they don't demand blood, sacrifice of reputation, and constant tears. This is primarily what keeps prepared, capable people from seeking office.

My wish is that the newspapers of our city, state, nation would put out a large, highly visible series of articles to educate the general public as to what politics is, not what it is not. That the general public would recognize that its leaders are doing them a direct service by putting order in their lives, and that any needed improvement in services must come from individual participation.

Leadership classes, involvement with organizations proven to work for the good of all people, and the continuing desire to educate oneself and one's family are all necessary toward that improvement and the advancement of Galveston's citizens. Freedom is never really free; the price we pay must be negotiated.

CHAPTER THREE
POLITICS: OUR VOICE

Turn-of-the-Century Politicians

Early African Americans of Galveston understood the price of freedom, and rose to the challenges — whether the struggle was for better jobs, housing, or whatever need. The Reconstruction period gave them opportunities unparalleled thus far in our history. Politicians in Galveston had a goal, a destination, and did not rest until it was achieved. The best-known African American politician in Galveston was without equal: Norris Wright Cuney.

Norris Wright Cuney

The son of a slave mother and a white plantation owner, he was born in Waller County, Texas, in 1846. He was one of eight children, all of whom were given their freedom and educated. He attended school in Pittsburgh, Penn., before settling in Galveston to "read Law." He and his wife Adelina had two children, Lloyd Garrison and Maude, an acclaimed concert pianist.

The following information on Galveston's best-known African American politician came from The Texas Trailblazer series, sponsored by The Houston Place Preservation Association of Houston, and my grandfather's account:

Cuney's first political position was in 1871 as president of the Galveston Loyal Union League. (The Union League of America was formed during the Civil War and spearheaded Southern Republicanism.)

Politics: Our Voice

The next year he received his first of several federal posts, and for four years beginning in 1873 Cuney was inspector of customs at Galveston.

Cuney became secretary of the Republican State Executive Committee. White businessmen, impressed by Cuney's efficiency and dedication to public welfare, invited him to deliberate with them in the Galveston Cotton Exchange over the city's future; his nomination as a mayoral candidate, running against a well-known Democrat in the 1875 election, was the result. Though he was defeated, he was admired by his opponents for his race for the office. When for political reasons he was dismissed from his post as inspector of customs, the new mayor -- his former opponent -- and 100 other people demanded that he be reinstated.

He was elected temporary chairman at the state Republican Party convention in 1882 and elected chairman two years later. Blacks far outnumbered whites as delegates to that year's state convention in Houston. As a delegate to the national convention in Chicago, he was elected vice president of the Republican National Convention.

By 1883, Cuney was elected alderman in Galveston, a first for his race in the city. He won his Twelfth Ward seat again in 1885. The prominent Galvestonians running with him were Henry Rosenberg, Charles Fowler and J.G. Goldwaite. Because he could not hold two public offices at the same time, he resigned his federal office as inspector for the local post. He remained on the Board of Aldermen until 1887, when he was appointed to the Board of the Commissioners of Water Works.

Cuney also served as school director for Galveston County, and as the first assistant to the sergeant-at-arms of the 12th Texas Legislature.

Cuney also operated a stevedore business and was the first to hire blacks as dock workers in Galveston; he established the state's first organization for black longshoremen.

The highlight of his career then came when President Benjamin Harrison appointed him in 1889 as Collector of Customs in Galveston, the most powerful government job held by a man of his race in the South. Forced to resign as Grover Cleveland took office in the White House, he died two years later in 1898, and was buried in Lakeview Cemetery in Galveston.

To honor his contributions to the Prince Hall Grand Lodge of Texas, as Grand Master of the Negro Masons of Texas, a monument was unveiled in Galveston circa 1964. Cuney was a member of Reedy Chapel AME Church and his name is still etched on the cornerstone of that historic Galveston monument. A historical marker in front of Galveston County Court House also recognizes Cuney's contributions, and [Wright] Cuney Park was dedicated in his honor in 1937. A town in East Texas bears his name, and the Cuney Homes Housing Project in Houston was named for him when it became the first public housing unit for Blacks in 1940.

William H. Noble

William H. Noble, born in 1876, was editor of *City Times*, the first Black newspaper in Galveston. A well-educated man, he attended the University of Chicago and the University of Saint Louis, Mo.

Noble was interested in improving the self-esteem of Galveston's Negro population. Every year he helped to sponsor an event called "Children and Old Folks Day." This event was held at Cotton Jammers Park at 37th Street and Avenue S, to promote appreciation between young and old. Literary, athletic, musical and beauty contests were among the activities. Merchants throughout Galveston participated in the festivities by donating prizes. Noble felt that this event would help Galveston Blacks see themselves and their community in a better light.

Noble was also known and respected throughout the South. In 1904, he was elected recording secretary for the Southern Negro Congress in Mobile, Ala.

He died in Galveston in January 1930.

George T. Ruby

George T. Ruby was born in New York in 1841. He first worked as a correspondent for a Boston newspaper. Ruby and the newspaper advocated complete separation of Negroes from whites in the United States.

The start of the Civil War brought Ruby back to the United States from an assignment in Haiti. He arrived in New Orleans in January 1864 and began working towards the education of freedmen, as the principal of an elementary school. Soon he was appointed school agent for Louisiana. In this position, he visited and established schools throughout that state.

In 1866, George Ruby moved to Galveston to continue his work in Negro education. He established the *Galveston Standard* in 1871, and the newspaper was issued semi-weekly through 1873. Accounts by other newspapermen gave him credit for a neat-appearing journal.

He soon became involved with politics and the Republican Party in Texas. He was active in organizing Negroes to vote Republican. The Republican Party was influential in Texas throughout the Reconstruction period, although factions within the party disagreed over its aims and

Island of Color

goals. Ruby was active in a radical segment of the party that worked to prevent Texas from returning to antebellum practices.

The first African American congressman from Texas, Ruby was twice elected to the state Senate during the early 1870s where he was active in a variety of committees. He actively pursued civil rights issues in the Legislature.

<u>During his political career, Ruby introduced the bill that incorporated the city of Galveston.</u> He also helped to get tax exemptions for educational and religious organizations, which had a huge impact in relation to the University of Texas Medical Branch. He was also one of the leading forces in getting a free public school system created.

In 1873, the Democrats took control of the Texas Senate, and Ruby's influence was reduced greatly. In 1874 he returned to New Orleans.

Doc Hamilton and the Lone Star Cotton Jammers

In 1898, the Lone Star Cotton Jammers of Texas, a Black union, received its operating charter. Cotton jammers, or screwmen, were the longshoremen who loaded cotton into the Galveston ships. The more cotton on a ship, the more profits for the owner, thus the art of the cotton jammer developed. The Lone Star Cotton Jammers were famous for packing more cotton into a ship's hold than was thought possible.

Because space was at a premium, cotton jamming was very important to Galveston shipping and commerce. Large screws forced cotton into the hold. Cotton jammers also placed more bales aboard a ship by building an arch of bales in the hold, removing the braces and jamming the cotton against the hull. If water poured on the bales stayed on top

Politics: Our Voice

without soaking through, cotton jammers knew that they had succeeded in packing the bales tightly.

Another Black union was formed in 1913: International Longshoremen's Union Local 851. This union was a counterpart of the Lone Star Cotton Jammers. The Jammers loaded cotton and Local 851 loaded general cargo. The lists of officers for the two unions overlapped and eventually ILA Local 851 absorbed the Cotton Jammers.

Doc Hamilton, president of this local from 1930-37, is credited with establishing Local 851 as an important force in the Galveston ILA. Not only was Doc Hamilton the first Black man to be elected to the District Executive Board of the South Atlantic and Gulf Coast District ILA, he also served that board as vice president and was elected to the vice president's position on the International Executive Board.

Doc Hamilton died in 1939 and his funeral was held at City Auditorium. This is thought to be the only funeral ever held in that building.

These biographical sketches of Norris Wright Cuney, William Noble, George T. Ruby, Doc Hamilton and The Lone Star Cotton Jammers illustrate the leading thrust of politics for African Americans in Galveston at the turn of the century (19th to 20th century).

But the struggle continued.

Suffrage and Other Political Efforts by Women

From the time of the Emancipation Proclamation to the 1900 Storm, 42 African-American men served in the Texas Legislature. Ruby of Galveston was among them. Another man, W.H. Holland, among other noteworthy work, sponsored a bill in 1875 to establish Prairie View State

College. The last African American to serve in that century, Robert L. Smith, left the Legislature in 1899.

In 1902, whites regained enough control to pass the infamous poll tax as a requirement for voting. The attempt to discourage, even prevent, African-Americans from voting, is well-known.

And here in Galveston, instead of joining hands with their darker sisters, white women even used the poll tax to advance the women's suffrage movement over the right of both Black men and Black women to vote.

Dr. Elizabeth Turner had the courage to reveal this in her research: "In the meantime, southern states began their systematic campaign to disenfranchise black voters, ending with the poll tax in Texas in 1902. Texas women supported the poll tax through the Texas Federation of Women's Clubs, which endorsed it and educated women to its advantages. The tax, they argued, would improve the electorate and purify the ballot by removing poor blacks, poor whites, and Mexicans from voting."

I remember so well when this group forced my mother's organization, the Texas Federation of Colored Women's Clubs, of which she had been president for five years, to change their name after over half a century of good works. They were challenged in a court of law just because of this other association's claim that the name was too much like a derivative of its name, and so the name was changed to the Texas Association of Colored Women's Clubs.

Politics: Our Voice

Texas Federation of Colored Women's Clubs

Receptions for State Officers (l to r) Mrs. H.E. Williams, Mrs. A.E.S. Johnson, Mrs. Ada Bell DeMent Mrs. C.H. Christian, Mrs. W.E. Brackeen, Mrs. Viola Scull Fedford, President

It was bigoted reasoning like this that led this group of women to pursue keeping "undesirables" from voting. The inference was even more insulting to Mexican-Americans -- they didn't even bother to use the word 'poor' in connection with them, as though none of them would then be able to vote. Watch out – in the near future, there will be much romancing the Hispanic vote, you can believe.

Turner gave another reason for the success of the poll tax effort, a selling point I can vaguely recall hearing when I grew old enough to pay the tax and vote at age 21, in 1950. The poll tax cost $1.50, and $1.00 of that was supposed to go to education. However, most of that was spent on white schools, far more than was fair percentage-wise. The tax gave most benefit to those who most did not need it.

"Thus, the question of black male voting was effectively eliminated, raising hopes for a woman suffrage movement that would be 'for whites only'."

Even as African Americans saw some advances in their segregated economy, in those years before the Depression hit both whites and blacks, they were plotted against.

Since this movement was succeeding so well elsewhere, Galveston soon had a white women's suffrage movement with delegates to the executive board in Houston, including the daughter of a woman who started a free kindergarten here. <u>The Galveston News</u> reported that 74 women and 7 men became charter members of the Galveston Equal Suffrage Association during a meeting at the Hotel Galvez in February 1912.

Two different state suffrage societies flourished, then died when other interests prevailed, such as city improvement. (For instance, the Women's Health Protective Association in Galveston replanted the island with trees and shrubs killed by the grade raising, and inspected and reported on the conditions of streets, alleys, markets, bakeries, restaurants, dairies, and housing.)

After World War I started, the national suffragist movement was in high gear in Washington D.C., and active with Negro intellectuals. Despite the bigotry often found in the movement, most of the Negro women leaders continued to support women's suffrage efforts because they believed that

Politics: Our Voice

only through political equality could Negro men and women be raised out of obscurity.

The National American Woman Suffrage Association (NAWSA), trying to get the Susan B. Anthony amendment passed, sponsored a march on the evening before Woodrow Wilson was inaugurated as president. The participating Negro women were members of Delta Sigma Theta Sorority, newly founded in 1913. These courageous young women were asked to bring up the rear. They included our own Jessie McGuire Dent, of Galveston, with the other Texas founders of Delta Sigma Theta Sorority, from the Howard University campus in Washington, D.C.

In 1917, the Texas Federation of Colored Women's Clubs endorsed suffrage, and in this same year the Negro Women's Voters League of Galveston was founded.

These dedicated women's activities were seldom documented, but the year 1932 saw Negro women working in a special club to support a man named Quinn in the race for sheriff in Galveston. These women were also going from house to house talking to the voters, evidently having quite a bit of success.

In addition to political activism, Negro women's groups' displays of patriotism date back to World War I: selling bonds, tending victory gardens, working with the YWCA, Red Cross, and providing other services such as USO dances for the servicemen. Ruth Winegarten's research noted that in Galveston, Mrs. L. A. Pinkney, president of the Progressive Club, organized women to prepare "comfort bags" for the soldiers who were leaving soon.

And the joined effort of community and political work went on. In 1941, thanks to the Texas Federation of Colored Women's Clubs lobbying the Texas Legislative Board of Control, Texas finally appropriated $60,000 to establish a State Training School for Delinquent Girls. It was not coincidence that this happened in the first legislative session after the U.S. Supreme Court granted African Americans in Texas the right to vote in the Democratic primaries.

The president of the Texas Federation of Colored Women's Clubs, then known as the Texas Association of Colored Women's Clubs, was Mrs. Viola C. Scull Fedford when the first students were admitted to the Brady State Training School for Negro Girls in 1947. She served from 1943 to 1947. My sister married in 1945, and had Mother's first grandchild in 1947.

Women of color had their families and their people in mind when they took on the work they did. These women fought for their brothers' rights, for their children's rights to live as decent citizens, and for their own rights as women of destiny.

Certainly there were other significant characters, but too many to mention. And for a detailed understanding of women's ventures into Galveston political life, in an era when they were not permitted to take active roles in government, I would refer you to <u>Women, Culture and Community</u>, by Dr. Elizabeth Turner, and <u>Black Texas Women</u> by Ruthe Winegarten.

Much more of the Galveston African Americans' political fight, detailed later, followed the end of World War II, when African American men and women returned from serving their country, determined not to be subservient to the people whose lives they had saved directly and indirectly.

Politics: Our Voice

Without the political and voting activity described in this chapter, many developments good for all Galvestonians couldn't have happened. And yet, increasingly, so many people who have not had to pay one single price for their freedom ask, "Why vote?" It would do me so much good just to see the ground eroded right out from under these pitiful, apathetic people. They have no earthly idea of the high price paid for them, by those who died for the right to vote their convictions, whether or not their candidate or issue succeeded.

Evil as the policy was, I will never forget the pride I felt when I was finally allowed to pay my poll tax at age 21. Then I voted every time.

Solidarity and Leadership

As stated before, Galveston in origin was naturally integrated. It was when laws of segregation were passed and enforced in 1885 that the churches, schools, and most public buildings were then separated by race.

It was a condition born in absurdity. Mrs. Amelia Curtis, a friend of my mother's, recalled how often they sat alone in the otherwise empty balcony for Galveston Opera House performances, even those by Black entertainers. What a colossal waste of money it was to keep anyone else from sitting with them, and what courage and love of the arts these ladies had, to pay to sit in isolation to enjoy the music.

But it was a condition that gave birth to solidarity. In these times of segregation, unity within the African American community only grew, due to the spirit of the Galveston African-American. There was no irony in the timing of this community's emergence. It was because of our poor treatment that we pulled together more.

The average person facing segregation did not expect anything else from those who opposed him, and so we more or less ignored whites and built our own world. As a child who grew up in this atmosphere, I can say honestly that we never even thought about white culture, although we were familiar with it.

It was part of the landscape, much like the everyday view of fish jumping out of the Gulf. You don't really notice them unless you want to fish, you enjoy sitting and watching sea life, or you're checking for signs of a storm -- in this case, a storm of racial trouble.

As a community within a community, we learned to laugh, cry, plan, work, celebrate within our own means. When we were yet children, encircled by the love of family and friends, we felt we had everything we needed, for we did not miss what we had never had.

But as adults we did not accept segregation and a downsized way of life, just as Adam and Eve were no longer happy being naked once they ate from the tree of knowledge and their eyes were opened. The difference, however, is that Adam and Eve truly lacked nothing they needed. We continued to support the growth of our community, even as we lifted our voices to call for the end to the limits our community faced.

It is plain, I repeat, that *politics* is only a dirty word if you don't participate. Early in this new millennium, we can truthfully say that things have generally improved for the African American. But we certainly know that much must be done first within our own ranks, and then in connection with the other "races" of people with whom we live.

Politics: Our Voice

There will always be leaders who will put themselves in danger to achieve a goal, a just cause, that is well worth the cost, although most of the people being helped may not understand what is done, let alone follow this leadership.

The advent of single-member voting districts in the city, school district, and county has meant more representation of African Americans in political life. Until this development, there have been so few representatives of our people as to make some progress hopeless. There must be more improvement still.

We must train our people in well-structured programs for civic development. We must be prepared before we file for office. Our people must realize that they will always be scrutinized more than those of other races, and be prepared for the scrutiny.

Politics are not evil by nature. Politics are simply utilized for evil purposes by so many who do indulge themselves. At any given time in history, leaders have risen above the swill, and given political direction that has saved our very lives, and certainly the quality of all of our lives.

CHAPTER FOUR
EDUCATION: OUR JOURNEY

African Americans' effort in Galveston to access learning for their people has its roots in humble circumstances – tiny facilities, few and ragged supplies, Spartan salaries. But the goals pursued were noble: those of self-improvement and socioeconomic advancement for family and community.

A Map To The Early Years

During Reconstruction, the Freedman's Bureau was responsible for bringing many Black teachers into the South. A glimpse into those early years is allowed by the records made by Papa -- my wonderful, spiritual, faithful, dedicated maternal grandfather, who gave his entire life to formal and informal education. He was far-sighted enough to record his memories, including educators' names and the location of facilities. They serve as a map to the little-known past:

"Just after emancipation there were a number of private teachers trying to instruct children [African American]. In the East End we first had Miss Reedy who was a daughter of Rev. Reedy then pastor of Reedy Chapel A.M.E. Church. Change of ministers took her away.

Education: Our Journey

East District School

A man named Gomy then opened near 10[th Street] and Ave. H. Later Mr. A. Cook a northerner who used a cowhide whip quite freely ... then Mrs. Flynn a white widow with one son about 12 years old. She was one of the best teachers up to about 1870. In the West they [were] Mr. Mormest, Mr. Stevenson, Mrs. Stevenson, Miss Elward.

In 1872 the Public Schools started up with Miss Dora Mayo in the East assisted by Miss Narr. In the West Mrs. Francis wife of D. Francis custom house officer. Miss Annie Narr. Later Mrs. Webb, Mr. Webb. Mr. Joseph Cuney were East [I think he meant to add another name here].

Island of Color

Faculty of East District

Miss Elward at 20 street and K and Miss Mayo and Mrs. Francis and others at 28 street and Avenue L.

In the Spring 1875 money gave out and schools closed down April first -- Politics changed and most of the teachers went back to the North. Now Rev. Randolph pastor of Reedy Chapel Methodist Church opened school in the church where he taught for about three years.

In the West Miss Barber who later became Mrs. Cuney taught school in Barnes Institute [at] Avenue M and near 29th Street, assisted by Gertrude Potts and Virginia Ross. Several smaller schools were running in other parts of the city.

In the neighborhood of Broadway and 10[th Street], the people got together with H. Scull, Henry Ballinger, Oliver Perry, R.A. Scull, and others and built a schoolhouse on J between 9th and 10th streets. Mrs. Patterson taught there from 1878 till the building and opening of the present system of schools [in] 1882."

Education: Our Journey

Public schools for African Americans were opened in Galveston in 1881 and reorganized a year later.

"Miss Barber married Mr. Cuney. Mrs. Patterson, Miss Gertrude Potts, Miss Virginia continued with the new order of schools.

The September of 1882 found two colored schools in operation -the East District - F.H. Mabson, principal, J.R. Gibson, Mrs. Patterson, Miss Potts, Miss V. Ross, Mrs. Patterson's niece, Annie Ashe. West District [at] Ave. M near 29[th:] F.J. Wall, principal, W.N. Cummings, W.D. Donnell, Miss Fannie Harding, Miss Sadie Patton, and W.A.L. Campbell who I should have stated -- had been teaching a school at 25[th street] between Ave I and J ? see further.

There has not been many changes in the teaching force of the Galveston schools except by deaths and marriages."

The Freedman's Bureau recognized Black marriages in 1869, but they were not legalized in Texas at that time. This may be why so many teachers who came to Galveston before 1900 never married, unaware when this ban was lifted, if it ever actually was.

My grandfather, who was hired in 1883, and his sister, Clara E. Scull, who was hired shortly afterward, were at that time the only African American teachers in the island's public schools who had been raised in Galveston.

Island of Color

Clara Scull

Most of the African American teachers came from other locations, remaining on the island for many years. As my grandfather noted, there was little faculty turnover except due to marriage and death. Such losses included faculty members claimed by Galveston's storm of 1900:

"At the death of Mr. Webb about 1896, Donnell became principal of West District School, where he served until September 8, 1900 when he was drowned in the great storm. ... In the 1900 Storm, East District School

Education: Our Journey

was destroyed and Misses Ada Rowe, Florence Holmes, E.W. McDade, Hattie Rowe, Mr. W.D. Donnell and wife, Mrs. Evelyn Whitteby Donnell were drowned."

Near the end of his manuscript, Papa provided further details on Central High, East District and West District schools. When I was growing up, these were all of the public schools for our people. We had no junior high school, no eighth grade. The East and West District elementary schools offered the first seven grades – we used a high and low grade system -- and then we entered Central High's four grades.

In my day, the high seventh grade was in an annex across the street from Central High School -- between 27th and 28th streets, from Avenue M to Avenue N, right on the southwest corner of 27th and M – where Courville Stadium is now.

Booker T. Washington

Both elementary schools, later named Booker T. Washington and George W. Carver by 1939, sent students to the High Seventh Grade Annex, where they were first taught by more than one teacher. After the

Island of Color

high seventh, we went directly to Central High School, on Avenue M between 26th and 27th streets.

My grandfather notes the creation of the first high school for African Americans in Texas:

"CENTRAL HIGH SCHOOL

The first high school began in the Fall of 1887 at Avenue L and Sixteenth Streets with C.J. Waring as principal, who had four other teachers with him -[including] W.A.L. Campbell [and] Miss Bell Love.

Old Central

This school was later moved to Ave. N and Fifteenth in a place used by the white East End School which had previously been used as a soldiers' barracks.

At the close of 1889, C.J. Waring went to Chicago, and Gibson became principal of Central High School. In the [meantime], N.W. Cuney

Education: Our Journey

got busy with the power in control of the schools and the Brick building for Central High was created on Ave. M and Twenty-sixth Streets."

Principal J.R. Gibson & Teachers

Papa's writings allude to the political effort behind the school's creation. (Cuney, who taught in the island's African American schools, later served as collector of U.S. Customs at Galveston.) He further details the facilities that were made available to African American students:

"WEST DISTRICT SCHOOL

At the organization of the schools in 1882, Mr. F.J. Webb was made principal of the West District School, assisted by Messrs. W.N. Cummings, W.D. Donnell, W.A.L. Campbell, Misses F.O. Harding, Sadie Patton. ...

Island of Color

West District Faculty

The West District was taught in a two story brick building on Avenue M near 29th Street, that contained six rooms. ...

About 1888 several classes from this West School were moved to M ½ and 35th streets to some small buildings made vacant by white pupils. Later on the large frame building used up to 1932 was built, and all W. District pupils moved to the 35th street school. ...

The storm of 1900 drowned W.D. Donnell and damaged Central School, so both Gibson of the high school and Cummings of the East District doubled up at West District the Fall of 1900. In the Fall of 1901, a house at Avenue M ½ and 13th St. was rented for East District School and three teachers and four grades were placed there.

Misses Sims, Huff, and R.A. Scull remained there one year till the East District School of four rooms was built ... when H.T. Davis was principal with Misses Harris, Huff, and R.A. Scull as teachers."

Education: Our Journey

H.T. Davis, R.A. Scull, Jeanie Mabson, & 2 unidentified ladies

The information recorded by my grandfather precedes the Galveston public schools' oldest records, which date to 1880. After that point, school records as well as city information archived at Rosenberg Library are largely in concordance with his account. I am grateful for the kind assistance of the Galveston school district's longtime secretary, Mrs. Veronica Paul, in accessing the original minutes of the school board for the island's public schools. It is my hope that these records will be preserved on microfilm or with other technology before natural deterioration makes them useless.

Reviewing in those minutes the establishment of separate public school systems in 1881 for the whites and African Americans of Galveston reveals a familiar story that would be laughable if not so very true, a story that is in fact heartbreakingly pathetic. As was happening all over the South, white people in Galveston could not pay those of their own race or those of the colored race what they deserved to earn as educators – the salary for principals was $80 a month; teachers earned from $40 to $70 a month -- because of the costs of a dual system of education.

Faculty West District Elem.

If they had not had to build two of everything necessary and pay two sets of salaries, the city might have fared much better. Certainly, the students could have been afforded a better education.

Of course, the city never completely provided two of everything. Often when there were not enough leftovers for the colored – leftover buildings, leftover books – colored students just had to do without.

Like everyone else of my generation and those before me, I well remember those leftovers, such as the worn books we received on the first day of each school year. Well aware that we never received anything new,

Education: Our Journey

we seemingly took it in stride, like the last children in a large family of modest means who know that they will seldom if ever have new clothes.

Sometimes there was still writing in the books from the last white child who had defaced them, and we read of their social lives, likes and dislikes. African Americans have always known more about Anglos than they knew about us. We were supposed to be invisible. But it really didn't work like that in Galveston for long, because we eventually made our presence known by the excellence we created. In our community, in addition to enjoying church outings and lavish public activities of all kinds, we held school parades and games to which the other race came in large numbers because they were truly spectacular. We were in our own world, hardly caring what the other folk did. Thank God for competent, resourceful leaders, who transformed meager means into splendid results. A school board minutes excerpt dated March 2, 1883, notes such means:

"The petition of Horace Scull for the loan of ten or twelve of the old benches in the yard of Broadway School was read and loan granted, subject to the order of the Board, upon his giving a proper receipt to the Secretary. It was moved and carried that the Committee on School Property be authorized to have the old cistern on Avenue M1/2 and 35th street repaired, and put up at Avenue L and 31st St. school."

We received what we could beg and plead for -- with the proper documentation, when it could be spared. But not new equipment; just what was not used or needed by the white schools at the time. Galveston was considered "good" to its colored folk. (And some of our people talk about not needing affirmative action.)

School board minutes from 1885 note appropriation of facilities funding -- $20 to $30 to rent rooms for the "East Colored School" – and funding for educator salaries. I appreciate an entry listing newly hired African American teachers with the titles of "Miss" and "Mr.", which was not often the case where my people were concerned. But the greater surprise here is that the amount funded to pay a new colored principal was the same as the sum for the whites: 80 dollars a month.

In those days, you could get a day's groceries for about a dollar. From that time to the era in which I taught, increases in the Galveston area of the cost of living and salaries for educators were both restrained. Even half a century later, I could buy a loaf of bread for a nickel, milk for about fifteen cents, vegetables for a quarter, a pound of shrimp on the wharf for a quarter, and so on. And in 1948, my starting teacher's salary in Bay City was about 80 dollars a month.

Interestingly, the payroll listing colored teachers for November 1887 shows that regular teachers were docked about $10 a day when they were absent, although substitute teachers were paid only $2 a day. It seems that in these days preceding provision for sick leave, they had better not have gotten sick, or they could not pay their bills.

Still, the teachers in our small, tight-knit community served long, and their names are dear, an integral part of our history. Faculty members listed in 1887 are Mr. J.R. Gibson, Miss Fanny Harding, Mr. W.N. Cummings, Mr. Joseph Cuney, Miss G.A. Ballinger, Miss Alice Dunn, Miss M.I. Daniels, Mr. F.J. Webb, Mr. George Hamilton, Mr. R.A. Scull, Mr. C.M. Nichols, Miss Florence Holmes, Miss A.E. Floyd, Mr. C.J. Waring, Mr. W.A.L. Campbell, Miss Clara Scull, Miss J.A. Patterson, Miss Eva M. Webb and Rev. S.H. Burford. Listed substitute teachers are Miss Anna Howard, Lucy Campbell, Grace Carnes, Virgie Sanford, Lillian

Education: Our Journey

Mitchell, Sarah Campbell, Mrs. M. Germain, Miss Levy Jenkins, Laura Williams, Minifee Daniels, Georgia Ennis and Ada M. Rowe.

West District Faculty #2

Road From Segregation To Integration

Other information on the public education of blacks in Galveston was compiled and organized by Leon A. Morgan, who had once planned a book like this one. He and Mr. Bert Armstead, who researched our people's church heritage, both died before they could complete their work. Morgan notes that the need to educate the newly freed children of color prompted organization of an organized system for the white race as well.

Morgan states, "Efforts to establish public schools in Galveston began as early as 1838, but no matter who tackled the job, the end results proved disappointing, in instance after instance. ... "The people were often disheartened about their schools, both private and public. In 1868, one of the recurrent epidemics of yellow fever evidently put an end to the brave start at public schools which had been made in 1865-66. The first really effective Public Schools for Black children were opened on November 1, 1881, in rented buildings." For the Barnes Institute and the East Broadway Colored School, "the rentals were $22.50 and $20.00 per month respectively."

"Colonel W.H. Sinclair, board member in 1881, when considering a Black [or] White person for a principalship expressed one point of view when he said: 'A competent person should be assigned principal regardless of color.' The entire board further expressed their desires for quality education for Blacks when they authorized the superintendent on October 15, 1881 to give notice that they would select the teachers for the Colored schools without regard to color. On the other hand, the idea of segregated schools still existed on the Board. The president expressed it when he said during the October 15th meeting... 'I am in favor of putting colored teachers in colored schools.' All Black teachers were employed for the two schools for Blacks."

In view of my own experiences in Galveston, I am of mixed emotion at these statements. On the one hand, I am very proud that a board of Southern White men had sense enough to see the need for quality education in the days when our people were just out of slavery, that they were willing for teachers of both races to be used in our schools. On the other hand, I am so very glad that all of our teachers were Black, since they knew more of what their people felt and needed than those of any other race could possibly have known.

Yes, I supported and still support full and equal integration, with quality teachers. However, when African American children are taught by immature and uninterested teachers who, coming from a different culture,

Education: Our Journey

are often unaware of our children's needs, I prefer the old segregated system, which allowed only teachers of color.

Sure, we want equal facilities and supplies, and equal opportunities, but we lost the caring manner, the honest criticism, the push to excel, and the direct contact with the home, that we had with high-quality African American teachers. They did not just relate to their students, they felt their pain.

Surely, there have been unethical misfits of our own race who have taught and will teach our children, and those unscrupulous principals who have wielded unnatural control over their staff because officials outside the race chose not to interfere. They remain an argument for integration.

And I by no means ignore the wonderful teachers of all other races who do their level best every day to reach one and teach one, as the saying goes. I have worked with fine dedicated teachers of other races who made me proud to call them co-workers, some I still count among my cherished friends.

But I maintain that the struggles of our race continue with those teachers who do not care whether the poorer, disadvantaged students learn or not, as long as they get a paycheck and cherished time off. The debate as to which was better, integration or segregation, rages on, behind closed doors.

Regardless, our schools before desegregation reflected the pride of the community. Our proudest educational institution was Central High School. Morgan detailed its creation:

"In the year 1885, when the children had reached the sixth and seventh grades and showed by their inclination a strong desire to go further in the line of study, they were permitted to enter the 16th and Avenue L School - Central Colored School, later to be called Central High School.

Champion J. Waring of Dartmouth College, who had been elected as a teacher on October 4, 1883, was designated principal ... and held the position until he was dismissed in October 1888. Waring was succeeded by John R. Gibson, a native of Ohio and a graduate of Wilberforce University in that state.

The Central High School and grades 6,7 and 8 occupied a structure at 15th Street and Avenue N from 1889 to 1893. The next momentous step was taken when real estate was purchased for a permanent location. Lots at the corner of 26th street and Avenue M were sold to the school district by J.L. Boddeker, Vincent Ceaccio, Nora Craver, and Nona Smith and a two-story brick building was erected at a cost of $13,500.00 by contractor Thomas McHenry from plans by Nicholas J. Clayton and company, architects.

The purpose of the high school for Black children had been spelled out quite clearly in school board deliberations as an organization for: ... 'providing higher educational opportunities for Colored in a free public school in the City of Galveston, Texas'.

An indication of the worth and esteem in which the school was held by the community as a whole came in 1904. This milestone was reached when Central High School was selected as a site for a branch of the Rosenberg Library. This took the form of cooperative action on the part of the Public School Board and the Public Library to furnish library services to students and adults of the Black population. ...

It was on January 11, 1905, that the Colored Branch of the Rosenberg Library actually opened. It is said in the Handbook of Texas that this was the first of its kind in the United States. The one-story structure for housing the branch was attached to the Central High Building at a construction cost of $6,000.00, financed by the Rosenberg Library

Education: Our Journey

Association. A generation later, the Rosenberg Library was to report in its 'Negro Branch' a collection of 4,303 volumes, and 210 registered borrowers.

(Morgan also noted the high school's damage "in the great 1900 hurricane and tidal wave." His is the only written comment I have seen that bears out my mother's observation to me years ago that a great wave accompanied the storm. She said that as a 12-year-old girl, at her home near the water's edge on that fateful day, she looked up and saw a huge wave rolling toward them. Her father called to her to come right away; they were leaving for shelter immediately. The sky wasn't even fully cloudy, she recalled. And she never forgot the awesome sight of the wave.)

Morgan goes on to describe the grade raising of Central. He notes that the building constructed to house the new addition to the school and the one-story library is the only part of the old Central that stands today -- the Old Central Cultural Center, on whose board I sit.

Old Central Cultural Center

But the rooms of my high school days are those in my fondest memories. The mighty Bearcat Band, directed by "FESS" Huff, practiced on the stage that is still there, although renovated. I had chemistry class under the brilliant Mr. Hall "just call me Hell" Dansby in the upper corner room of the building facing Avenue M. And my sweet Latin teacher, Mrs. Jessie McGuire Dent, taught me in one of the rooms facing east upstairs.

As we walked down the upstairs hall, we could see the basketball games being practiced down in the gym, and much social action happened in those halls. Around the corner was Mrs. Martha Cort Jones' room, and although she was my mother's best friend and a familiar sight to me, I still followed the stern decorum enforced in the area around her English classroom. Not to mention Miss Eloise Sterling's math class at the other end of the hall; it was businesslike, with no horseplay by the fellows in that area either.

Morgan spells out the exact purposes of the new addition to Central:

"The 1924 additions and improvements to the Central High School were quite extensive. They included facilities for two well-equipped Science laboratories, a homemaking laboratory, a Gymnasium-Auditorium, four additional classrooms, lavatories for boys and girls, teacher lounges, an administrative suite, and a spacious library. The school board handled this in a package with changes in the building housing San Jacinto at a cost of $164,671.58. The contractor was M.W. Bowden of Galveston, Texas.

The quality of the Central High School program was somewhat enhanced by the fact that in 1926 the school was accredited by the State of Texas. Such action permitted graduates to enter colleges in this State without taking examinations to prove eligibility. It was in 1933 that Central

Education: Our Journey

became affiliated with the Southern Association of Secondary Schools and Colleges (a regional accreditating agency).

In all the schools for Black children, ...1940, Music, Health, and Physical Education were added [to the curriculum]. At this time, Homemaking and Industrial Arts were added to the high school program."

Although Morgan, who came to Galveston in the latter '30s, is probably correct about the curriculum becoming official then, we had competent teachers in the schools teaching us music, health and physical education well before 1940.

As Central grew, the architect Nicholas Clayton was brought to the foreground of our history for its replacement. It is sad that this classic building could not have been preserved by the shortsighted board of education in those days. We have only pictures, but I well remember going to classes in old Central. New buildings are good, but proper use of such an architectural treasure could have been so important to a sense of community pride and cultural advancement.

Morgan continues: "In recognition of the need for upgrading facilities, Central High School was given a new campus and new school plant in 1954. Three square blocks were purchased from 30th to 33rd Street between Avenue H and Avenue I, and a new 133,379 square foot building was constructed. The school's address was listed officially as 3014 Avenue I. It was provided with an auditorium seating 1,000 and a gymnasium seating 1,000. The cafeteria seated 400 at one sitting."

Central High School was a member of the Colored Interscholastic League of Texas, and won many awards in the competitions of the League, especially in Band competitions, and Sports, as well as in academic activities. The school placed much emphasis on social and civic responsibility, and as a result of this emphasis received a major award by the Freedom Foundation in 1955, as well as an award from the Industrial Education Conference of Prairie View A&M [University] in 1966. More than 40, 125 students attended the Central High School during the years 1885 - 1967 and there were 7, 529 graduates. In the community many of these students have provided outstanding leadership and fellowship.

Central High School as an institution ceased to exist in 1968, when its students were merged with the Ball Senior High School in order to achieve complete integration of the public schools in the City of Galveston. As an institution Central High School no longer exists, but in the minds of many people it will always remain as an emblem of pride and achievement."

Shortly before Central's merger with Ball, the prevailing perception in Galveston's Black community had been that administrators planned to move Central north of Broadway, and west of 25th Street, to "keep us all in one place, in case of integration." The housing projects were already over there, and the alleged motive was to school all the Black people there, in case of school zoning. But for the racially backward people in power, the courts were the reckoning force, mandating full integration.

The main mistake they made was failing to keep the name of Central in the new integrated high school, even in hyphenated fashion. Many persons of color, and some who were not, were very dismayed at the prospect of losing all of our traditions. We were absorbed, not integrated. To have the first high school for our race in the state of Texas be simply ignored was more than most of us have been willing to swallow.

Education: Our Journey

Violence over the snub was avoided by overt manipulation, including moving Dr. Morgan from the position of principal of the high school to a position in administration. He was replaced by James Sweatt, who succumbed to many demands for compromise.

Such demands ranged from the material to the symbolic. I recall when the Central High School Glee Club, under the direction of Mrs. Rose Mary McKinnis, was forbidden to sing a selection for graduation in the last year of Central High. It was a selection I wrote for the occasion, *Metamorphosis*, about the developmental change we were all going through, to emerge better and bigger. Because of misconceptions, after Mrs. McKinnis and I had taught the work to the enthusiastic students, Mrs. McKinnis was told to scrap it. Even the students cried.

Members of the African American community organized to maintain the proud history of Central. On October 23, 1973, the board of directors for the Old Central Cultural Center received its state certificate of incorporation. Morgan was the board's executive director and the president was Mr. Robert Hoskins. Members were Mrs. Lucile Alexander, Ms. Gloria Haywood, Mr. Bert Armstead, Mr. Theasel Henderson, Mrs. Helen Ayachi, Mr. Gerald Hoskins, Mrs. V.J. Beninati, Mr. Lucius Humphrey Jr., Ms. Rose M. Bennett, Mrs. Howard Krantz, Mr. Peter Brink, Ms. Eula Lyles, Mr. John H. Clouser, Mrs. Robert McClintock, Mr. Thomas H. Dent, Mr. A.W. McDonald, Mrs. Vera Dever, Rev. R.E. McKeen, Mrs. Gloria Ellisor, Mrs. Lucy Ramirez, Mrs. Rose Forcey, Ms. June P. Ross, Mrs. Reita Fugger, Rev. James Thomas, Mr. William Harris and Mrs. Susan L. Walsh. In the years after integration, their mission was to prevent the loss of our people's history. But integration still had its emotional costs. The process was very painful because of the ignorance of those who were in control of it in Galveston, particularly at the high school level.

Before and after integration, administrators have had the opportunity to effect both harm and good in educating Galveston's African Americans.

Morgan paid tribute to the African American administrators who served in the segregated system, noting that there had been too many dedicated and prepared Black teachers to list in his document. Administrators for the Barnes Institute/West District and George W. Carver were:

F.J. Webb, 1881 – 1894; G.W. Hamilton, 1894 – 1897; W.D. Donnell, 1897 – 1901; W.N. Cummings, 1901 – 1927; T.H. Love, 1927 – 1932; H.T. Davis, 1932 – 1940; L.A. Morgan, 1940; T.H. Warren, 1940 – 1968; and C.W. Moore, 1968.

He also listed principals serving the East Broadway Colored School/East District and Booker T. Washington Elementary; the first named was White; the others were African-American:

W.F. Missplay , 1881; Jennie Patterson, 1882 – 1884; F.H. Mabson, 1884 – 1887; J.R. Gibson, 1887; Joseph Cuney, 1888; W.N. Cummings, 1889 – 1902; R.A. Scull, 1902; H.T. Davis, 1903 – 1932; T.H. Love, 1932 – 1934; T.H. Warren, 1934 – 1940; R.F. Sterling, 1941 – 1957; C. Harris, 1957 – 1970; and E. Clay, 1970.

In listing African American administrators after integration, Morgan included those that led Galveston's junior highs and middle schools, noting also that Galveston phased out its junior high schools in the years that followed integration: "School building occupancies and principalships have changed somewhat since racial integration. The Sam Houston Junior High School which had been built for Black students in 1965 became a part of the Ball Senior High School complex in 1968, the

Education: Our Journey

Central High School became the Central Middle School and the old Goliad became an elementary school again.

J.L. Sweatt, Jr. became principal of Goliad Elementary School in 1966, where he remained until he was transferred to Central High School in 1967. C.W. Moore became principal of the Goliad School in 1967, but was transferred to the Carver Elementary School in 1968, and J.L. Sweatt, Jr. returned to the Goliad Elementary School and remained there until he retired in 1973.

Edgar Collins became principal of the Goliad Elementary School in August, 1973, and remained until November, 1973, when he was transferred to the Guidance Center. Jewel Earles Banks became principal of Goliad Elementary School in November, 1973, and remains there, as of 1976."

Mrs. Banks, my dear friend, was the first African American woman in this century to become a principal in Galveston. She was principal at Goliad until the new L. A. Morgan Elementary School was built. She became its first principal, and stayed there until transferred to San Jacinto, where she remained until her health gave out. She retired shortly before she passed away.

LA Morgan School

Island of Color

"The first principal of the Goliad Junior High School was R.F. Sterling in 1957. He was principal of the Sam Houston Junior High School and the Central Middle School until 1968, when he was moved to Central Administration [the Administration building]. At this time, F.W. Windom became principal of the Central Middle School where he remained until 1972, when he was moved to the Administration building and R.F. Sterling was returned to the principalship of the Central Middle School. Mr. Sterling retired in June, 1975, and was succeeded by McKinley Davis, who remains there in 1976."

Mr. McKinley Davis remained as principal of Central Middle School until the mid-1980s. He retired, came out of retirement to head the Alternative School, and retired again in the mid-1990s.

As for other African Americans who have served Galveston schools as administrators, no African American has been principal of Ball High School since it was integrated, but there have been some African-American assistant principals, such as Reginald Pope, Tommie Dell Boudreaux and Ennis Williams.

Before retirement, Mrs. Boudreaux held head principalships at Austin Middle School and Weis Middle School, returning to Austin as principal. Other principals since Morgan's writing have been Elbert Clay; Dr. Patricia Williams (Rosenberg Elementary School), then administrative personnel director, and curriculum director, now personnel director of GISD; Barbara McIlveen (L.A. Morgan), Connie Herbert, Errol Garrett, Agnes Barefield, Barbara Myles, Dr. Zachary, Harriet Fields, and the hardest-working assistant principal the current GISD has ever known, Mr. Manuel Thomas.

Education: Our Journey

Those in administration shortly after integration made some attempt to gauge its effect on the students of those years. In addition to his records on African American educators, Morgan also contributed a study on "The Impact Of Desegregation On The Black Child: A Study of the School Year 1967-68 to 1969-70."

Conducted with Dr. Ernest S. Barrett of University of Texas Medical Branch, the study was limited to male students and offered little conclusive work. But I found it interesting, to say the least. It is presented as a "study of the Effects of Racial Integration on Academic Performance and Attitudes among high school males," in which a total of 1,268 males in grades 9 - 11 during the 1967-68 school year were tested. Compared was the achievement of two groups of academically "better" and "poorer" white students, before and after racial integration, with that of black students.

"Many studies, including the Coleman Report have indicated that there were no significant changes in the 'mean' level of performance of white students before and after racial integration." Several standardized tests were used to measure academic performance.

As for attitudes toward school, those who attended Ball High School all three years showed no appreciable change, though it is important to note that when compared with students at "a private high school," their attitudes were "poorer." Yet the attitudes of Central High School students did change significantly.

While they were still at Central High School, the students' attitudes were positive, not much different from those students in the "private high school." After they started at Ball High School, their attitudes became more negative, more like that of other students already attending Ball. Most of their written complaints were about the lack of air conditioning and proper lighting. The next most common complaint was made about teachers, with the request for better teachers with more enthusiasm for their work. Less than 5% of the students during the third year of the study wrote any complaint about racial matters.

No significant difference was noted in the achievement levels of the three groups in reading and numerical competence, or in study habits or personality traits. Ability level scores showed no big change (only a small increase in the spatial relations score for the Central High School students).

So two findings were important: The attitudes of Central High School students shifted significantly, from being positive toward Central to being negative about Ball, much like the attitude of other BHS students. And integration did not affect reading and numerical skills among any group of students during the first two years after integration.

To plan for integration at Ball and other schools in Galveston, in July 1955 Galveston's school board appointed a biracial committee with 26 members -- 17 were white, nine were Negro. The panel addressed administrators and teachers; the student population and physical facilities; comparative knowledge levels; traditions, customs, mores, health; and the athletic program. It issued a statement declaring that "...the principle of desegregation as decreed by the Supreme Court of the United States be applied to all schools and all grades in the Galveston Independent School District, commencing in September, 1956."

GISD adopted a plan of gradual integration, intended to begin in September 1957. But from 1957 to 1963, state laws required that an election on integration be held in which "only qualified voters" could cast their votes, preventing further plans by the GISD Board. It was on Jan.

Education: Our Journey

15, 1964, that minutes show the board voted that "GISD be integrated on September 1, 1964 as far as physical facilities will permit."

On the secondary level, integration was not completed for years. Although Weis Middle School was far west of most African American homes, the African American students from the housing projects were bused in to provide the right numbers for the racial quota reports. Then all the reports from Weis showed African American students as inferior to the other students. Of course, nothing had been done to equalize educational levels, other than giving the same homework and expecting the same results.

Central had become a junior high, then a middle school, and was moved north of Broadway, west of 25th Street, to a predominantly African American neighborhood, effectively segregated by location. No students were bused into Central until the district, seeking a separate campus for the city's eighth-graders, sent all of them there. Central later became a middle school again, with 6th, 7th and 8th grades, and mostly Black students attending.

Out east, Stephen F. Austin, where I taught for 19 years, began as a junior high but has frequently shifted levels among the sixth through ninth grades; Weis went through similar changes. After integration, Austin, which began with Anglo and Hispanic students, grew to become evenly divided among Anglo, Hispanic and African American students, and its demographics continued to steadily change. Before I left in 1984, it had became half African American, 1/4 Hispanic, and 1/4 Anglo and Asian.

Although Alamo, Burnet, Bolivar, Morgan, Rosenberg, San Jacinto, Scott, Parker, and Oppe Elementary Schools remain, Travis and Goliad are gone. Lovenberg Junior High is no more, and Ball High is the only public high school remaining. And at Ball, what was once a graduating class of about 650 fell at one time to only 300-plus, due to ongoing dropout problems, but it now averages under 500.

To the credit of all personnel there, there has never been an outstanding student racial problem at Ball High; its sometimes poor reputation elsewhere is only hearsay. As much credit should go to the traditionally African American security staff as to the multiracial teaching and professional staff; the security guards protect the students from themselves as well as each other, going above and beyond the call of duty to guide students out of trouble, counsel them and occasionally play nursemaid or boxing partner.

We have had 40 years or so to get this integration act together in Galveston, and it is not right yet. But it has been a lot smoother here than in many Texas locations, simply because of past amenable associations and alignments. Notice I did not use the word "friendships," because some of these alignments were forged out of necessity. But there have also been real friendships, which are crucial to a state of ease in any situation. As we laughingly say, "Some of my best friends are ..."

Nevertheless, many of my friends in adulthood of other races far surpass the friends I had of other races as a child. Because Galveston has such diversity on this small island, partially due to the medical complex, and largely to the island's role as a deep water port, we have learned to exist closely and profit from each other for a long time.

Education: Our Journey

...

My Conversation with Charles McCullough
On Radio Station KGBC, February 19, 1991

This man, a Caucasian, had written a very nice guest column for the newspaper having to do with race relations and the history of our people, African Americans. I called to congratulate and thank him, and he invited me to be a guest on his radio show. A partial transcript of the show with comment follows:

"This is Black History Month and none other than Izola Collins, one of our finest community leaders, is here to join us and talk about what that means to all Galvestonians and Americans. And, Izola, thank you for taking the time to come out."

"Thank you for inviting me," I said.

"Izola, why was February originally instituted as Black History Month? Why the month of February?"

I told him that every month should be regarded as Black History Month until we have no need of a special time to celebrate the history of any people of America. But, I told him, since February is the month of the great presidents' birthdays, and a special time for love as the month of Valentine's Day, it is appropriate to have that month for brotherhood and learning to love others.

He asked, "Mrs. Collins, I guess role models, heroes are needed; is this a need more now than before?"

I talked about Black men being threatened -- the history of abuse in slavery and abuse after slavery -- and the demeaning of Black men in their own families as well as by other people. He asked, "One in four are

Island of Color

in prison – why? Is there a loss of identity? Where are whites missing this in understanding?" I replied, "Many think problems are on the streets. Not so; it's in the boardrooms where decisions are made affecting us all."

He then stated that white men are blamed for all ills, and asked, does that excuse reverse racism? I replied that African Americans did not come here by choice; some did come as indentured servants, but most did not. History does not fully show their contribution to the nation's welfare and achievement.

Is that racism? he asked. He mentioned TV shows that perpetuate stereotypes. And he asked, is white racism always to blame for all misunderstandings?

The term *race* itself bears a story that people your age and even older don't always know, I said. What makes you a certain race? Miscegenation laws perpetuated what was once enforced as slave mentality. And today racism takes many forms.

He asked about terminology. "Why are you called so many different designations? Why African Americans? Why not just Americans? Why so many different names over the years?"

I was just "chomping at the bit" to talk about this point, because it is a pet peeve of mine, and one I am always ready to argue, discuss, fuss and tear open with just about anyone who will venture into these waters.

The changing of titles came from misuse of them in the print media as well as by the oppressors themselves. This applies to the gamut of names, from the word "colored" through "coloured"; "Negro", purposely mispronounced until it was brutally misused, and spelled with lowercase "n" rather than given the distinction of a proper name; "Black," embraced by all except those who insisted on using lowercase "b," and those who had little dark pigment in their skins and so could not really relate to this category. And so on.

Why all the derogatory designations? We are all Americans. The need for separate identifications came from slave owners' misuse of our American title. They are the ones who made it law that any person with even a drop of African blood would receive one of the above titles denoting racial separation.

In proud defense of self, and in a bit of backlash, persons of color writing in their own print media decided that anyone not proud to be so designated would be considered a traitor to the race. I have always thought that people who make acceptance of slave identification a loyalty test are akin to our Gulf crabs who, once placed in a pot, violently pull down any crab who tries to get out of the boiling water.

I explained on the air that what you are called really depends on what part of the world you are in. Many of us have several categories of blood in our veins, and have had the experience of being called different names by different people. In Acapulco, Mexico, my friend and I were considered Mexican by one of the native women there, who walked up to us and asked us something in Spanish that had both of us replying,"Huh?"

Once at a Texas timeshare resort, while working on this very book, I took part in a water aerobics class, and was uncharacteristically very quiet. This was only because I was preoccupied, didn't know any of the women in the class, and really wanted to learn the movements to get the benefit of the exercise. One lady in the class asked me curiously, after I had been quietly following instructions for two days, "Habla espanol?"

I thought she was addressing someone else. Frowning, I heard her say, "Or do you speak English?" I mumbled, "English," as I tried to catch

Island of Color

up mentally to where I was supposed to be. As full realization hit me, I wanted to laugh out loud. Of course, I didn't, since I would have seemed to be making fun of her. These ladies all knew each other --. all were Caucasian, and from the resort area -- and she was trying to be friendly.

Because I have lived in this area all of my life, and been categorized under one of the titles above by all the people I meet, I was exuberant at being visible and still uncategorized. (Although, if I had answered her in Spanish, she probably would have classified me as Hispanic.) In a sense, I had finally found freedom. Freedom to be whoever I wanted to be!

Mentally laughing at myself as I left, I thanked God that I have always been free to be whomever I wanted to be. We all are as spiritually free as we wish to be, and as free as we let our education in life's classroom make us.

Another incident happened to me years ago, as I was driving some children in my sixth- grade choir class home after rehearsal at school. It was late afternoon, and five or six of these young ones had no transportation home. As I drove silently, tired of talking, I listened to their conversation. I had a pretty good reputation with this bunch. Our class operated without racial reference, and we had won the respect of the musical world, with our trophies to prove it. In the class were Anglo, Afro, Asian, Hispanic children.

As one comment was made about an African American entertainer on TV, I interjected my opinion, using the pronoun "we." Because my skin is light brown, I was shocked to hear one of the Anglo children in the car ask me seriously: "Are you Black, Ms. Collins?" This being the accepted term that year, I laughed and replied, "Sure -- what did you think I was?"

The answer came back slowly: "I dunno."

69

Education: Our Journey

That was probably one of my proudest moments socially. They had not thought about it, because it never was necessary to identify me in that way. I was just their teacher, director. Amen.

I have digressed long enough.

After I briefly explained my position on the radio, the station took a news break. When we came back on the air, McCullough asked about my personal background. I told him about Papa, and Papa's journal dating back to 1865. We talked about the lack of instruction in the history of my people, to people of all colors. My history knowledge came, I told him, from association, as well as college classes.

McCullough asked why Galveston was spared the evils of most of the South. "How did Galveston escape Deep South mentality?"

I told him that as a port, a harbor for so many races and nationalities, Galveston was more like the rest of the world – its residents were not so narrow in their perception of other people. We talked of the neighborhoods that had never been segregated, and how many places were so hate-filled because of their isolated beliefs, fears, and prejudices.

McCullough asked, "What was it like here in the '60s?"

I gave the example of the city of Atlanta, so different from the rest of the state of Georgia. Traveling with the all-girls orchestra in 1945, I had been so aware of the poverty and pitiful look of Georgia as we drove through to Atlanta. Once we were there, the city was like an oasis -- like Las Vegas in the middle of a hot, summer Nevada day.

I told him that education was the answer. Education made Atlanta stand up away from Georgia. And education, as well as the geographical reality of the waters that separate us from the mainland, made Galveston

Island of Color

stand away from the rest of Texas -- formal, informal and practical education.

McCullough talked about how people once had to turn to the library to find truths about Black people, to discover that many famous figures of the past were dark-skinned, "Negroid in appearance. No mistaking, these people were <u>not</u> Caucasian."

Appreciating this White man who knew truth, and wasn't afraid to share it, I noted that the books available in the past had been written by people with their own prejudices, their own limitations, but that the situation is improving, with education improving people's perceptions. I noted that most white people are not racists, but just don't know about black people, and they absorb wrong impressions.

McCullough asked, "What was the goal of the civil rights movement? Was it the end of segregation?" With the problems of integration, "would Martin Luther King, seeing today's results, still have gone to all that trouble?"

"Separate but equal was the problem," I answered. "Separate is never equal. I know what we lost -- but I know what we gained. I still think it was a necessary step to where we want to go."

I told him what statistics reflect about life for Black men, that there are more economic than social problems today.

McCullough was not finished with controversy. "Asians face the same problems as Black people, but they still succeed. Why?"

Not through educating, I explained that many factors do not allow comparison. First of all, Asians who come to our shores were not forced to come here. They come with the desire to get ahead, be somebody, succeed in the new world. They come motivated to improve upon their past situations, ready to make any sacrifices to conform to the world to which they come.

Often Asians have already become professionals -- doctors, businesspeople -- in their own country, but seek another setting, mostly for financial reasons. They represent the "cream of the crop" of their country, not those of borderline intelligence or slow thinkers. And they already know what to expect, because they have learned about our language, customs, environment before deciding to make the trip. They are also free to return whenever they wish, to the culture to which they are accustomed. And Asians often have the support of a tight family network – unlike Blacks who as slaves were often separated from their families.

Motivated, educated, prepared and supported, it is no wonder that they advance over the average Americans who grew up here and take for granted what is available.

There are many reasons for lack of success. Some have to be recognized as our own fault. Others cannot.

"Are whites deprived of understanding from their own history?" McCullough asked. I said that they too have a poor history education. But I disagree that they are deprived. No, if they want to understand more, they can.

McCullough then asked why Black boys start out as enthusiastic students in the first grade, and later "shut down" by the fourth grade.

Most boys have the problem of feeling claustrophobic in a classroom atmosphere, I said. But racial implications also exist for boys of color. A teacher can cause a child to feel inferior in ways beyond spoken words. "Good" behavior, as deemed by the teacher, is rewarded. "Bad" behavior – outspoken, extroverted behavior that is valued differently in the

Black culture -- is punished. Isolated and excluded from various activities, left out of small classroom rewards, the male child of color learns to retreat, compensate in other ways. He doesn't fit in, he soon learns, and acts out his frustrations.

"Only a Black man can teach a Black boy properly, some say. Why?" McCullough asks.

As a role model, I told him. "Before you can be a racist, you have to be prejudiced, prejudge by what you're accustomed to, or not accustomed to. Some Anglo teachers don't mean to be, but give out racist signals in their normal behavior."

"What do we do about this now?"

"These boys have to have some goals given to them, both directly and indirectly, in their home environment/daily surroundings."

I wanted to elaborate on how they just need to be appreciated, respected, and given the expectation that they will succeed in life.

McCullough asked about the problem of drug abuse.

My reply: "Simple but complex solution. Cut it off at the source." I am aware of what all the law enforcement community knows and cannot enforce: The drug problem is a money problem. Top elected officials and top government leaders are captive to the fact that big money is made at the expense of the poor hooked guy on the street. At any given moment, the drug traffic could be stopped, wiped out. It would kill the economy of our land, but the moral decay can and will be stopped when it becomes expedient to do so.

Since that doesn't seem about to happen, educate children so they won't become victims. Dry up the demand, and you at least slow down the supply.

Education: Our Journey

McCullough brought up Louis Farrakhan, and how he does so many good things, but says so many harsh things. Seeking agreement from me – but not getting it -- that our people blame whites for all their problems, McCullough then shifted gears and asked me, "When do you see the first Black person being elected president (of the United States)?"

I spoke of encountering Barbara Jordan once in 1971 in Houston, and that, although the official reason given for her not seeking presidential office was her "health," I think more than that discouraged her and kept her out of the picture.

McCullough mentioned that Jesse Jackson is viewed cynically by Blacks as well as Whites, and asked me to identify what candidates could come from the Black race.

I told him, very truthfully, that leaders could come from anywhere. That we're not just preachers and teachers anymore. That a new leader wouldn't have to start out in the political arena at all.

McCullough asked, "Do you think some leaders have already been 'Black'? We just don't know they had 'black' blood?" I laughed out loud, and said I had no idea, but it brought out my original point: What difference does it make, anyway? I added, "Isn't it still true that it matters what you know and how effective you are -- not who you are?"

This closed out the interview. He thanked me for coming on the show, and I thanked him heartily for having invited me, for having given me a voice to tell the public the truth that I know.

CHAPTER FIVE
EDUCATION: OUR LANDMARKS

In the early years of Galveston school integration, well before the political struggle was resolved, my husband and I decided to send our firstborn child to Rosenberg Elementary School, which became the island's first fully integrated elementary school. Born in 1954, the year that segregation was outlawed in public schools, June Viola Collins became a pioneer in the fight for equal education in Galveston by attending Rosenberg's first grade.

(Integration officially began with voluntary high school enrollment at Ball High, and then in first grade at Rosenberg Elementary.)

I was a foremost advocate for integration, and we did not have the violence then that is so possible now, but my husband and I weren't sure that we were playing it safe with our first child. I dressed my daughter in her color-coordinated finest clothing, and took her to school quite early that first day. As we registered in the school office, I began shaking. I gave my daughter a bright, happy "let's do it" smile, put my hand around her shoulder, and started the long walk down the hall to her new classroom. Before we got halfway there, a kind white face came into view from her classroom, looked at us, and said, enthusiastically, "This must be June Viola!"

I knew that this teacher, Mrs. Alice Guest, was all right. She was ready to call my daughter by name though we had never met. June was not her only Negro student, although she was one of few. For her to know

Education: Our Landmarks

and say June's name as we approached, realizing we both would need encouragement, was a blessing.

Mrs. Guest encouraged her all the way -- setting the foundation for the confidence June later showed in leadership through junior and senior high school, where June was the first African American student to do many things. June's friendships with her classmates have lasted through their recent 25th reunion, and we still keep in touch with Mrs. Guest by mail. I will never forget her as one of the unsung heroes of Galveston.

It is the personal memories like these and personal profiles that I add to the facts of the educational development of our people -- from the earliest schools to the trauma of desegregation, to the present struggle to receive equal access to the educational process.

We recall the educators -- the people who were in life and memory both the landmarks of our community.

Students' Memories

I include the accounts of over a dozen Galvestonians of diverse backgrounds; many more had stories to tell. There was consensus among them that Galveston offered a unique climate for African Americans, in which we were not ashamed of our status or apologetic. We did not need Jesse Jackson's appeal to our folk in the 1960s; we *knew* we were "somebody," and it just irritated most of us that everyone else had to figure this out. Their words give you the spirit and the warmth, the love, the tears and heartaches behind the cold facts.

Reverend Hanley Hickey

Reverend Hanley Hickey, who graduated from Central in 1931 with classmates that included Dr. Leroy Sterling, Mr. A.D. Harris, Mary Twine, Hilda Bolden Hunter, and Charleston Jenkins, is now a retired presiding elder of the 4th Episcopal District, A.M.E. Church, in Xenia,

Education: Our Landmarks

Ohio, and president for 10 years of Payne Theological Seminary. He spoke of the early years:

"Your mother taught me in the second grade ... I went to West District and Central." Recalling other educators, he said Mr. Gibson was principal, and Mrs. Gaston was his music teacher.

The white superintendent " ... would request for the students to sing 'Old Black Joe.' We'd resent that. Mrs. Gaston was our music teacher, and would play it because our principal asked her.

In one assembly, we decided we weren't going to sing it. We arranged our signals among ourselves, that on a certain count, we decided to cross our legs, right over left. On another count, left over right. He said, 'What's going on down there?' twice. When it came time to sing, we just wouldn't sing it."

We all laughed, proud of the innovative ways they compensated in his day, when there was no other recourse to express their indignation at being purposely humiliated as a race. But we did learn to look at the lighter side, laugh at our own troubles. We have thereby survived. We realize that real strength comes from forgiving and making life better than we found it. Hate destroys the hater. Forgiving love in action brings not only healing, but hope for the future, and salvation itself.

He also mentioned such teachers as the Cummings and the Mabsons.

"When the older Mabson got on the streetcar, she'd sit up front," he said. Mrs. Mabson looked very Anglo, as did many of our first professionals who were considered to be "colored," and he was recalling what was known as "passing." We talked about the wide diversity of skin colors in being "colored," and how that range began with the slaveowners' decision that one drop of Negro blood made one a Negro, a practice retained in defense by our own people though such a practice means denying all your other heritage, which is also unfair.

Recalling when he played first violin in the early orchestra that became the first school orchestra, he said, "Our rehearsal time was 7:00 at Central High, and I loved to skate. And I'd bring my violin and set [it] in the corner, and skate till they got there. I skated too long once, and Mr. Coleman took my violin inside, and gave me a good scolding. He was that type of disciplinarian ... he'd stomp his foot until they got it right! But those six violins were so beautiful -- I can hear those violins now."

We talked of many other things, but Rev. Hickey returned to his education, and the role a wood shop teacher played: "My daddy started me out doing carpenter work when I was about 12. Remember Mr. Charles Johnson teaching shop? I was good with wood. He got me a scholarship ... actually got me a scholarship to Radcliffe University in Washington. Blacks didn't go to Radcliffe. My name was Hickey, [so] they didn't know ... Black folk weren't named Hickey," he said. He didn't mention that he also looks more Anglo himself than African American.

(I spoke to Mr. Johnson too, who said he became Central's manual training (shop) instructor in March 1918; he taught on staff with my mother for a long time, and his wife and my mother had been friends since long before either had married.)

He continued, remembering help from Jessie McGuire Dent, Central's Latin teacher at the time: "I had studied Latin for four years in high school. And believe it or not, when I was in graduate school, in the University of Pittsburgh, [and] I was trying to know more Latin ... I wrote Mrs. Dent about the problem I was having, and you know she sent me two grammar books in Latin? She was a sweet person. So, I managed to pass the entrance exam, through Latin and German, to the doctoral program...."

Hickey's remarks on his experiences in a generation ahead of mine are testimony that people of color raised in Galveston were educated by superior teachers, and left the island well prepared to become professionals and compete with others, even in a segregated society.

Mrs. Evelyn Jones

I spoke also with Mrs. Evelyn Jones, another of my elders:

"I went to East District, West District, Catholic School [Holy Rosary], and Central. ... Your grandfather was at West District. I enjoyed my school years, every one of them. Mrs. Butler was my teacher at West District. ... I know two of them [who] taught me: Ms. Mabson ... when I was at West District; [and] Mr. Scull taught me.

Every morning, he'd say, 'I will lift up mine eyes unto the hills from whence cometh my help,' and he was serious! If you acted up, he'd say, 'I'll file you out of here.'

"Your mother taught me at East District. I remember Ms. Gaston at East District. She put on small plays. On Fridays, we had programs. And the football games -- it was more like families. You had rallies, then after the games we had entertainment, got together. And everybody knew all the players, out-of-town players, too. You didn't have police and all of that. The biggest thing they had [to do] was running people off the campus that didn't have no business there. They'd come by at 12:00. They didn't carry no knives or guns or stuff like that, or fighting. [It was] more of a family school.

"We had playchildren -- [in seventh grade] we'd pick a playchild. You could go to any teacher and talk to them -- you can't do that now."

She continued recalling her teachers: "I remember Ms. Cort at Central, [and] Ms. Anona Smith." Mrs. Martha Cort Jones was my mother's best friend and my sister's godmother. "And please don't forget Miss McGuire -- Mrs. Dent. She didn't teach me, but she was good! Our teachers were our friends. You could talk to them after school or anytime about anything!"

Mrs. Gertrude Elizabeth Siverand

Another elder, Mrs. Gertrude Elizabeth Siverand, born in 1899, said she came to Galveston with her parents after the 1900 storm. At West District School, her teachers were Mrs. E.B. Mabson and both Mabson daughters, Effie and Eugenia. She entered school at age 5, and she said that in the first grade, my mother, Viola Scull, taught her how to sew and cook. Other teachers she named were Addison Bridge; his wife, Mrs. O. Bridge; Ms. Smizer; Mrs. Smith; my grandfather, Ralph Scull; my aunt, Miss Clara Scull; Mr. T.H. Love; and Mrs. M.I. Daniels McCoy, whom she recalled as her sweetest teacher, who taught her in the fourth or fifth grade. Mr. Cummings was her principal; she said he had long feet.

And then she mentioned a teacher feared in her day, who was still very much feared in my day also: Mrs. Odelia Shelton. Mrs. Shelton had a reputation we both recalled the same: "They said you could hear a mouse tipping on cotton in her classroom. It was just that quiet all the time. I remember being almost afraid to breathe in there."

I laughed out loud; it was the first time I had heard that from someone much older. I remember that too, just as I recall the learning that also went on there, like the miniature village we students built in a sandbox table in her room, with many of the activities in our city represented.

Mrs. Siverand recalled the Central High principal in her day, Mr. J.R. Gibson, and his often-repeated slogan: "Study and prepare yourself, for someday, your chance will come!" He would raise his right hand and shake his forefinger at us as he said those words. Although in my day he had retired, he came back for assemblies and special occasions, and all the students would say the slogan with him, we knew it so well.

Mrs. Siverand thought of other teachers: Mrs. Hagler at West District, Love at Central, and Ms. Lola Thomas was her music teacher at Central. She said Mrs. Sadie Hathaway taught her sewing at Central, and may have also taught her children. She mentioned Eunice Victor; and said that Mr. McCoy taught her at West District.

M.I. Daniels McCoy

She thought that Mr. and Mrs. McCoy made a sweet couple; I told her how Mrs. McCoy ate dinner with us every weekday after her husband died. Interviews like this were like visiting with loved ones, as we spoke of those in our community who have passed on.

Mrs. Melinda Price

Mrs. Melinda Price was 101 years old when I interviewed her at her Hitchcock home in 1998 and still quite sharp mentally. She said she began school at age 8, in Cuero, near San Antonio. After moving to Hitchcock, "we were transferred to Central [High School] by the milk truck."

Her account pointed to our community's family-like atmosphere. "They picked the children up, along with the milk, and carried them into Galveston. And at that time, everybody loved one another, didn't they? And they took care of those children, the dairymen."

Mrs. Audrey Lee

Mrs. Lee, in her 90s, showed me a picture of her aunt, Lola Thompson, who worked as Central High School's librarian. Before moving to Chicago, her aunt apprenticed Lillian Davis to replace her; I knew Miss Davis very well, for she held the position for many years. We spoke of Addison Bridge, who taught third grade at West District, and how well he played the violin. Of Miss Annie Williams, a good friend of my mother's, who taught at West District. Of Miss Alice Antone, valedictorian in her class, who as a teacher took the time to teach advanced principles to a few of us in her senior algebra class during lunch – covering the work I faced in algebra class as a college freshman. My cousin, Fleming "Snooks" Huff, did the same thing for band students on his lunch period, teaching me some music theory before I ever got to college. God bless them!

Education: Our Landmarks

These are the things so precious to us that make Central so dear in our hearts and minds. Not just fun and rah-rah good times, but the devotion our teachers had to us, and their desire to see us learn all we could learn.

Andrew "Brother" Bess

I spoke also with "Brother" Bess, one of the kindest, humblest men I knew and a lifelong family friend. He recalled school days in Galveston: "I ... finished elementary school in Hitchcock, then came to Central. Before that time, they had to come by cross-country bus." He also recalled that elementary students were required to buy their textbooks when the school year began. He also recalled watching commencement exercises upstairs in the old Central High School as a little boy.

"I remember Class Day at Reedy Chapel. Everything was at Reedy Chapel, " he said, referring to African American community activities and ceremonies. "That's where they got their diplomas. The girls were so pretty; they looked like brides." In my mother's pictures, they wore beautiful handmade dresses of fancy, lace-trimmed material, and carried flower bouquets. Graduation was a very grand occasion.

"There used to be blue and white flowers ... oh, it was so pretty ... and they had commencements downtown, Harmony Hall ... whites and colored. But it looked like the colored kids would excel the whites, so they stopped it. Gave the orations, and they excelled the whites." There were many examples of how whites in the community did not want to acknowledge the superiority of the education received by the "colored" children as compared to that of the "white" children. Because I lived through the days of segregation, when Galveston was a leader in education,

I can offer them myself, as have others. African Americans in Galveston knew that their schools were better staffed -- with more seniority in the teaching staff, and more sincere efforts to teach -- than the other schools.

The "white" schools had a fast turnover of teachers because of the medical school in town. Wives of white medical students came into town looking for work to support their husbands in training. They took the teaching jobs at a lower salary, as beginning teachers, and left after their husbands graduated. This meant little carryover of tradition or excellence for the white students. Because the colored teachers could get few skilled jobs, teaching was more important to them. Teaching was a profession of pride in those days. It was respected highly by the colored folk in the community, and the parents supported the teachers' efforts. Most of the parents had been taught by the teachers of their children, and the children obeyed without question. This whole "village" of segregated Galveston raised its children.

Andrew "Brother" Bess and I talked about the All-City Musicals that all the schools in Galveston used to have in the spring. These were held in the City Auditorium and well attended by all "races," for the music was good, and it was a chance to see how your child compared with others in other schools -- not just for racial pride, but for school pride.

Each school used to perform a selection or two, and some years the schools combined for a selection. Of course, the combining was segregated also in my school days, but was integrated later.

I recalled how the "white" groups were not as well prepared as the "colored" groups, and it caused much resentment that we children felt, although it was never openly expressed. We could see it in their faces, in the way we were ignored as we passed by them to set up beforehand.

Education: Our Landmarks

But the good people of both races would always applaud the results enthusiastically.

I remarked to him: "Ball High Band wouldn't even play. Snooks [Fleming Huff] would have Central play, and that was the climax of the evening."

Bess added, "Mary Lee Sweatt would have the elementary kids play violins, etc. They made the others look so bad, they stopped having them [the musicals]. They got so jealous."

This I remember still. I was teaching in Bay City shortly before they ended. GISD's music supervisor was Paul Bergan, and he was trying to upgrade the district's music programs. So he had introduced a string program into the schools for both races. My nephew, Theodore Henderson, played the viola. And both of the "colored" music teachers in the elementary schools – at Booker T. Washington was Mrs. Bernice Hightower; at George W. Carver was Mrs. Mary Lee (Canada) Sweatt -- had learned from a string teacher how to teach the children the basics for playing the instruments. Both teachers had done a very creditable job, and the children did sound superior.

Bess remarked, "Same way with athletics. Ball High would play [football] and no one hardly came. Ball High didn't have anything but the pep squad, didn't have all that other. Central played -- everybody was there."

Central High always took to the field with at least three major performing units: the band, the Blue and White Battalion drill team, and the drum and bugle corps. Later they added a dance group and flag carriers. I attended the major games played by Central, especially the championship games, even after I was grown, and the stands were always crowded with all races. We just had more exciting games; the team wasn't the only attraction.

I also remember that the non-district season always started with the Catholic high school team, called Kirwin High School then, playing Ball High. Ball High would always win, having many more players than Kirwin, and it seemed so unfair to me. Without saying these things aloud, we just knew that the pride of Kirwin kept the series alive. There was no chance to beat Ball High, with their dominance in team size, supplies, and the whole bit.

However, when some of the Central players sought to play the Ball High team, they were flatly refused. The reasons given had some truth to them, but no one wanted to admit that Central would have beaten the (expletive deleted) out of Ball High, if allowed the opportunity. Many sports-minded "whites" really wanted to see a good matchup, but it wasn't going to wash with the diehards who wouldn't take the possibility of creating mayhem. So it never happened. Poor Kirwin was the yearly sacrificial lamb to the pride of the "whites" in the community. And we continued to take pride in our own traditions. Then desegregation eliminated them.

Mr. Joseph Arnold Banks

I spoke also with Joe Banks, my neighbor and my husband Roy's close friend, raised like a brother to him. He was godson to my husband's parents and is godfather of our youngest, Cheryl. In addition to a beautiful personality, he has a sharp memory, remembering not only what he has experienced but much of what his grandfather told him as a young boy:

"So I asked him, 'How far did you go in school?' and he said, ' I went to the fourth grade in Catholic school, and my teacher was Mr. Ralph

Scull, at the old East District School, at 10th and Broadway, in Galveston. Mr. Scull was an amazing person. In addition to being an early educator, he later was a preacher. He preached at a church on Strand. And when he preached down there, he also brought education to the Blacks down there that hadn't gone to school.' "

Joe Banks and my husband went to a private Catholic school, Holy Rosary, before transferring to public school in the fifth grade.

"Tom Warren, principal of East District School when we were attending it, also was principal of West District School for a while, and was a classmate of Mrs. Marguerite Collins," my mother-in-law. My mother, Viola Fedford, became their teacher.

Reflecting, Joe continued, "Mrs. Fedford had a piano moved up to the room where she taught. Every day she would play a march. As we fifth-graders came into the room, we marched around like soldiers. We'd stand stiff, then take our seats. Now she taught us many, many things about our Black heritage. She taught us about the contribution that our Black Civil War soldiers made to this country. And she taught us this little song. This was a Black Civil War song that was sung for inspiration by the soldiers.

" 'I have taken up the flag. It will never touch the ground. And I'll fight my way to honor. Oh, yes, I'll fight my way to honor. And a soldier's royal crown, a royal crown. ... '

"Now, you know it's amazing that you can remember that after all these years. But it's the teacher that does it.

"For instance, Mrs. Fedford would tell us, 'Now to spell Missouri, just say Miss - ou - ri.' And when I was 60 years old, and had to spell 'Missouri,' I still remember that." He also remembers much about many other things most people have forgotten.

Robert and Ada Simmons Butler

Other neighbors, Robert and Ada Simmons Butler, are a longtime Galveston couple who have children and grandchildren here. He mentioned changes in discipline: "Kids didn't go where they wanted to go without their parents' permission . I didn't get to go out like that. I'd better be at Fred Robinson's house if I said I was gonna be there. Problems started in school when they took segregation out. Mr. Love [in earlier times] sent me out to the cedar tree, to get two switches ... [They] just didn't want the Black teachers whipping the White kids...."

The Butlers named the teachers they could recall: Low Fourth, Mrs. Nettie McCullough; High Fourth, Mrs. Shelton; High Fifth, Mrs. V.C. Fedford; Low Sixth, Miss Loleta Anderson; High Sixth, Mrs. Gertrude Brown; Low Seventh, Mrs. Emma Nan Foreman; and in High Seventh, Mrs. Mable Boone Jones for mathematics and science, Mrs. V.C. Fedford for language arts, and Mr. A.W. McDonald for social studies. (There was no eighth grade; we went on to Central High after that, where the freshman year was referred to as Low First, not the ninth grade.) It was years before this lineup of teachers changed; the same people stayed in the same grade levels for ever so long. It was one reason they were so good at what they did: They knew the subject matter thoroughly and enjoyed the security of knowing what they were going to do, year after year. But they did not become stagnant, because they kept up with the latest teaching methods -- though they did not need the multiple ways to motivate children that are used now. The students came to learn, and there was no nonsense if they "didn't feel like it."

Education: Our Landmarks

Other teachers in the early years that the Butlers remembered were Mrs. Carrie Johnson, first grade; Miss Alecia Victor (Urquhart}, second grade; Miss Clara Scull, third grade, Miss Fannie Butler, fourth grade.

Those Who Taught

Bernice Davis James and Lois Davis Tyus Martin

Mrs. James and her sister, Mrs. Martin, were teachers who lived across the street from me while I was growing up, at 819 Ave. K. Their father, Henry Thomas Davis, was a longtime principal at West District Elementary School, succeeded by Thomas Warren after he passed away.

Their mother, Daisy Davis, was a devoted homemaker, and they were two of six children: After Bernice came Henry T. Jr, Granger, Leona, Lois and Daisy Addice. Daisy Addice, who was like a big sister to my sister, Florence, passed away at age 13 from meningitis. The life span of the average person in my youth was much shorter. We don't really appreciate the strides that medicine has made.

As a young single woman, Lois Davis was my very first public school teacher. I wanted no part of school, but I was very fond of her. When she married and left Galveston, I mourned her leaving for a long time. And in later years, after her first husband and my mother had died, I asked her to be my "play mother." Though I was a grown woman, she never thought it silly. "You're right to call yourself my play daughter; your mother actually gave you to me, when you first started school, when you were six years of age. You started school in the third grade. ... [She] told me, 'Lois, she's all yours now.'

Adding insight on the employment picture for African American teachers, she recalled the response when she left Galveston to be with her husband: "Back then, for somebody to send in a letter of resignation, you had to be crazy, they thought. It was so hard to get on."

Yet the education provided in Galveston seems to have prepared graduates to go anywhere in the world, because our graduates of Central certainly went all over the world, and made very successful livings wherever they went. Lois Tyus Martin said she lived in New York for 24 years; her first husband, Randall Tyus, worked for Fisk University as alumni secretary and also served as executive director of the United Negro College Fund. While in New York, she served as regional director of Alpha Kappa Alpha Sorority and "taught all kinds of children: Russian, Orientals, Jews, practically all white. One time, I was at a silk stocking school. Governesses would come for interviews at the school, because the parents were usually in Europe, or some such place."

Reviewing her own education in Galveston, Lois Martin said, "My aunt, Carrie Harris Johnson, taught first grade to practically everybody in the East End. When you got to the sixth grade, Mrs. Lucas was the art teacher. Freckles in her face, Ms. Shelton frightened everyone whom she taught."

Even as a fellow teacher, she acknowledged the fear mentioned earlier that Ms. Shelton inspired. It wasn't because of her freckles, but that awesome stare she gave you. I can see her in my mind's eye now: She stared at you full-face, never smiling that I could remember. I think she was probably a very nice-looking woman, if you got past the stare.

Lois Martin spoke of her affection for Ms. Lucas and Mrs. Emma Nan Foreman. Lucy Haller and Florence Lawton were Mrs. Foreman's sisters. Mrs. Foreman "would not allow her [Lawton] to call her 'sister' in school; [Haller and Lawton were] in my class."

Education: Our Landmarks

I recall a similar experience with my sister. She once taught Mrs. Dent's senior Latin class as a substitute, shortly after graduating from college. I was in the class, with a handful of students, and we knew Florence only too well. To keep some discipline, Florence had told me not to dare call her anything but "Miss Fedford." We kids were amused, but not disobedient. In our day, students would not dream of disrespect to anyone in authority -- nothing compared to that seen from the "good kids" of today.

Mrs. James also spoke of her teaching career. She graduated from Central, and then from Fisk University with an English degree, returning to Galveston to teach language arts. She taught for about 43 years, becoming head of the English department when Mrs. Martha Cort Jones died, and remaining at Central until retirement.

She married Costello James in 1932, who taught science at Central. Active in various community organizations, Mrs. James was a faithful choir member, and Mr. James, a skilled gardener, was also a very devoted member of Reedy Chapel A.M.E. Church, where he served as a longtime trustee in financial affairs and as unofficial caretaker of Reedy's aging pipe organ. A music lover, Mr. James played the alto saxophone in the summertime park band under the direction of Mr. Fleming Smizer Huff, who taught in the science department with him.

They could be counted on for faithful attendance at church, school and all related functions, and to almost always be the first ones there. The two, who had no children, were known for extreme punctuality, arriving a half-hour to an hour before a scheduled event, often before the building was even opened. They celebrated their 50th wedding anniversary shortly before Mr. James passed away.

Island of Color

Central High School students certainly had role models for the conduct and behavior we were taught. This we miss more than we can express.

Mr. Frank Windom

Frank Windom Jr.

Mr. Windom was a legend in his own time. He was the longtime assistant principal of Central High School, and certainly should be credited with doing all the hard work of administration at Central. He was a very stern disciplinarian to those who disobeyed the rules, but he was a dear friend to those who needed his advice and assistance in their daily life at Central. He could joke with the students and still keep their respect and devotion, because he gave them credit for having good sense, and inspired them to do well.

He had only one arm, and kept the sleeve of the other arm tucked into his belt. But he was absolutely the strongest human I have ever seen, physically and mentally. He was a large man, and with his one arm could pick up a teen-age boy and flip him. And he meant business. As the saying goes, he didn't have to chew his cabbage twice. If his warnings were not followed immediately, he took immediate action. He seldom had to prove his superiority.

He could control any disturbance, individual or mob. But he never mistreated anyone; the students knew him to be fair. He would give them every chance to justify their position before taking action. Without saying a word, he commanded silence and order.

Mrs. Irma McCullough Ward

Mrs. Ward, my mother's first cousin whom we knew as Aunt Irma, also taught in the Galveston schools, and she referred to the disparity in pay for male and female teachers, recalling an example. "They said the teachers were to get a raise. Mr. Cummings said, 'I'm going to recommend you for $5.00 a month raise – John [Clouser], $10.00, because he has a family.' " As reflected in school board minutes, female teachers, especially if they were single, were paid less, even if they did more. And yet they persevered, often for lifetimes of service.

Another cousin, Jeanette Ward, lives in Houston; she is a graduate of Central and one of the very few regular teachers at the old Central High who are still alive. She began as a very young science teacher while my mother was still teaching, and credits Mother with teaching her so much about handling adult circumstances and student challenges.

Mrs. Viola Cornelia Scull Fedford

My mother was a BOI (Born on the island) and resident of Galveston for all her 85 years. Her father's father, Horace Scull, came to Galveston at the end of the Civil War, with his wife Emily and children including her father, Ralph Albert, only 5 years old at the time. She was educated in Galveston's public schools, Prairie View College, and Roosevelt College in Chicago, Illinois; a language arts major, she returned to teach for 47 years.

In 1923, she married Brister Marshall Fedford; their two daughters were Florence Carlotta Fedford Henderson and Izola Ethel Fedford Collins.

In addition to being a devoted mother, homemaker and teacher, she was a tireless church and civic leader. A lifelong member of Reedy, she was active in many organizations there from childhood until her last illness. She was also a very conscientious community worker, holding various local, regional and state offices in the Texas Federation of Colored Women's Clubs. When she presided in the early '40s, the federation opened a long-desired Texas facility for delinquent Negro girls in Giddings, and organized three clubs. And she spent long hours assisting ill children in her efforts for the federation's local Hospital Aid Society.

She sought to minister unto others without concern for praise or recognition. I often wonder how she kept our home clean and comfortable, cooked wonderful meals, and still maintained a full-time career as a teacher,

Education: Our Landmarks

church worker and community leader -- all in the days before the modern appliances we now take for granted. I remember our wood stove; the ice box, cooled with a 50-pound block of ice; the No.2 wash tubs on the wash bench; and the cistern in which we caught rainwater because we preferred it to tap water for drinking. (I also recall the gas stove that came later, as well as a new Servel refrigerator, one of the island's first telephones, the Model T and Model A Fords, and one of the early hot-water heaters.)

Because we grew up before the marvelous age of television, our mother taught us how to play checkers and many other games, and we learned to make many of our toys from things around us -- bottle dolls, mud pies, and writing ink from the berry bushes by our house. We learned to be more creative and resourceful than the children of today, with their thousands of manufactured toys and computer-generated pastimes.

People still alive today can testify to the love for children she showed long before she had two of her own. She regularly picked them up for picnics she provided, and in the summertime took them daily to the nearby beach. Relatives recall that she allowed them to enjoy her prize possessions: They played on her furniture and with her blankets and good china dishes, in turn learning to respect and appreciate what they used.

With mandatory retirement from the school system at age 70 in 1959, she did not slow down in service, especially to children. One summer, in addition to caring for her grandchildren all day, she served as Reedy Chapel Bible School superintendant. But after Bible School ended, while attending a Texas Association meeting as a delegate, she suffered a disabling stroke. She then lived with me for 11 precious years after that, enjoying watching her grandchildren grow up. Though her doctor advised us to expect changes in her personality, only her speech was affected, never her sweetness.

She did not receive a long list of awards. But testimony to her greatness comes from not only her family but also the many who remember with gratitude her regular, unselfish kindnesses.

Miss Alecia Victor Urquhart

Another teacher who was very close to my mother and spoke of her as a model for behavior was Miss Urquhart, a native Galvestonian who lived in her family home at 828 Ave. L until her death. She stood as a witness at my wedding; I didn't find out until I married that she was also my husband's cousin.

Education: Our Landmarks

She attended Holy Rosary School, and transferred to East District in the fourth grade. Her first public school teacher and counselor was Miss Jessie McGuire, later known as Mrs. Dent, who also became her English teacher at Central, and inspired and encouraged her to pursue a teaching career.

After Miss Urquhart graduated from Prairie View College, she began teaching English in Galveston at age 20 -- first at East District, then Central, where she became a colleague of Miss McGuire, her childhood idol. She received a master of education degree from Texas Southern University, and did postgraduate studies at the University of California at Los Angeles (UCLA). She also succeeded Mrs. Dent as a counselor at Central, serving for 14 years. Including the years she taught language arts for the high seventh grade in Central's Annex (with Mr. Windom and Mr. McDonald as other subject area teachers), she spent 45 years teaching in GISD.

I was in her English class in Central; she was one of my favorite teachers because she explained things in a way that allowed you to learn while you thought for yourself as well. She once stated that the reward for a teacher comes after the job has been done, that achievements cannot really be measured.

As she approached retirement in 1969, she began planning how to spend it: devoting her time to volunteering throughout her community and in her church, Holy Rosary. She enjoyed sewing, cooking, and reading historical novels. But even more she loved serving people and thoroughly enjoyed working in her church. There was no time for self-pity; she was too busy giving herself to others. "Retirement doesn't mean sitting in a rocking chair," she said.

Island of Color

Her groups ranged from the Galveston County Child Welfare Board and Mayor's Commission on Mental Retardation to her many church organizations. She tirelessly attended the bedsides of the sick and went to most funerals in the community. In her last years, she assisted Holy Rosary School as a counselor for grades K-6. We never know how people like this manage to do it all. She died suddenly in 1973 of a heart attack.

Miss Urquhart was a respectable Christian, admired and loved by many. She is remembered as one of the finest and most self-sacrificing persons. She never wanted to be a great person, but humbly contributed great works toward humanity, doing God's will. She did all with a smile on her face and a cheerful attitude. She never complained.

Holy Rosary holds its annual mother-daughter breakfast in her honor. Another program once held in her honor was called "The Power of a Virtuous Woman." That title well sums up her life, and points to the example our finest educators set.

John Henry Clouser

Another of our examples was Mr. Clouser. Born in Velasco, Clouser moved to Galveston as a boy, attended West District School and graduated from Central in 1918. He said that his graduating class was the largest that Central had graduated at that time: 14 African American students -- six boys and eight girls. He received bachelor's and master's degrees from Texas Southern University and began his teaching career in Matagorda County. By 1922 he had returned to teach in Galveston. He taught at the West District and George W. Carver schools for many years, and was a tireless worker in the community.

Education: Our Landmarks

Clouser started the Volunteer Health League in the 1930s, a Galveston organization designed to promote good health practices among Negroes through education. The league sponsored health clinics and neighborhood clean-up campaigns in Galveston. During the league's National Negro Health Week, school classes, exhibits, radio shows, newspaper articles, lectures, clinics, health pageants and a parade demonstrated the importance of good health to people of all ages. This project helped dispel Black people's fears about doctors and hospitals.

Known in the community for his dedication to health, education and youth, he worked with the Boy Scouts as a Scout Master, participated in church and NAACP activities and served as director of the Mayor's Youth Opportunity Council in 1969. He also worked with the Galveston Community Action Council. He helped found a credit union with Charles Scott Jones that is very solvent today.

Clouser was also a major worker at Holy Rosary Catholic Church -- recognized by the pope, and honored in a display at San Antonio's World Hemisfair Exhibit.

He spoke of his teaching career. "Your mother and Miss Jeanie Mabson came in the evening and taught us music. I liked music, but I wasn't very interested in playing, singing it.

I started teaching out in the rural in 1919 -- what your mama taught me. ...

"When I came back and started teaching here, she was right across the hall from me. After the 1900 storm, we had three rooms upstairs and three rooms downstairs -- six classrooms, wide spacious halls. Miss Effie Mabson, who taught second grade, moved to Central when I started in October 1920. Miss Jeanie [and] I was with your mother until she retired."

Speaking on books and journals that influenced him, Clouser mentioned <u>Black Reconstruction</u> by W.E.B. Dubois and <u>Freedom Road</u> by Howard Fast. He then moved on to African Americans in education that he remembered as having positive influences in Galveston life.

Clouser cited Dudley Woodward as a good mathematician and W.J. Mason as a good mathematics instructor. Mr. Mason had succeeded Mr. John R. Gibson as principal of Central High School, who Clouser said had identified himself as a top-quality principal, and was recognized all over Texas.

Mr. Clouser also mentioned how Theasel Henderson, while on the school board, tried to advocate use of Early Childhood programs to prepare minority children for school, and how whites supported by Theasel abandoned him for fear of white backlash.

Other good leaders in the schools he mentioned were Mr. Cummings, Mr. H.T. Davis (whose family lived across the street from us, between 8th and 9th streets on Avenue K), Mr. Love, Mr. Thomas Warren, and Mr. Webb, who was killed in the 1900 Storm. Clouser stated that Mr. Webb received special recognition in the field of education, and got into top colleges without an examination. Clouser also mentioned Wright Cuney as a superior leader, prior to 1900.

Recalling the times in which they taught, he spoke of the Negro Teacher's Convention in 1920 in Houston, Clouser said, when the Ku Klux Klan paraded in the streets. They organized whites into a police force to intimidate Negroes, but also Jews or Catholics, "who caught most of the hell."

As for teachers' economic situation, Clouser said that teachers in his day dreaded retirement, because there was nothing to retire on. The largest monthly salary was probably no more than $125.00. A teacher's life then certainly was one defined more by service than reward.

Mrs. Jessie McGuire Dent

Mrs. Dent, a very wonderful, service-focused woman, was born around 1892. She was close in age to my mother – my oldest photograph of Mrs. Dent is in the bridal party on my mother's wedding day. A January 1913 drawing shows her with the other Howard University founders of Delta Sigma Theta Sorority, in their senior-year caps and gowns.

Mrs. Dent began teaching in the public schools after graduation, most of that time teaching Latin. Solidly fixed in my mind and those of others taught at Central during those years is the sight of her at her door between classes, speaking to everyone softly and sweetly, smiling, encouraging them, admonishing them, and inquiring how they were getting along. She was always interested in what each student was doing, and had a kind word to say about whatever progress was made. You knew she really cared.

If she suspected a male student was getting into some mischief, she would call him over and counsel him. She would go the extra mile to help him, especially if he was around the age her son would have been, had he lived to high school age. Many of them borrowed lunch money from her, and she would tell them, "Now, don't hurt your mother/father by doing that. They would feel so ashamed of you." Mrs. Dent told my husband that several times; he was about her son's age. When Miss Anona Smith, the girls' dean, passed away, Mrs. Dent was asked to take her place, because she had such a special way with the students. Three years later, in 1947, she passed away.

One of her major accomplishments was in fighting for equal pay for teachers of our race. At the time of her tenure with the Galveston school system, records show that African American teachers who qualified with credentials and experience equal to those of the white teachers were paid 20% less. With her husband, attorney Thomas Dent, she went all the way to the United States Supreme Court and won the case for equal pay for all teachers, irrespective of race, creed, color or gender. Teachers of any minority owe this couple for their fight.

And the debt goes back a generation further, to the father who provided the funds for the education that allowed her to teach. Young Jessie's father, Robert "Bob" McGuire, was an entrepreneur whose hack stand business, transporting people across town in horse and buggy, earned him the funds to build a bathhouse, which operated for at least a generation in the late 19th century and early 20th century. (More on his legacy follows in Chapter 8 on Employment and Businesses.)

Education: Our Landmarks
Jewell Earles Banks

Jewell Earles Banks

Educators with an eye to the future served Galveston's African Americans in my generation as well. Jewell Earles Banks was born in 1927 in Galveston as one of 7 children. She attended East District, Booker T. Washington and Central High School, graduating in 1945 with honors.

She always had a burning desire for more education, and a love of knowledge. Unable to afford college at first, she did domestic work for a time, then worked as an insurance agent and in the transportation department of University of Texas Medical Branch Galveston until she could finance her education at Texas Southern University in Houston. She received a bachelor of science degree in education and began teaching at Booker T. Washington. She had one son, Christopher Banks.

Inspired by some of her teachers to excel, she was determined to better her condition and that of those around her. Deeply committed to the children she taught, especially those who were underprivileged (now called "at-risk"), she worked in their behalf for most of a 24-hour day, everyday. She also joined the Galveston Alumnae Chapter of Delta Sigma Theta Sorority and held several responsible positions in this organization, always striving to "make a difference."

Jewell Banks went back to school on evenings and weekends and earned her master's degree in education from Texas Southern. She then continued her training, earning administrative credentials. Because of her dedication, she was appointed principal of Goliad Elementary School, succeeding Charles Moore.

When L.A. Morgan School was completed, Jewell Earles Banks became its first principal, and redefined the word *exemplary,* seeking every avenue of improvement possible for her "little Black babies," as she lovingly called her students. It was quite possibly the high level of stress that she endured in promoting her school's needs and requesting funds often denied that was a factor in her cancer illness. She frequently appealed to parents to attend school board meetings to support the causes she espoused, in her effort to help her school's children catch up to those who had more exposure to all of life's learning experiences. She suffered through the lack of parental support and community interest and fought the children's battles anyway.

Education: Our Landmarks

    Thanks to her innovative ideas, the concept of a private school without red tape and legislative restrictions was born. Garnering support, Susan Lynch resigned from GISD and started Satori School in Galveston, giving Jewell Banks full credit for her vision.

    A lifetime member of St. Paul United Methodist Church, Jewell Banks was a dedicated worker in many departments. She sang in the choir, and of course, the children in the church were a priority. She did her best to expose them to the best training and opportunities for growth.

    She was transferred as principal to San Jacinto Elementary School, where she started a special Career Day and a student council, to give students incentives to stay in school, the desire to "be somebody."

    She succumbed to her illness on March 30, 1985, a few days after making it to church once more. For her exceptional dedication to effective education of the least advantaged children of the district, the Alamo School annex for physically and mentally challenged students was named the Jewell Banks Annex, with the school board's approval of my nomination.

Theasel Henderson

Theasel Henderson

Another Galvestonian to make his contribution to education on the island was Theasel Henderson. He was born in Hope, Ark., on July 22, 1921, and shortly after his birth, the family moved to Fort Wayne, Ind. He graduated from Central High School there, then attended Indiana University.

Education: Our Landmarks

The entrance of the United States into World War II took him from college into military service. His subsequent military assignments included a year at the Galveston Army Air Base, where he met my sister, Galveston native Florence C. Fedford, whom he married on June 14, 1945, while stationed in Tallahassee, Florida. Three days later, in the Medical Detachment of the 1869th Engineer Aviation Battalion, he began the journey to Guam, where he spent the rest of his tenure in service.

After his honorable discharge in March 1946, Henderson resumed his education at Indiana University, then graduated from the newly designated Texas State University for Negroes, now Texas Southern University, in 1949. He served as principal and interim mathematics teacher at Oakland Vocational Schools in Palestine and then Waco. He and his young family returned to Galveston, and Henderson pursued additional graduate study at Texas Southern University. He began a 19-year career in the U.S. Postal Service, then turned in 1970 to the field of life insurance, training with New York Life Insurance Company as a field representative.

Throughout military and civilian life, Henderson was involved in community affairs. He joined Reedy Chapel A.M.E. Church in 1947, holding several church offices and remaining very active in church activities the rest of his life. While with the Postal Service, he was active in the National Alliance of Postal and Federal Employees, serving in various local positions, as well as participating in regional meetings.

The first African American to serve on the Galveston school board, he was appointed to fill a vacancy in 1968. Elected and re-elected for six terms, he served 18 years before retiring. During that tenure, he served in each of the offices of the board: secretary, vice president and president.

He served on the Workmen's Compensation Board at the state level of the National Association of School Boards, and as a Texas delegate.

Before his service on the school board, he was active in the Parent-Teacher Associations of the schools his children attended. He and his wife were the proud parents of three children -- Theodore, Diane and Janice, all honor-roll students who graduated from the public schools of Galveston. He was also a member of Citizens for the Advancement of Public Education.

After his retirement as an agent of American General Insurance Company in 1990, he remained an active volunteer in community work, until his death in an automobile accident on Aug. 6, 1999.

He was avidly involved in the NAACP, and also served on the Galveston County Memorial Hospital Board, Galveston Association of Life Underwriters, Sunshine Center Board, Communities in Schools Board, and Galveston County Coalition of Black Democrats. With each of these organizations, he served as president. Other organizations in which he held membership included the Galveston County Park Board, Old Central Cultural Center Board of Directors, and Kappa Alpha Psi Fraternity.

His commitment to community work was extensive and lifelong. At the time of his death, in addition to serving as NAACP secretary, he was chairman of the Civil Service Commission, and foreman of a sitting grand jury.

Florence Henderson

His wife, Florence Henderson, was born on March 13, 1924, in Galveston and educated in its schools. Because she had accompanied her mother, a teacher, to school until she was old enough to start officially

Education: Our Landmarks

at the age of six, she was advanced to the third grade at that time, and in 1939, she became one of the youngest students to finish Central High School.

In high school, she was a member of the Blue and White Battalion, a marching unit that supported the football team during football season. This all-girl unit was organized and directed by Mrs. Frankie Sheppard, wife of football coach Ray Sheppard. Along with the band and the drum and bugle corps, this organization was known statewide for its snappy dress and maneuvers.

She graduated from Prairie View A&M in 1943, returning to Galveston to teach. She began at Booker T. Washington Elementary School, and ended her career at Central Junior High, as it was known after integration. When she retired in 1984, she had served as head of the mathematics department for several years, and had been elected as Teacher of the Year by her colleagues.

Her love of children has also led her to care for many children when their parents needed assistance. And she has been active throughout the community, preferring more often to assist others in community work rather than take leadership positions.

A life member of Reedy Chapel A.M.E. Church, Mrs. Henderson has been active in several church organizations and committees, as well as serving as director and musician for the youth choir. She was initiated into the (Galveston) Gamma Delta chapter of Delta Sigma Theta Sorority, Inc., shortly after it received its first charter in 1943 with the initiative of national founder Mrs. Jessie McGuire Dent. A member of the Galveston Education Foundation Board of Directors from its inception, Mrs. Henderson served a term as president in the 1990s.

She has also been especially active with ecumenical organizations, such as the Church Women United, and sung for many years with the Galveston College Chorale.

She and her husband Theasel celebrated 50 years of marriage in a service at Reedy Chapel, with many family members and friends present.

She is well known for her optimism, her ability to be in harmony with everyone, the evidence of her faith in God and the goodness in this world, and her teaching excellence.

Izola Collins

For my sister and myself, education has been a family tradition that reaches back generations.

In that tradition, on April 9, 1986, at the Galveston Independent School District Administration Building, I was sworn into office as a new member of the GISD Board of Trustees, after my brother-in-law, Theasel Henderson, issued a brief goodbye statement as an outgoing member.

At my request, Leon "Maggie" Banks, a longtime buddy of my late husband, swore me in. Mr. Banks was a notary public and the precinct judge in one of the precincts that turned in a very high percentage of votes for me; I know he talked in my behalf during the campaign.

"I, Izola Ethel Fedford Collins, do solemnly swear or affirm ... that I will faithfully execute the duties ... of the office of ... member of ...the School Board of Trustees ... of the Galveston Independent School District ... of the State of Texas ... and will preserve, protect, and defend ... the Constitutional laws ... of the United States ...and of this state. And I further solemnly swear or affirm ... that I have not directly or indirectly ... paid, offered, or promised to pay ... contributed nor promised to contribute

Education: Our Landmarks

... any money or valuable thing ... or promised any office or employment ... as a reward ... for giving or withholding a vote ... at the election at which I was elected...so help me, God."

The applause as I ended the oath meant a great deal -- that a lot of people not only approved of my seating, but cared enough to come to witness and support my taking office. Praise God!

The value placed on education by African Americans in Galveston has for many, many years been high. As for myself, I had decided at the tender age of six years old that I was never going back to school again.

Nosiree! It was an etched-in-stone determination in my mind that very first afternoon that I walked home from school. I cried and lay across the bed. It was too confining, too regimented, and too quiet an existence for this soul who had been a noisy, fun-loving and imaginative being. I had also had my mother as playmate, instructor and caretaker, all rolled into one, all to myself, until that day. Now I had these various adults telling me what to do, and children ignoring me, and -- oh, it was awful! Well, with such determination, I am still rather amazed that I spent the next 58 years in the education system.

First, I did learn to love my teacher, Lois Davis. Then I did learn to conform and make friends with some of my classmates; there is a little snapshot I cherish of five of us girls with locked arms, hands on hips, frowning into the sun, on the playground of East District School, in about the fourth grade. I then went on to Booker T. Washington's seventh grade, the annex for high seventh grade, and then a wonderful and exciting four years at Central High.

Our grades were organized differently, but we were on a par with or above the brightest students from the main metropolitan areas when we reached college.

I was salutatorian of my class, and went directly to Prairie View A. and M. College for training in mathematics, then music education; I received my bachelor's degree in music education with, like all Prairie View students, a minor in education. After a year in Bay City, teaching band at Hilliard High School and first grade, I enrolled at Northwestern University, where I earned my master's degree in music, with an applied major in piano.

My teaching career in Bay City lasted five years. My band grew in numbers and quality, and I was offered a band instructor position in Corpus Christi – it would have been a step up at a larger school, in a larger city. I instead married Roy Collins and came back to Galveston to live.

I settled there without a regular job, as I completed my master's.

After five years of substitute teaching, and brief employment with the YWCA, I applied to start a band at Lorraine Crosby School in Hitchcock, which was still segregated. This was 1958-59, when integration was slowly taking place across the land, as Southern diehards realized that they needed the federal government's money and had to obey the law. They were also slowly admitting that it cost a lot more to run dual school systems than one good system.

Hitchcock began gradual integration, grade by grade. It was really hard for all of us to adjust to not only the regular graduation of our top students, but also the departure of a whole grade of kids we had learned to care for and taken under our wings. We tried to prepare them for a new set of standards, new realities. We told them to listen carefully and take great notes, because no one at the new school would give them the extra help that we had -- pushing them to turn in work that they had put off doing, etc. But we strongly encouraged them to get the best education they could get, with such benefits as having new supplies. They were not to view this as a step down, but the start of a better day for all of us.

As firmly as I still believe this was true, although the kids at Hitchcock High School had an easier time of it than elsewhere -- my last band students even received their new uniforms before transferring to Hitchcock High -- the difference in how they were treated caused many of my former band students to leave the band program at the new school.

I felt very badly about how African American fire and fervor left the band program in both Hitchcock and Galveston. My students who had achieved top rating in band never did so at Hitchcock High, where I taught in the integrated band program as an assistant to the new first-year white band director.

Many parents and people in the community had wanted to demonstrate and demand that I receive the position of head band director. I refused to cooperate with those plans for only one reason: As school started that year, I had not told anyone outside my family that I was pregnant with my third child, and I was physically unable to go through such changes, or deal with the emotional stress. Also, my mother at that time was an invalid in my home. And it would have been too much.

God always answers prayer when it is time to do so. As my needs at home became more acute, Mr. Jack Sweatt offered me an opening for a music teacher at the recently opened Goliad Elementary School in Galveston. It was then December holiday break, and he assured me that he knew I was expecting my baby in January and that he was willing to wait until my doctor released me about six weeks later.

I prayed and consulted my husband and family. Roy said, "I want nothing to do with this decision, Izola, because I don't want you to ever regret leaving band and blame me, but I do know that people teaching regular music classes live longer than band directors." Mr. Blick, the band director at Central, had recently died of a heart attack. After his none-too-subtle comment, I decided to take the position. So began my Galveston teaching career, which lasted until 1984 in the public schools, ending successfully with retirement from Stephen F. Austin Middle School, formerly a junior high.

After retirement, I heard that Galveston Catholic School needed a band director. After talking with the principal, I worked part time there. But after organizing and training that band to performance quality, I could not keep up with other obligations to my satisfaction, so I resigned. I had been recruited to run for the GISD Board of Trustees by my brother-in-law, Theasel Henderson, who thought that 18 years was long enough for him in Position 2 of that board. We organized a committee and spent long hours on the campaign. Against opposition, I won city-wide. In the process, I learned to make new friends, appreciate my old ones even more, and started a new life. This new life did not leave much time for teaching, so I had to let the teaching go.

I spent nine very fruitful years on the board. I have laughed with close friends and family many a time about the remark from one young lady who was astonished to learn that we did not get paid for serving on the school board. She exclaimed, "You mean you did all this work to get elected to get no money?" Although no material gains were sought or

Education: Our Landmarks

received, many a day after that I have seen the direct and indirect benefits of the contacts and knowledge I gained.

After serving as president of the board, I resigned in 1995, to put my latter-day energies into recording Galveston's African American history and otherwise creating -- more music, poetry, stories, more of myself in some form or other.

After 58 years, I finally left school.

CHAPTER SIX
OUR CHURCHES

Church life has always been an integral part of the African American experience, for which the reasons are as varied as the people themselves. Primary, however, are the facts that our Christian faith dates back over 2,000 years to our African ancestors; and that, left few resources after slavery, our people have long depended heavily upon that faith to sustain them.

Just as some people of color today are unaware of African Americans' history of celebrating freedom on the Fourth of July and Juneteenth, some African Americans misperceive Christianity as only the device intended by the white man to pacify the slave. But most continue to rely on the proven help of a loving God.

In Galveston, the conscientious leaders of the African American churches have played a major role in the lack of violence, as well as the presence of brotherhood and tolerance, in this city, as well as the amount of respect given to members of this "race" who live here.

Not that in Galveston our people have "rolled over and played dead"; there has not been in Galveston any stereotypical head-scratching, shoe-scuffling Black presence as has been said of some parts of Texas. To tell the truth, I identify with those Whites who claimed in Galveston's early days that we were not a part of Texas at all, but our own Republic. We have an island mentality that might be blamed for many negative behaviors, but the ability to get along with each other to survive all of our

Our Churches

problems is our main continuing trait, particularly for original BOIs (those Born on the Island).

It needs to be said that you don't know African Americans, and their interests in Galveston or anywhere else in America, unless you know something about how they worship, why they worship, and to what extent they will go to worship freely, and how much they trust those worship leaders to tell them the truth about what they experience.

Galveston has a very rich history of many faiths and their offshoots. This contradicts the title bestowed upon the city by those jealous of how it flourished -- Sin-City of the South -- and several other names that played up its prostitution, gambling, and other vices. These vices were more enjoyed by wealthy Whites than poorer Blacks; due partly to income differences, the Galveston known by whites was not always the Galveston known by non-whites.

In our African American community here, as in others countrywide, the church and its leaders have been more believed and supported than any other agency or organization for hundreds of years.

It is known that the African American churches in Galveston were the first in Texas, and they were most likely the first in the South. It is fitting then that the news of freedom, having been proclaimed in Galveston, spread about through the churches first. The encouragement to former slaves to seek a living for themselves and families came from the churches first. The church was not only a spiritual source of strength for these newly freed individuals, but also a social agency.

Today, the churches that still serve this function are the ones that have survived over the years in Galveston and continue to grow. Galveston's first official African American church setting was, according to records kept, the Avenue L Baptist Church, which still has its doors open today at 27th Street and Avenue L. It was established before emancipation by the First Baptist Church, an Anglo church still present in Galveston. One of the next African American congregations to begin in Galveston was Holy Rosary Catholic Church. More Baptist, Methodist, Catholic and Episcopal churches followed, to be joined later by other denominations. The sampling of religious community life that follows reflects no intent to omit the rich history of many of the churches not discussed here.

Reedy Chapel African Methodist Episcopal Church
2013 Broadway

Reedy Chapel

Our Churches

Reedy Chapel is the mother church of African Methodism in Texas, the first of its kind organized in Texas and much of the Southwest. It was to this church that a procession marched to proclaim the South's first official message of slaves' freedom to the public, on Jan. 1, 1866. And when the Civil War ended, the church housed the area's first school for African American children.

Reedy was the site of change -- from ignorance to education for African Americans, and from slavery to free and independent worship. Centrally located on the city's main street, accessible to members lacking transportation, it still stands at 2013 Broadway and is listed on the National Register of historic buildings.

Reedy grew out of an effort by white slave owners to provide a place of worship for their slaves.

"X-raying Galveston and the Mainland," an article in the July 9, 1878, edition of the *Informer,* an African American newspaper in Houston, says a blacksmith shop was once on the Reedy site.

The property upon which the church stands today was purchased by white trustees of the Methodist Episcopal Church-South, from the Galveston City Company, through their representative, Gail Borden, on March 8, 1848. Originally, the property was used as an open meeting area, with the addition of a small structure where, before Emancipation, white Methodists Church would conduct Sunday school for the slaves. In 1863, a permanent churchhouse was built, later destroyed by a great residential fire in 1885.

The members of the white Methodist church later supported giving the former slave church to the African Methodist Episcopal Church, preferring that to turning it over to white Methodists from the North.

Lawsuits had been filed throughout the South by the Methodist Episcopal Church-North against the Methodist Episcopal Church-South, seeking to take over the property and ministry of the former slave churches. The book *Methodism in Texas* by Mrs. Bernice Watkins McBeth, chairperson of the Methodist Archives, further details the fight:

"The only Southern Church in Texas taken over by the Methodist Episcopal Church, so far as we have learned, was the one in Galveston in 1865, just as the war was closing. ... Before long, it seems, it was taken over by Rev. Joseph Welch, leader of the Methodist Episcopal ministers arriving in Texas. However, the Negro members of the Southern Church wished to become a congregation of the African Methodist Episcopal Church, whereas Welch evidently wanted them to adhere to the Methodist Episcopal Church. A lawsuit ensued in 1866 between Welch and Rev. Mr. Clark of the A.M.E. church, and the latter won. Rev. Horatio V. Philpott, pastor of the Methodist Episcopal Church, South, in Galveston favored the A.M.E. church in the dispute."

The matter was resolved when the courts ruled in favor of the Methodist Episcopal Church-South, which gave the property to the ex-slaves so they could establish their own churches. In 1866, the church and property were deeded to the African Methodist Episcopal Church, a denomination which arose in Philadelphia after the mistreatment of several African American slaves in a white Methodist church service.

The former slave church's first minister was M.M. Clark, an Afro-American missionary sent from Philadelphia in 1866. He served the church until the Louisiana Conference of 1867, when representatives of various areas of the South were appointed as officials of the church. One of those

Our Churches

appointed was Houston Reedy, also a missionary from Philadelphia, who was the first pastor after the former slave church became A.M.E.

Women's Day

The church was then named in his honor.

The first trustees of Reedy Chapel were Horace Scull, R. Winston, C. Essex, J.E. McPherson, G. Goodson, W. Fields, R. McPherson, F.Z. Miller, S. Warren, and Ralph A. Scull. B.G. Chisholm was the architect. Contractors were Todd and Campbell.

Entering the ministry from Reedy's congregation were Wilson Nichols, Robert Mason, A. Viney, Thomas Anderson, R.P. Chamberlain, H. McKenna, J.H. Martin, G.W. Hamilton, Buford, and Ralph Albert Scull.

After fire destroyed the first building in 1885, the present building was constructed in 1886 on the same site. This was during the pastorage of Rev. J. E. Edwards, with masonry laid by Norris Wright Cuney, who was a member of Reedy. This structure was severely damaged by the 1900 storm, but was completely restored. It also suffered damage from other storms through the years, which weakened its structure.

It was completely renovated in 1947 by B. Marshall Fedford, contractor, and member of the A.M.E. ministry as well as Reedy. Rev. R.C. Walker was the pastor. The building committee included Mrs. M.A. Love, Mr. T.H. Warren, Mr. J.W. Coleman, Emile H. Fatha, and McKinley Brown. There were additional building changes in 1957, with Rev. C.B. Bryant as pastor, and again in 1976.

When Trinity Episcopal Church in Galveston purchased a new pipe organ in 1910, they traded in their smaller organ, which was then purchased from Henry Pilcher and Sons on April 15, 1913, by the following trustees of Reedy: George W. Hamilton, J.E. Cobb, J.E. McPherson, George W. Thomas, H. Malone, W.N. Cummings and Ralph A. Scull.

This organ, recently restored by Roy Redman of Fort Worth, is one of the only two remaining tracker organs of its type in the nation.

Our Churches

Reedy Chapel A.M.E. Church Pipe Organ

They were formerly water-powered, but now are powered by electricity. The other organ of this type is in the Smithsonian Institute. The

Reedy pipe organ was played for many years by Mr. J.W. Coleman, whose wife was the musician for the Avenue L Baptist Church, and in later years by me as well.

JOHN W. COLEMAN
BORN: November 30, 1880
DIED: July 11, 1957
Orchestra Conductor
and
**Organist of Reedy Chapel A.M.E. Church
Galveston, Texas**

To date, 40 ministers have served the church.

Our Churches

The longest tenures have been by the Rev. R.C. Walker, the Rev. A. I. Henley, and the Rev. Robert Louis Jeffries. Under Rev. Jeffries' leadership, Reedy entered the National Register of Historic Places in 1984, purchased a parking lot on adjacent land, started a child guidance center in the annex earlier used as a parsonage and multipurpose room, and received grants for a complete renovation.

Reedy Chapel is in the 10th Episcopal District of the A.M.E. Church connection. Presiding bishops of the districts have changed many times, but its period of real prominence was under Bishop John Adams. His knowledge, wisdom and finesse were soon recognized by the entire general conference; he became chairman of the Bishop's Council of the entire A.M.E. Connection soon after leaving the district. And one of the longest-serving presiding elders of Reedy has been Rev. X.L. Williams, now retired.

1. Clark, M.M — 1866-1867
2. Reedy, Houston — 1867-1868
3. Reed, John — 1868-1871
4. Haywood, Richard — 1871-1872
5. Carson, W.R. — 1872-1873
6. Hammitt, R.E. — 1873-1878
7. Bates, Hammon — 1878-1879
8. Armstrong, J.H. — 1879-1882
9. Edwards, J.E. — 1882-1885
10. Bradley, J.F.P. — 1885-1889
11. Reynolds, L.H. — 1889-1894
12. Taylor, Green — 1894-1896
13. Moody, M.D. — 1896-1900
14. Beamer, W.R. — 1900-1903
15. Trapp, H.L. — 1903-1906

16. Hamilton, G.W.	1906-1910
17. Rhone, J.H.L.	1910-1913
18. Lee, J.R.L.	1913-1917
19. Edwards, J.E.	1917-1920
20. McDade, J.W.	1920-1921
21. Young, H.A.	1921-1924
22. Butler, J.B.	1924-1928
23. Jackson, B.J.	1928-1929
24. Johnson, W.S.	1929-1930
25. Carr, W.A.	1930-1933
26. Womack, P.E.	1933-1934
27. Williams, Fred	1934-1935
28. Cooper, H.F.	1935-1936
29. Brown, G.E.	1936-1939
30. Walker, R.C.	1939-1949
31. Barker, E.F.	1949-1953
32. Jackson, C.F.	1953-1954
33. Young, L.C.	1954-1956
34. Bryant, C.B.	1956-1958
35. Henley, A.I.	1958-1971
36. Green, S.L.	1971-1975
37. Rice, M.E.	1975-1979
38. Jeffries, R.L.	1979-1997
39 Ferguson, Arthur	1997-2000
40. Payne, Brenda	2000- present

Biography of Reverend Brenda Payne

Elder Brenda Payne was born in Washington, D.C. to Attorney Eugene McDonald and Mrs. Mary Alice Beckford. Pastor Payne received her undergraduate degree as a registered nurse in 1974 from the Alma Mater of her father and grandfather, Boston University. In 1986 she also completed studies in the Master of Divinity program at Boston University School of Theology, majoring in Pastoral Counseling.

Pastor Payne accepted the call to the ministry in 1979. She was ordained a Deacon by the African Methodist Episcopal Church in 1982, and ordained an Elder in 1984. In her years of traveling, Pastor Payne has preached throughout the First and Second Episcopal Districts and now in the Tenth Episcopal District. She has served as a member of The New England Annual Conference Board of Examiners; New England Conference Director of Stewardship; and as the Assistant Pastor of the 1,000 member St. Paul A.M.E. Church in Cambridge, Massachusetts.

Pastor Payne is founder of Clear Lake African Methodist Episcopal Church in the Clear Lake City area of Houston, Texas. She has served as the Assistant Pastor of St. James A.M.E. Church, Dickinson; has been a member of the Texas Conference Board of Examiners since 1989; coordinated for two years the South Houston District Retreat; preached numerous revivals and taught in the Houston Women in Ministry city-wide conference.

She is currently pastoring full-time at the the Mother Church of Texas, Reedy Chapel. During her tenure there Pastor Payne has led the renovation of the sanctuary, and the membership is growing spiritually.

Pastor Payne delights in the fellowship of the saints and ministering to the unsaved and downtrodden. She is committed to a life that reflects the words of Paul:

*I, therefore, the prisoner of the Lord, beseech you that
ye walk worthy of the vocation wherewith ye are called. (Ephesians 4: 1)*

Our Churches

Profile of a Reedy Member: Bernice Gardner

A Galvestonian since the age of 3, Mrs. Bernice Gardner is the widow of General Gardner and mother of Dr. Frederick Tillis, a retired university professor and probably the best known trained music composer of any race who has been born and reared in Galveston.

She and her husband were Reedy's oldest living members and have served our church for almost 70 years -- over 80 for Bernice Gardner, who has spent all of her years in Reedy. Part of a rich family musical heritage, Mrs. Gardner said she always loved to sing, and that she sang in Reedy's choirs from the time she was a very young child. I knew her as a very bright and capable adult soprano soloist. She hit her peak while singing under Mrs. Barker, an accomplished musician who directed Reedy's choirs while her husband was our minister. I recall being thrilled to hear Mrs. Gardner sing *Italian Street Song*, at a time when our choir was at its finest and its performances in various places included some favorite secular selections.

It was after a rather grueling concert schedule that Mrs. Gardner lost her singing voice, permanently. She endured a form of laryngitis that kept her hoarse all of the time. Eventually, she was able to talk again -- sometimes with trouble, but at times understood very clearly.

Bernice Gardner also remembered playing and singing for my grandfather's services, down in his little mission church in the poorer district of Galveston. She said that Papa worshipped at Reedy on Sundays, and held his services on weekday afternoons after school was dismissed. (I had often wondered how he had been active in both churches.)

She came from a musically talented family. "All of us could sing, everyone in the family... My mother's sister played for different churches; they didn't have services every Sunday."

Because she "couldn't just sit," preferring to remain active, she joined Reedy's Usher Board in the '50s and asked her father, Frank Hubbard, who was on the board, to teach her how to usher correctly. She has served there as an usher ever since.

Avenue L Baptist Church
2612 Avenue L

Ave. L Baptist Church

In 1840, the First Baptist Church organized its five slave members as the Colored Baptist Church. In the 1850s, slaves were worshiping in a separate building that became known as the African Baptist Church, at 26th Street and Avenue L.

Our Churches

The Rev. I.S. Campbell became pastor in 1867, organizing the church as the First Regular Missionary Baptist Church. In 1871, he helped organize the Lincoln Baptist District Association, serving as the first moderator.

In 1891, a new church building was erected, and Rev. Ambrose Hubs replaced Rev. Campbell. The Rev. P. A. Shelton became minister in 1898. The Rev. S.W.R. Cole assumed leadership shortly thereafter and began rebuilding the church after its destruction in the 1900 storm; he died in 1903. Rev. Shelton served again from 1903-1904. The present name, Avenue L, was adopted under his pastorate.

The Rev. H.M. Williams served from 1904-1933. His first task was further rebuilding the church. In 1905, a frame building was erected at the cost of $7,500; by 1915, the congregation had outgrown it. The Tanner Brothers' Contractors and Architect, a Black company, began construction on the present brick structure in 1916, laying the cornerstone on Dec. 10. It was dedicated on Jan. 7, 1917. Many fund-raising activities were held to build the church, which cost $18,000 and included art glass window panes; a furnace supplying steam heat; semi-circular gallery; pulpit; baptizing pool; and space reserved for an organ. On Dec. 29, 1919, the church celebrated the end of its debt by burning its mortgage papers.

And in March 1921 the congregation installed a new pipe organ, built by the Estey Organ Company of Vermont, o.p. 1859, at a cost of $4,860. (It was removed in 1956.)

Rev. Williams organized the Ladies' Ushers and other groups for the church. He baptized over 1,500 people into the church and ordained over 50 ministers. He was also moderator for the Lincoln Baptist District Association for 23 years. He died in June 1933.

Rev. G.L. Prince

Rev. G.L Prince served from 1934 to 1956. He was president of the National Baptist Convention of America for 23 years. Rev. Prince also served as vice president of the Baptist World Alliance, and president of Mary Allen College in Crockett. He traveled all over America, Africa, Europe and Asia for the cause of Christ. And at the church he organized the Brotherhood Union, Junior Mission, Choir No.2, Junior Choir, Benevolent [Society], and a Mary Allen College Club. He was 86 years of age at the time of his passing in 1956.

The Rev. R.E. McKeen was the pastor from 1957 to1978. Rev. McKeen served as moderator of the Lincoln Baptist District Association, belonged to the Mary Allen College board of trustees and the Missionary General Baptist Convention, and took part in many civic activities in Galveston. Rev. McKeen was the first at Avenue L to conduct a radio

Our Churches

ministry, with many evening services broadcast to Galveston County residents. He attended the Baptist World Alliance in Rio De Janeiro, Brazil, in 1960, and Stockholm, Sweden, in 1975.

In 1973, the church began a $150,000 renovation; an air conditioning and heating system was installed later. In 1977, the stained-glass windows were refurbished, and protective glass added. In September 1978, Rev. McKeen died at the age of 80.

The Rev. Ralph J. Cummins, who had been president of the Galveston Ministerial Association and had been ordained by Rev. McKeen, served as interim minister until he was elected minister in 1979. In 1980, a new public address system was installed, and the church's renovation was completed.

Avenue L Church was designated a landmark on Feb. 28, 1982, and received the Texas Historical Commission marker (medallion); the Brotherhood was the original contributor.

In 1983, Dr. James McGlothlin, pastor of the First Baptist Church, presented Ave L with original slave documents of the early church. These documents were donated to the Rosenberg Library Archives, to add to the Avenue L church files, on Aug. 15, 1983.

After Hurricane Alicia struck on Aug. 18, 1983, a new roof and main entrance were completed.

Rev. Cummins resigned in April 1984, and delivered his farewell sermon on June 3, 1984. The Rev. Andrew W. Berry was elected pastor, becoming the youngest pastor in the history of the church. He caused quite a stir of interest in the city, bringing in many members and making several changes in church procedures. To everyone's astonishment, he died suddenly while serving there.

A member who became the new minister, the Rev. Clifford Thompson, has had a rather low profile. But I recall how he ignited the audience with a practical, common-sense speech at the Old Central Cultural Center Board banquet during a Juneteenth celebration in 1999, and his fine bass voice has graced a choir I have organized occasionally.

Like Reedy Chapel, Avenue L Baptist Church has shown a love for fine music over the years. Very good musicians at Avenue L have included members of the Thomas family.

Profile of Avenue L Church Members: The Thomas Family

All of the Thomas family had musical ability, and formed several singing groups. I saw a picture of one such group at the home of Ruth Thomas Hall.

Mattie Peachey Thomas, Ruth's father's mother, was born in 1880 in Galveston, and was one of Avenue L's biggest workers; she served as president of the church's Missionary Society until her passing. Another family member, Mattie Edwina Thomas, played for various churches, including Mt. Olive. (Other musicians at Mt. Olive Baptist Church have included Faye Boutte and Beatrice Hill.)

In the years immediately after the Civil War, many independent African American congregations organized, often with assistance from the Freedmen's Bureau.

Our Churches
The Thomas Family

THE THOMAS FAMILY - 1958

Seated: CARRIE BELL THOMAS & EDWIN HARTWELL Standing L to R: RUTH THOMAS HALL, SARAH THOMAS TATUM, OCTAVIA THOMAS, EDWIN H. THOMAS JR., JAMES B. THOMAS, R to L: DUMBAR J. THOMAS, LAWRENCE THOMAS, PAUL S. THOMAS, CARRIE BELL THOMAS, Top: MARIE THOMAS GOLSTON & GEORGE W. THOMAS

Thomas Family

The Thomas family has long been a very musical family. Roland Thomas was one of Texas Southern University's top band directors. His cousin, George Thomas, is still in Houston today, as a name synonymous with great jazz. George has also sponsored educational camps for young aspiring jazz players.

But the backbone of the family, still active after almost 70 years in church music, is their aunt, Ruth Thomas Hall. She has played the piano and the organ at Avenue L Baptist Church for many years. She has pursued harmony in getting along with all sorts of differing musical tastes over the years, retaining her likable ways and still setting an example in quality music.

Her great-nephew Lawrence Thomas, who was in the famous Grambling University Marching Band, has started more than one musical group here in Galveston: first a community band that rehearsed at Wright Cuney Center, then a band at Rosenberg Elementary School. And most of her family members, more than I can name, are active in musical circles.

The Reverend BRUCE A. AUGUST, Sr.. had the largest funeral of anyone born and raised in Galveston, in my experience. One reason was that he was so young, the same age as my son, at the time. He was only 46 years old. We were all so shocked because most of us knew nothing of any health problems that he had before his sudden death. I will write from his obituary to include pertinent facts. Since he was not only my son's classmate, but also fraternity brother, and fellow minister, I knew him well. He came through Austin School when I taught there. He was a very loving, positive man, and he was loved by so many. I remember that he never failed to give me a big hug when he saw me, along with a big smile, and told me "You will always be one of my favorite teachers. You taught me so much by just watching your life." Spiritually, we are not supposed to question God's actions, but you do wonder why he was taken from us when he had so much to offer, especially to the youth in his family, and the community at large.

Bruce was born December 31, 1956 in Galveston, Texas to the late Wilbert Sr. and Velma August. He was a graduate of Ball High School Class of 1975, and went on to further his education by attending Sam Houston University in Huntsville, where he received his Bachelor of Science degree in Business Administration. While attending Sam Houston, he also became a member of the Alpha Phi Alpha Fraternity, Inc, where he served as chaplain of the local chapter.

Our Churches

Bruce was a long time member of the Avenue L Baptist Church where he served as an associate minister, working with the Youth Department and was assistant superintendent of the Sunday School. He was employed with the Texas Department of Correction, where he served in many supervisors' capacities, rising up to the rank of assistant warden at the Jester III unit. He was affiliated with the West Ft. Bend County Heart Association, Pecan Grove Athletic Association, and volunteered with many other youth organizations. He really had a passion for kids and tried to be a positive influence on their lives He will be greatly missed.

He left a loving and devoted wife, Kathy August, four sons- Bruce Anthony Jr., Stephen Bradley, Kristen Joseph, and Brandon Joshua August, all of Richmond (texas). Named as surviving relatives also were a stepmother, brother, three sisters, and other uncles, aunts, and hordes of friends. I was welcomed up into the choir stand where I sat for about an hour before time for the service to begin. Anyone coming within the hour had no place to sit left. The huge crowd was testimony to his popularity and genuine love for people. This included so many co-workers from the prison and even inmates that were allowed to attend.

We are reminded that is the quality of time we give in service and not the quantity that matters to a divine creator.

Wesley Tabernacle United Methodist Church
902 28th Street

Wesley Tabernacle

The Rev. Peter Cavanaugh founded Wesley Tabernacle United Methodist Church in 1869 in a one-room house on Broadway between 38th and 39th streets, with a handful of members, including Irvin Claborn, Abe Woods, John McClean, Mrs. Elsie Mosely, Mrs. Esther Ashe, Mrs. Lydia Striltman, Mrs. Louise Valentine, Mrs. Louvenia Cavanaugh and Mrs. Mary Bland.

As the church began to grow, the present location was purchased for $1,200 by George Terry, George Ashe, Matt McKinney and Wash Green, trustees for the congregation. The little one-room house was moved to 28th Street. Under the leadership of the Rev. George Ashe, a former Presbyterian church on 14th Street was purchased and moved to the corner lot at 28th Street and Sealy.

Our Churches

Jesse Shackleford served as pastor for one year and was succeeded by the Rev. V.M. Cole. Under the Rev. Cole, the congregation continued to grow.

During Cole's pastorate, the church and the parsonage burned. Cole, however, refused to move from the corner lot, and held services under an arbor of brush. A foundation was laid for another church building, which was completed under the leadership of the Rev. Peter Morgan. The great storm of 1900 destroyed the newly constructed building. The Rev. William Bartley rallied surviving members of the congregation, and built a one-story church.

In 1921, the Rev. E.W. Kelly was appointed to Wesley Tabernacle. In 1924, the church was remodeled -- the existing one-story building was raised, and a new first floor was constructed.

The addition included Sunday school classrooms, a kitchen, pastor's study, and new restrooms. The construction gave the building, which remains today, a unique combination of architectural styles. The simple lines of the Craftsman-style porches contrast with the traditional Gothic Revival peaks and flourishes on the original church's roofline.

The church, under the leadership of pastor Rev. Perrie Joy Jackson, continues to serve the needs of the congregation and community.

Profile of A Pastor: Rev. Perry Joy Jackson

Valedictorian for Central High School's 1953 class, she received her bachelor's degree with highest honors and earned a master's degree in education. After about 10 years of teaching, she earned a master of theology degree. She founded the very first United Methodist Church at Prairie View, and was sent to three other area churches before she was assigned finally to her home church, Wesley Tabernacle, which she has pastored the better part of a decade.

Rev. Jackson has served on the Board of Global Ministries of the United Methodist Church, traveling to Port-au-Prince, Haiti, and the Methodist Conference in Dublin, Ireland. She has served at various U.S. mission locations, including New York, Atlantic City, Chicago and Atlanta, during her other assignments.

Rev. Jackson is the worthy counselor of Southern Beauty Court #61, Order of Calanthe, and a member of Sarah's Court #1, Heroines of Jericho, PHA. She is also on the Board of Missions of the Texas Annual Conference, and on the Board of Ordained Ministry of the Texas Annual Conference; each year, she leads the morning devotion of the worship service at the conference. She is also an ordained elder, among the first women in the United States ordained for the Itinerant Ministry of the United Methodist Church, and has several published works to her credit.

She has received many awards, but does not like to list them. She is also very interested in youth, always making a place in the church's program for young people.

Rev. Jackson initiated Wesley's Saturday Chapel Service for the infirmed, for those unable for health or job reasons to attend Sunday services, and started a neighborhood breakfast program in the church area, where there are many needy; free breakfast is distributed to about 70 people every Saturday morning. Other projects maintained by the church's small membership are the Food Pantry, the Clothes Closet, and the Emergency Fund of the Society of St. Stephens.

Our Churches

Under the dedicated leadership of a woman who lives the life she preaches about, her church is moving forward to perpetuate the principles of Jesus Christ.

St. Paul United Methodist Church
1425 Broadway

From Reedy Chapel came two other churches, founded by other pioneers of African American religious life in Galveston: another African Methodist Episcopal Church, Shiloh, at 29th Street and Avenue M; and the St. Paul Methodist Church, now at 15th Street and Broadway.

St. Paul's Methodist

The history of St. Paul is tied so with my own church, it is like giving a report on family. I grew up with these members as close to me as those in my own church. For a while I also played the organ there regularly at the request of a member, Jewell Earles Banks, one of my dearest friends. And there I played for her funeral, within a week after she made that last request.

This is just one of my precious memories about St. Paul, having attended quite a few services there before and after my service to the church. My godmother and one of my mother's dearest friends, Mrs. Mandania Lemons, was a faithful member.

The oldest records we have show St. Paul to have been established about 1866, not long after Reedy Chapel became an African Methodist Episcopal Church. After Reedy's sale to the AME Church, those who did not want A. M. E. affiliation began St. Paul.

Founders of St. Paul include Matthew Henry Earles, George Terry, Rev. J.L. Smith, Robert Cambridge, Ephram Hunter, Harriet Scott, Amanda McKinney Hayes, Fanny Butler, The Russells, Ms. Maze, Abb Johnson, Archie Harris, The Dorseys, The Mannings, Sarah Spencer, Millie Matthews, and the Wrights.

"Old St. Paul was located on 8th and Avenue H, the second lot on the odd numbered side. There were two structures on this lot. The buildings were destroyed by the 1900 Storm, and all records connected with the beginning of our church were also destroyed.

The first new historical record book for St. Paul, after the storm, was not purchased until December 4, 1903.

After the 1900 Storm, the congregation decided not to rebuild on the original site. With the help of their present pastor, Rev. Frank Gary, the

Our Churches

members purchased a lot on the corner of 15th and Broadway, and erected the beautiful structure that is now known as St. Paul United Methodist Church."

This information came from a history of the church printed for St. Paul's 122nd anniversary, in 1988. The headline read "The Small Church With The Big Heart."

"In 1919, Pastor L.V. Harrison changed the Sunday School hour from 9:30 a.m. to 12:30 p.m., and this was said to have increased attendance and collection of money. During this same year, broken windows described as "art glass" were replaced, and new screens added." (Stained glass was not readily available then; I used to hear the old-timers talk about the stained-glass windows St. Paul used to have that I did not see there.) Wooden racks for hymn books and bibles were also placed on pews.

"In 1921, the first Community Center was purchased, under Reverend G.E. Belcher. Miss Naomi Hunter held her kindergarten class in this two story structure.

"Rev. R. Hightower (Dec.1927 - Dec. 1930) was a great leader and builder. During his tenure as pastor, the present parsonage was built at a cost of $8,999. This structure was a splendid complement to modern architecture.

"Through the thirties and forties, St. Paul continued to grow, and in 1953, the Conference sent Reverend Ruben White. Under his leadership, we paid off the mortgage on the parsonage, and advanced the youth department.

"Reverend Fredrick Price was sent to us in 1954. In 1955, Sister John T. Williams willed St. Paul property on the corner of 28th and Avenue

K. The church sold the property and purchased the now standing annex, which is known to our members as the Sister John T. Williams Education Building. During this period, we also purchased concrete steps for the north and west sides of the church, and enclosed the rear property with a cyclone fence."

In the anniversary history of church achievements, Samuel Osbourn is listed as the founding pastor, beginning his service in 1867. Other notables include J.B. Scott, who pastored in 1917 and went on to become bishop, and J. Leonard Farmer, who pastored from 1918 to 1919 and became dean of Wiley College

As for church improvements, Frank Gary served as pastor from 1896 to 1899, and returned for another term from 1900 to 1901, during which he rebuilt the church. G.E. Belcher, pastor from 1920 to1922, oversaw creation of the community center. W.H. Hightower, who served from 1927 to 1930, helped build the new parsonage, and Ruben H. White, 1953-1954, helped pay off the parsonage mortgage. Freddrick Price, 1954-1956, added the Williams Education building.

W.H.B. Tapp, 1960-1964, saw to it that the church was painted; Hubert Liedy, 1964-1967, oversaw placement of new carpet in the church. Under Matthew Lamb, 1971-1975, window air-conditioning units were added. Lonnie Flanagan, who is listed as starting his service in 1980, helped oversee placement of a new roof . (I recall him, however, as pastor in 1979, consoling my husband after his mother passed. I played for the church while he was pastor.) Under Leroy Hall, 1981-1982, central air conditioning was installed. And Freddie Shaw, 1982-1987, oversaw renovation after 1983's Hurricane Alicia.

Our Churches
Holy Rosary Parish, Roman Catholic Church
1422 31st Street

Holy Rosary

Because segregation in the Deep South prohibited whites and non-whites from sitting together, and therefore worshiping together, the Roman Catholic Church's administrators enforced that prohibition, even as the church stated that all men were regarded by God as equal to each other -- there was no practicing what one preached. At first, the non-whites could be in the same church, but were relegated to sitting in the rear, behind the whites. Then the faithful of the darker race were allowed to raise money to build their own church, Holy Rosary. They were also allowed to build their own school. So, the children could be taught the ways of the Roman Catholic Church, but only under their own roof.

Holy Rosary was the first African American parish in the South, with Texas' first Black Catholic school. It was the church of my husband's family, where he belonged and attended all of his life, and I have served as musician at their masses for several years. This is the history supplied in 1996 by the church:

"In the 1880s there were many African-Americans living in Galveston. The Most Reverend Nicholas A. Gallagher felt that a school should be established for their children. In 1886 he established Holy Rosary School in a small cottage at the corner of 12th and Avenue K, with 13 students in attendance.

The Dominican Sisters cooperated with the Bishop and supplied the teachers. This was the very first Black Catholic school in Texas, and Holy Rosary Church thus became the first African-American parish in the South. Larger numbers enrolled and it was necessary in 1888 to erect a new school at 25th and Avenue I. There were four classrooms and they could accommodate 50 students.

On December 21, 1889 Father Phillip Keller, a native of Germany, was appointed the first resident pastor of Holy Rosary Parish. He found there about 45 parishioners and the school, but no church or rectory. He lived at St. Mary's Cathedral and began construction which was blessed by Bishop Gallagher on October 1, 1893. All the while the school was meeting with increased success. On September 15, 1898 the school was taken over by the Sisters of the Holy Family, founded in New Orleans in 1846. The Sisters proved themselves the worthy successors of the dauntless Dominicans. With the arrival of the Holy Family Sisters, Father Gallagher built and organized Holy Rosary Industrial School, where the children were taught dressmaking, cooking, housekeeping, and other useful work. It was a very successful school.

Our Churches

No one in Galveston can forget September 8, 1900. Holy Rosary was not spared. The Sisters opened the convent doors and the school to every man, woman, and child who sought shelter and assistance. About 8 o'clock in the evening , at the height of the storm, the building twisted around and all thought the end was near. But the sturdy structure, though it rocked like a ship at sea, remained intact and did not suffer the fate of similar buildings. At about 11 o'clock, with waters rising to the second story, the wind changed, and the battle against the elements was won for the occupants of Holy Rosary Convent. The church, rectory, and school were damaged to the extent of $5000.00. While others suffered more, this was a severe blow to the struggling little parish.

Father Keller's pastorate at Holy Rosary spanned 24 years from 1889 until 1913. He resigned as pastor on July 1, 1913. The Josephite Fathers, members of the Society of Saint Joseph of the Sacred Heart, whose special apostolate is with the African Americans, were invited to take charge of Holy Rosary Parish. Father Charles Gately, S.S.J. succeeded Father Keller as pastor on August 1913, and served until 1917. Early in his administration, in 1914, Father Gately moved the church and all other parish buildings from the original site on 25th and Avenue I [Sealy] to their present site on Avenue N between 30th and 31st Streets. The original site of Holy Rosary building is now occupied by Galveston City Hall, and the Public Safety Building.

Father Charles Reilly, S.S.J. succeeded Father Gately as pastor in October 1918. Father Andrew Fitzpatrick, S.S.J. arrived at Holy Rosary in the fall of 1923. He discovered that the single Mass on Sunday adequately provided for active members of the parish. He decided to seek out the "lost sheep". He was so successful that it was necessary to add a third Mass to accommodate the growing attendance at Holy Sacrifice. He was helped during his pastorate with associate pastors among whom were Father Hugh Duffy, S.S.J., Father John Doyle, S.S.J., who served as associate from 1936 until 1941, Father Edward Hennessey, S.S.J., and Father John O'Shea, S.S.J.

In 1927 a high school curriculum was added to the school program. This was the first accredited Catholic high school for African-Americans in the state of Texas. The 1927-28 session was held in the parish hall. In September 1928, the students and faculty moved into a new and well-equipped building. The high school made gratifying progress for several years. In the late 1930s, financial problems arose and it became necessary to close the high school in 1941.

Father Fitzpatrick was pastor for 19 years. He left a permanent impression on the parish. Older parishioners recall his name and work with affection and admiration. He died on July 21, 1943, mourned not only by Holy Rosary parishioners, but by many in Galveston. The years following Father Fitzpatrick's death were rather unstable times. In the short space of five years, the parish had three pastors -- Father John Callery, S.S.J. in 1942-43, Father Roderique Auclaire, S.S.J. in 1943-44, and Father Narcisse Denis, S.S.J., who served from 1944-47.

Things began to stabilize with the arrival of Father James E. Finegan, S.S.J., who became pastor in 1947. He began planning for the construction of a new church. He wrote, "the older 60 year structure could hardly weather another hurricane." Ground was broken by Bishop Christopher Byrne on October 17, 1949. The dedication was conducted by a new Bishop of Galveston, Most Reverend Wendelin J. Nold, on April

Our Churches

16, 1950. The cost of construction was $45,000. Replacement value at this date in 1996 is estimated at $673,000. Things do change!

Father Finegan died on January 29, 1953, and was succeeded by Father George Reynold, who immediately set about to replace the old convent and school which were literally falling down. On September 30, 1956, Holy Rosary's parishioners proudly participated as Bishop Nold dedicated the new convent. One year later, on September 29, 1957, the Bishop returned to dedicate Holy Rosary School -- a two-story building with nine classrooms and lavatory facilities at the cost of $85,000, in 1996 worth $874,000.

Father Reynold's term of pastor expired in 1959. His successor was Father Thomas Monahan, S.S.J., who served until 1965. During his term, a new rectory was erected and dedicated. Father Joseph Turner, S.S.J. followed Father Monahan. He added a cafeteria, a classroom, office, and library to the parish school. A generous gift from W.K. Hebert, local undertaker and member of the parish, assisted in the cost of construction. In early 1969, Father John Doyle, S.S.J. returned to Galveston as pastor. He had been an associate pastor following ordination in June 1936. One crisis during his pastorate was the fire of December 31, 1975, that destroyed the sanctuary and attic of the church. Repair work was completed for Holy Week 1976.

Father Louis Saporito, S.S.J. became pastor in the fall of 1976. He introduced the Mardi Gras to the parishioners and the people of Galveston. The first Mardi Gras (for Holy Rosary) was held in Moody Center on January 20, 1978."

Mardi Gras had been celebrated since the last century in Galveston. This probably refers to a reintroduction of the celebration after a lapse in interest that began sometime after World War II.

"Holy Rosary school ran into serious problems in the school year 1978-79. On May 28, 1979, Holy Rosary School closed its doors. The parish suffered general sadness to see the Sisters of Holy Family leave after 81 years of dedicated service to Catholic education in Galveston.

In August 1983, Alicia roared into Galveston. Holy Rosary did not escape. Damage to building amounted to more than $50,000.

Father Saporito moved on in 1984, and was succeeded by Father Joseph L. Waters, S.S.J. He accomplished various improvements to parish property, including redecoration of the church sanctuary, the church doors, and paving of the school yard. He served until August 1992, when he was succeeded by the current pastor, Father Paul H. Banet, S.S.J, in September 1992. Since September 1994, he has been assisted by a parochial vicar -- his blood brother, Father Charles Banet, C.P.P.S., who had retired from an administrative post at Saint Joseph's College in Rensselaer, Indiana. Also in residence is Father Robert DeGrandis, S.S.J. who serves as a charismatic apostolate throughout the world.

As of October 1996, there have been 3977 baptisms in the parish since its founding, 785 marriages performed, and there are currently 438 parishioners."

Our Churches
Saint Augustine's Episcopal Church
1410 41ˢᵗ Street

1884 – 1984

St. Augustines

This information came from compilations by the Rev. Roderic B. Dibbert, lay assistant at St. Augustine. In a document entitled "Do the Clergy of this diocese have an obligation to minister to Negroes?", Rev. Dibbert reports:

"A few of the clergy of the diocese felt the obligation, but due to the upheaval of the War [Civil], nothing permanent was ever achieved, and the Negro did not enter into the actual life of the diocese until St. Augustine's Mission in Galveston was founded [in] 1884. It may be safely said that whatever foundations were laid before the War Between the States, nothing remained after Appomatox, and that there were no Negro missions of the Episcopal Church in Texas for about twenty years after Emancipation.

There were, however, two unsuccessful attempts to bring the Negro freedman into the fellowship of the Episcopal Church before 1884. The Rev. D.W. Chase organized a Sunday School class of eighty-five in Independence in 1868, but this is not mentioned in later reports. At San Antonio, Bishop Gregg helped establish a Sunday School for colored children in 1869. Thirty scholars were enrolled at that time, but by 1872, the number had dropped to twenty, and thereafter the school is not mentioned in the diocesan reports.

Bishop Gregg suggested a suffragan for the Negro race at the Council of 1874, and the question of a 'racial episcopate' was discussed at every General Convention from 1874 to 1916. Finally, in 1918, Edward Thomas Damby became the Suffragate Bishop of Arkansas, in charge of Negro missions in the Southwest. But, as Dr. Murphy points out, 'the whole arrangement was still in an experimental stage, and the problem itself was really no nearer solution in 1935 than it was in 1866.'

The committee for 'The Moral and Spiritual Condition and Wants of the Freedmen' appointed by the Diocesan Council in 1867 has become the diocesan bi-racial committee of today. But most of the work of the Church among Negroes remained on paper only.

Although both Bishop Gregg and Kinsolving were anxious to see the church grow among the Negro members of the population, no pronouncements were officially made during their episcopate, other than suggestions for a racial episcopate. Resolutions containing any amount of social teaching did not appear until 1935 (against child labor), and in 1936 (against lynching)."

Our Churches

In a Feb. 15, 1996, letter to me, Dibbert wrote: "The fact that not all African-Americans are members of the mainline 'Black' denominations has always intrigued me, and because I am White, I cannot possibly really understand why. ... I came to the conclusion that Black Episcopalians remaining in our denomination under serious handicaps (especially before civil rights and integration) must have had more faith and conviction of the truth of that faith, to see beyond prejudice and discrimination. ... I do not understand why Black folks stood for such indignities, and the only answer I can come up with, is that they had more religion than the Whites." His letter speaks volumes.

Father Dibbert also said, "The first real statement on racial equality appears in Bishop Hines' address to the Diocesan Council in 1947: 'I would like to see this Council go on record in establishing a policy that where white and Negro delegates cannot be served together at a common meal, the Council, as a group will forego that meal.'"

Below are the entries of most relevance from Rev. Dibbert's timeline, "The African American in the Episcopal church, a chronology of major events 1619-1957":

1889 - First Episcopal School established for Negroes in the State: The Mary Stewart Pinckney Industrial School at St. Augustine's, Galveston

1900 - Early progress halted by the 1900 Hurricane at Galveston, which destroyed St. Augustine's, and killed Fr. and Mrs. Cain, along with many parishioners

1906 - First ordination of a Negro held in rebuilt church, the second such ordination in the State. Subsequently, eight other men have been ordained at St. Augustine's

1954 - First ordination of a White man in a Texas Negro church - Father Sutton

1955 - St. Vincent's Chapel and Community Center opened

1956 - First Interracial Board of Directors organized for St. Vincent's House, Galveston, with representatives from all three Episcopal parishes in the city: Trinity, Grace, St. Augustine's

In this same document, Father Dibbert states, "In the Beginning: About fifty West Indian Negro Anglicans desired the services of their church. Not being welcomed at the regular services of the two then existing Episcopal Churches in Galveston, the rector of Grace Church offered them the only thing possible under segregation: separate services.

Accordingly, at Grace Church, the Negroes attended at 7:30 p.m. on Sundays and at 9 a.m. every Wednesday and Friday. Bishop Gregg ... secured a Negro priest from Kentucky to organize the work in Galveston, as a separate mission (William F. Floyd).

But yellow fever claimed Dr. Floyd's life only about two years after he had arrived in Galveston. ...It was the Bishop's will that he travel throughout the nation in order to raise money for a church building. ... 'I have on hand towards building: $296.95.'

And in 1889, a church building was secured, and by 1900 the diligence of the second vicar of the mission (Thomas Cain) had established an active congregation of 209 communicants and 400 baptised members. A parochial industrial school had been established, and the report for 1889 lists it with an enrollment of fifty-five pupils."

With this document were photographs of Father Cain, a Black man; a scene of the destruction of Saint Augustine after the 1900 Storm; and Mrs. Laura Taylor, who at age 91 was St. Augustine's oldest member

Our Churches

at the time of that writing, a member of the parish for over 70 years who could still remember the early days. Mrs. Taylor was confirmed by Bishop Gregg on May 9, 1888.

"Inheritance posed a legal problem in some states, and it was argued in court that a freedman could not inherit property left to him by his former master. But when the 1900 Storm struck, all citizens -- black, white, yellow, brown -- fought together for their lives against the angry waves, which seemed to bring them together for the first time as equals. In 1902 (Easter Day), a new church building was consecrated by Bishop Kinsolving for the Negro churchmen of Galveston."

He included a picture of the new 1902 church, showing it cost $9,000. It was erected and paid for under the third vicar of the church, Rev. Walter H. Marshall, from 1901-1910. The site was at 22nd Street and Broadway, where the church remained until 1940, when it was moved to its present location to allow expansion. Other pictures included the Rev. Fred W. Sutton, who was the 14th vicar and 1st Rector of the church, from 1953 – 1959.

I was very disappointed that there was no picture of the Rev. Bright-Davies, who served this parish for about 18 years, and was the only leader at Saint Augustine that I knew when I was growing up in Galveston; he was also the only African priest I can recall at St. Augustine. Among his children, his daughters -- Esther, my classmate, and Lamatsoi, my sister's classmate -- were also very active in the community. Rev. Bright-Davies was mentioned, however, in Dibbert's listing of clergy serving since 1884; his 18-year term of service was longer than any of the others. The list also included Charles M. Parkman, supply priest 1884-54, and William F. Floyd, founder 1885-1887.

He also supplied further details about Father Bright-Davies: "Rev. William Hastings Bright-Davies spent the first eighteen years of his ministry in Galveston. Born in Accra, Gold Coast Colony, West Africa, Fr. Bright-Davies came to Galveston in 1926, and served as layleader here until sent to seminary by Bishop Quin. He was ordained deacon in Dec. 1930 and priested in July 1931. The major projects during his long ministry here at St. Augustine's were the Annual Summer Conferences, the move of the church and rectory to corner lots at 41st Street and Avenue M1/2 (1940), and the construction of a cement block parish hall (1943-47).

It has only been a few years since the facilities of Camp Allen have been available to our people, and the Annual Conferences held at St. Augustine's, held from 1930-1948, fulfilled a real need for fellowship between Churchmen. These conferences drew people from Tyler, Houston, Prairie View, Beaumont, and elsewhere, and were led by a capable staff of clergy and lay people.

The first women's group at St. Augustine's was organized by Fr. Cain, yet an official branch of the Diocesan Auxiliary was not organized until 1931, under the leadership of Fr. Bright-Davies. Its first president was Mrs. Laura Taylor, who throughout her seventy years as a communicant of this parish did outstanding work.

The greatest change in the local situation took place when the church and rectory were moved from their old location on 22nd and Broadway to more ample grounds at 41st and M1/2. Unfortunately, war conditions hampered the construction of a parish hall as originally planned. For ten years the building remained in an unfinished state, until remodeled and partly rebuilt. It was dedicated in 1957, as the final unit of a larger

Our Churches

section of classrooms and rectory, built in 1955. All of this would have been impossible at the old location due to lack of space.

Fr. Bright-Davies resigned his work here in 1948 to take charge of St. Patrick's, West Palm Beach, Florida.

Further excerpts from Rev. Dibbert's material:

"Fred Walter Sutton, Jr. was a deacon...had just graduated from The General Theological Seminary when he arrived in Galveston as the new vicar. The first project undertaken was a Vacation Church School for the neighborhood children, thus beginning a characteristic note in Fr. Sutton's ministry here. ... The eventful year of 1954 closed with the ordination of Fr. Sutton to the priesthood by Bishop Hines.

On May 15th Bishop Hines dedicated St. Vincent's Chapel ... July 9th, breaking ground for the new classrooms and vicarage by Bishop Quin ... death on Nov.26,1956...completed building at St. Augustine's dedicated by Bishop Hines Dec.11, 1955.

In the summer of 1953, Fr. Sutton rented an apartment in a quiet neighborhood on the west side of Galveston...temporary, as the neighbors complained to the landlord of the frequent visits of children from the corner of 27th and Ave. H, about a mile and a half from the church...observing an 'open rectory' policy, his quarters soon became a hangout for boys of all ages. However, the problem of rent had not been solved satisfactorily, and then men of the congregation remodeled a portion of the unfinished cement block parish hall for a temporary vicarage..the children who had been frequenting the old grocery store vicarage lost contact with Fr. Sutton, and with 3 or 4 exceptions, they did not come out to the church. It was evident that no real impression could be made on the neighborhood down in that area unless a center was made available for permanent worship, recreation, and instruction.

Seven months later, it was decided to open the building on 27th and Avenue H as a community center...after the necessary preparations were made, it opened on March, 1955.

All this would have been impossible without the enthusiastic help of laymen from the various parishes in Galveston and Houston. Full time help was secured, and the parish staff now consisted of three layworkers as well as the priest. College and seminary students have also helped out with the children's program during the summers since 1955.

Later on, a board of directors from each of the Galveston parishes was established, giving St. Vincent's House real stature and official standing as a social service of the Episcopal Church. The old grocery store soon became inadequate for the program and plans were made to build a new building, which became a reality in 1958. The present St. Vincent's House is a modern building of steel construction, located at 2817 Postoffice Street, in the midst of the worst depressed area in Galveston. A full time athletic director and custodian lives in the convenient apartment in the rear of the building, and a full time program of recreation and worship is presently making some impression on the neighborhood.

Thus, the influence of St. Augustine's Parish has spread...not only in depressed areas, but in quiet neighborhoods also, in the formation of St. Joseph's Chapel, Texas City. This small congregation holds services at a local funeral home, but it is expected with the construction of the new church there, a considerable growth will occur, and make it possible to become a parish itself, in the near future.

Our Churches

At the 108th Annual Council of the Diocese of Texas, held in Galveston in 1957, St. Augustine's was admitted as a parish after almost 75 years as a mission.

There was a general feeling among many of the faithful that the Diocesan opinion was that the long history of St. Augustine's as a Black Church should close, and that the membership be encouraged to become members in the two white congregations in order to integrate them.

All the priests since Father Davies have not been white. But the days of Bishop Quin finding a Bright-Davies have changed. "Bright", as Bishop Quin fondly called him, had an English college education and was working the Docks in Galveston for 50 cents an hour! Advancing him to the priesthood is the legend that has been a rich memory in the lives of those at St. Augustine's that he has touched.

In 1967, Father Gammon Jarrell...assumed the duties of the Rector of St. Augustine's...he was, in fact, officially the director of the William Temple Foundation, a campus ministry of UTMB. Father Nettleton was Director of St. Vincent's House ...Gerald Hoskins, a Black Presbyterian minister, on Nettleton's resignation, was employed as the Director of St. Vincent's House, with a vision for a nonstipendary ministry that would lead eventually to reception and ordination in the Episcopal Priesthood. These plans, for various reasons, never fully developed and Gerald resigned. Father Jarrell resigned in 1976 and a period of no priest for St. Augustine's was once again a reality."

Also worth adding to his history is mention of St. Vincent's director Alfreda Houston, now retired, who has had a tremendous impact on this community.

Island of Color

ALFREDA BATISTE HOUSTON needs more space than I have now, to list all of the things that have brought her to the attention of Galveston. She was born to Woodrow L. Batiste and Ora D. Batiste on July 11, 1940 here in Galveston. But, at the age of six, Alfreda was cared for by her grandmother, Anna Bell Oakey. Alfreda was quoted in 1997 as saying "She (Ms. Oakey) was the fiber that held the family together She was known in Galveston as the person who would write the president or the senators and representatives and let them know exactly how she felt. I guess I get some of my starch from her."

Alfreda became director of St. Vincent's Episcopal House in 1975. She told of being a volunteer there first, from the age of 16, saying "I would go before school and comb hair. After school, I helped read stories.

Our Churches

They didn't have any staff." Alfreda went from an annual budget of $8000 to a staff of 13 and a budget of over $300,000 in 1997.

Mrs. Houston started her education here in Galveston, graduating from Central High School in 1958. All of her formal schooling after that was done in Social Science and Behavioral Science Supervisor training. This included Human Resource in Houston, Texas A&M University Services in La Marque-Texas City, Galveston College, Southwest University in Lafayette, LA, University of Houston, College of the Mainland. She received her Associate Degree and was certified by the State of Texas, Department of Human Resources Licensing in 1984.

Mrs. Houston is married to Samuel Houston, has eight children, many grandchildren, and counts all of St. Vincent's children, past and present as hers. Her awards have been numerous for her lengthy service with the underprivileged and underserved persons of Galveston. They include the first prestigious "Steel Oleander" award from the Galveston Historical Foundation in 1994, the 1989 Rabbi Henry Cohen Humanitarian Award, the Galveston County Daily News "Citizen of the Year" award in 1997, and awards from Zeta Phi Beta Sorority, Delta Sigma Theta Sorority, Inc., Sigma Gamma Rho Sorority, Omega Psi Phi Fraternity, NAACP, College of the Mainland, and KILE Radio Station.

Alfreda Houston is an active member of Grace Episcopal Church. I first knew about Alfreda through my husband, who was commander of the American Legion Gus Allen III Post 614 for a while, and Alfreda worked with the Post activities. Thanks to her awareness of Roy's leadership, she was instrumental in keeping a scholarship in his name active in the Legion for a time, after Roy passed away.

Retired from active service as executive director of St. Vincent's House, Alfreda has passed the baton to Michael Jackson who continues to do great things there.

Certainly, these are not all of the churches attended and supported by African Americans in Galveston, or even all of the denominations represented in our city, which is very diverse in its religious expression. These are the oldest churches, however, that remain active today, from the denominations representing most of our people.

Exemplifying the kind of church members found in Galveston was a lifelong neighbor, Mrs. Naomi Jacquot, who recently passed away. I cannot end this writing without paying tribute to her as an example of religious life here.

Mrs. Jacquot was very proud of being called the "Mother of the Church" by her church, which was Pilgrim Baptist Church, in the 3200 block of Broadway. I know that they will miss her, because she attended every service, went on all the church's out-of-town trips, and sang in the choir. Her church life was the focal point of her life. And in our neighborhood, she always kept me informed of what was going on, keeping a watchful eye out for our visitors, for trespassers, as well as collecting packages delivered when I was away. She also reached out to me when I became a new widow. God bless her.

During my walk on this earth, my lifetime on this island, I have known that hope sustains, even when rescue or support has not come, and I have witnessed that the faith that things improve with prayer carries many through the hardest times imaginable. African Americans in Galveston as elsewhere can credit survival in the storms of life to their religious affiliations.

Our Churches

WHERE IS THIS CHURCH TODAY?

from *If You Want To Enough* by Ernest C. Wilson

"In the summer of 1918, Rev. Ernest C. Wilson arrived from San Diego to pastor his first church in Galveston. The church had survived two floods; red brick, steeply pitched roof, a belfry, Gothic windows that merited stained glass, double entrance doors twelve feet tall and arched like the windows. He entered to face a wide foyer. Across it, half opened doors gave a glimpse of an assembly hall, with rows of folding chairs facing a stage at the far end. At either side of the entry were gracefully curved stairways leading to an upper landing. I opened the outer doors, ascended the right stairway, and faced more open doors to the sanctuary. Rows of pews faced a chancel. There was a pulpit to the left, and a lectern to the right. Two high-backed chairs occupied the center space of the rear wall. There was a simple reed organ near the wall back of the lectern. I walked down the center aisle, up the two steps into the chancel, and seated myself at the organ bench."

The description sounds to me like Wesley Tabernacle United Methodist Church, but it could be some other. One of the Unity Church's significant pioneers was Ernest C. Wilson, who started a church here in 1918. Rev. Wilson's mentor, John Ring, was the above described church's prior minister. But further details of this early church are missing. Anyone recognizing this description who has additional information should contact Rev. Gary L. Browning, at Box 3674, Galveston, Texas 77551, or call (281) 333-0665. Rev. Browning, a Unity minister, recently returned to this area to create the Unity Spiritual Center on the island. This is Rev. Browning's offer, relayed to me when I attended his Unity Church service:

The first person revealing the location of this church will receive a bouquet of flowers for their church from Maisel's Florist.

Compton Memorial

Live Oak Baptist

Shiloh AME

CHAPTER SEVEN
MUSIC: ART, RECREATION & WORSHIP

Music, my lifelong passion, has always been known not only to calm but to fire up emotions. That is why trumpets were blown in biblical times, at the outset of a battle. That is why the American soldiers in the Revolutionary War are depicted playing drum and fife, in the long tradition of drums rolling in times of war.

One of the early Negro spirituals, which told biblical accounts through song, is Joshua Fit the Battle of Jericho, which relates how God instructed Joshua and his people to bring down the walls of Jericho with music, not with weapons. Some wonder how sounding trumpets could bring down the walls of a city. Following God's instructions was the key to their victory. The method He outlined can also be understood by study of physics -- knowing the walls were made of porous clay then, and the physical power of sound waves, I see it happening quite easily. (Remember the Memorex commercials showing Ella Fitzgerald's high notes cracking glass?)

Music, like other forms of art, has the power to be used for good or evil. And Galveston African Americans have yet to tap it fully. We have such a strong heritage of having great ability to create, having large impact on popular culture, but this generation must follow through and perpetuate itself in those art forms. Yet I am encouraged by many things -- just the other day I observed my 10-year-old granddaughter using her creative powers on the piano. Not content to only be taught how to read the notes and play them well, she has developed skill at playing the melodies she hears around her, and varying them. Thanks to consistent exposure to music from birth by her mother, she loves it and has an easy sense for it.

Just as older civilizations in Africa -- like that in Timbuktu, which predated any European civilization – produced persons of color highly skilled in the arts, the African American community has produced many with natural gifts that surpass those of formally trained people of any color. Musicians like late pianist Erroll Garner, who innovated a method that cannot be written down in any conventional musical format -- playing the right-hand melodies in a jazz rhythm just slightly behind the steady rhythm of the left hand with highly romantic effect -- made history with their unique styles without learning to read a note of music. Such musicians learned to play by listening to others play and experimenting; others were privately coached.

From the deep roots of music in Galveston's African American community came so many more musicians, known not only all over Texas, not only worldwide, but beyond -- some of our music has even been heard in space. (What better way to communicate with the unknown?)

Heritage on Parade

My grandfather's record of the island's Cadet Band offers the earliest recorded history of African Americans' musical talents in Galveston: "From the sixties [1860s] Galveston had its brass and string bands. The colored Cadet band served the pride of Galveston for many years and were often employed at big white funerals and in street parades. The Cadet Band was the outgrowth of Civil War musicians. Charley Wall was manager. Cornetest[sic] Carrol Cage, James Hill, Bill Massey, W. Sykes and other(s). Chief violinist in string band was Vincent Scott.

Music: Art, Recreation & Worship

Linberg was a great bass horn player, John Wyatt the kettle drum. Sam Robinson on alto horn and number of others. Old members and recruits from time to time -- Allen, Lawrence, J. Smith, Holland."

Not only were there musicians who were well trained on instruments not commonly associated with African Americans -- the violin, the kettle drum or tympani drums, for example -- but they were so good that their oppressors preferred their music.

Referred to as a Cadet Band, performing after the Civil War, they had evidently come together in the military. They might have learned to play together while awaiting combat training-- training often not received by colored soldiers sent to fight the South's enemy. Whatever the case, Papa said that these men of color in Galveston were in demand for many celebrated occasions.

But most examples relate to our own community's occasions. With public pride in their community heritage, Galveston's African Americans over the years staged many of its own festivals, parades and holiday observations -- occasions in which music played a large part.

Dr. Elizabeth Turner's research describes a 1903 Labor Day parade with a brass band, ending in Gulf City Park (possibly Cottonjammer's Park, a park cited by many old-timers I interviewed), followed by a celebration at Sea Wall Pavilion -- most likely the name given to Bob McGuire's place on the Seawall -- described as 'the best pleasure resort in town for colored people'.

In August, another parade and festival were sponsored by the city's Black newspapers for the children and the older folk, at a time when many could not afford vacations away from the summer heat and routine. As many as 1,700 fun-loving people were said to enjoy the picnics, with food, soda water, entertainment and prizes donated by merchants of both races.

Organized by a women's committee, Juneteenth activities included a parade, musical selections, speeches, and the reading of the Emancipation Proclamation. One year, after the proclamation was read, Everlena Anderson read a paper while costumed as the Goddess of Liberty. Turner mentioned that the women always handled the symbolic portions of the festival, while the men did the barbecuing and executed other activities. There was an old fiddlers' contest, fishing, crabbing, boating and bathing excursions. And people over 50 years old received free barbecue.

Although other communities started their own celebrations, Galveston's festivities drew large crowds from the surrounding area. It seems that the Juneteenth festivities received so much interest that white employers started giving their workers the day off by 1919. The parade was so large -- including a grand marshal and team, floats with May Pole Girls, the Goddess of Liberty and Maids of Honor, five divisions of mounted police, Black military men, decorated vehicles showing the progress of Black people in the fields of industry, education, commerce and labor -- that it ended in celebrations in two parks.

Turner noted the use of the Statue of Liberty in the parade: "Black women understood the power of the symbol, manipulated it to give meaning and substance to the freedom earned by ex-slaves, and to the promise of freedom for themselves and their children ... Juneteenth reminded Texans that freedom in any era is worth celebrating. ..."

Recreation, Celebrations, and Church & Concert Music

The people I interviewed provided further information about recreation, celebrations that included music, and other events that took on the face of African American culture in Galveston dating back to the early part of the century, as well as the music provided for church services and concert music.

Mrs. Della Rivers Sims

Mrs. Sims was 101 years old when I interviewed her. She remembered several fun activities here, such as church suppers and hayrides. The most exciting time I had as a young child myself was on a hayride on West Beach. She happily recalled, "We would go down to the beach, take a furnace along, fry fish, carry a container of ice cream, go down West Beach. Some would go in bathing, singing and clapping. Rev. King, minister of St. Paul, went on some of the hayrides with us."

She added that the Nineteenth of June picnics, as she called them, included taffy pulling. They would often do this at their homes at night, using lamps. And families would pop corn. She was old enough to remember riding the Interurban to picnics. The streetcars were mule-drawn cars. And to get to Tillotson College, one went to the Interurban station at 21st and Church streets, rode to Houston, then caught the train to Austin.

When I asked Mrs. Sims if she remembered the Little Susie Railroad, mentioned in Charles Hayes' book, she told me that her father used to ride on it. It was way out west, and they called it the Galveston-Houston-Henderson Railroad. The Henderson town, once planned for the west side of Galveston Island, never was built.

Mrs. Sims had fond memories that were still very detailed, and could almost make me see and feel what she described.

Island of Color

"Lamps stayed in bowls on walls in churches. People came through the dark with lanterns, hung them on the walls. Saturday nights, [there were] Eppworth League programs; [they] said speeches.

Best memories were 19th of June. Thanksgiving wasn't much.

White people would give the old people a calf or whatever to barbecue. Uncle Andrew used to barbecue. The old folks would sit at a table. The young folks had music -- a violin and a guitar.

Got to dance the two-step and the waltz. Arthur Jackson would wait for the square dance. They loved to 'swing your partner,' 'give your partner your right hand' ... [and at the] end of it, 'to the bar'. ... Whoever danced with you had to treat you to whatever was there; nothing over a nickel. ... If a boy had a quarter, you could buy two or three things, promenade on to the bar!"

As with all the others old enough to remember, the Dickinson picnics were her very favorite outings.

We "rode the train. ... All the churches met together, worked it all out ... West Point Baptist, got it all together ... just to ride the train was a treat itself ... Rev. Fred Williams, June Louise ... It was fun just to ride trolleys ... the church would charter a streetcar, make the belt around." They would ride the streetcar's full weekday route at night. "One large car would hold them."

Then she called the name of the McGuire Bathhouse, "at the foot of 29th Street and Beach ... that's why Negroes went to 29th Street to swim, bathe more."

Though she didn't know much about local bands or music for other occasions, she named the church musicians that she remembered. Some names surprised me. For instance, she said that Mrs. Gertrude Brown's mother, Mrs. Speed, played the organ. I knew Mrs. Brown, and her sister, Mrs. Martha Chase, but knew of no musicians in their family. She also named Joe Thompson as an organist. Effie Rogers and Frances Conway, an alto and high soprano, respectively, were in demand as singers. Pauline Bartley Collins (married then to Matthew Collins from Double Bayou, later to a man named Webb) was mentioned as a performer at Wesley Tabernacle.

Mrs. Evelyn Sanders Jones

Mrs. Jones, who mentioned some of the same memories as did Ms. Sims, added that they enjoyed movies and peanut hunts. She put new perspective on the Interurban by stating, "We lived on 25th and P. We didn't ride it, but we'd rush to see people get off it on Sundays and Tuesdays -- special Beach Days. They'd go back about 10:00 P.M. at night." This was from a time when arrivals and departures were events themselves.

Mrs. Elizabeth Bess Harrell

In answer to the question, "What did you do for fun here?" she said:

"We went kodaking [taking photographs] Sunday evenings. And we went to the Interurban station on 21st street between Church and Postoffice, got on the Interurban and rode to Virginia Point, between 59th and 61st Street. [We got off at] 61st street, and went clear across to Avenue S.

We went to the Cottonjammer's Park on 37th and S for picnics. Um-huh. Concerts on the sidewalk at 19th street between K and L. [We had] about 22 coaches for the Dickinson Picnic. The Southern Pacific train would stay on the track all day, wait for our return about 5:00 p.m."

Island of Color

She said her mother also liked to fish and occasionally went crabbing. It is surprising how few African Americans who live on this island enjoy fishing and crabbing, in a place many would love to inhabit just for the water activities. A lot of that stems from the days when African Americans did not feel free to go where they wanted to go on the beach without hostility from nearby business owners.

In answer to a question about which musicians played for churches, she said, "My classmate Janice Felder came from a large family, and played for St. Luke and Ave. L churches. There at St. Paul: Melvin Howard, and Claudell Williams," Tweezer's daughter.

Dr. and Mrs. Leroy Sterling

The Sterlings remembered riding the Interurban from the station Elizabeth Harrell described. The Sterlings said, "The depot was right across the street from the Martini Theater; it would stop at different places on Broadway, and would go to Houston, where you could get off at different places. Going to Prairie View, you could ride it, transfer to the Union Station" train.

For fun, they recalled going to the Mainland, where his father had a sister in Hitchcock. She had a white horse and a black buggy with the fringe on top and floor. Leroy said that he and his family would take along chinaberry branches to keep the mosquitoes off the horse's neck, but they had to endure the 'showers' (of mosquitoes) themselves.

Asked about other transportation, who had the first cars, they recalled, "Mr. McGuire owned some horses, as well as the Park, used to help Eunice Nash. The first cars -- neighbor Lizzie Phelps, a Model T

Ford. When Leroy was 14 or 15, the elders would let 'Dutch' take the car around. We had a car -- Graham Paige – 1925."

Asked about musicians who played for churches, they named Miss Laura Williams; someone whose last name was Gamble; Mrs. Mamie Richardson; Mrs. Hattie Freeman, and Mrs. Gaston. (Both taught me -- Mrs. Freeman privately, and Mrs. Gaston in school.)

Mr. Thomas Green

I asked him what he did for pleasure outings. He said that he remembered going into some type of recreational facility on 28th Street and Avenue Q, that it was an auditorium for African Americans, where they used to cook dinners. He remembered that Bob McGuire owned the park, and that the main part of the beach for Blacks was at 27th Street.

He also said, "Maggie Banks [Leon Banks' nickname] fought Jimmie Vacek for putting groins so close together to keep Blacks from congregating on that beach." Vacek was commissioner at the time. Green explained that placing the piles of rocks, known as groins, there caused such strong tides, such deep currents around them, that it was not safe to swim there.

"There were the Saturday night fish fries, church-related. They put a torch in front of each house where they sold them [the dinners]. I'd get a dime from Mother ... 5 cents for a sandwich, and 5 cents for ice cream. [This was] particularly around 29th street, during the early '20s.

Mr. Green also told me that he enjoyed going crabbing; he used to go to the beach and the bayou to crab. He told me that 61st Street was the best spot. This was in the days when we had no seawall beyond 61st

Street, because I used to ride down the 61st Street ramp myself, going onto West Beach.

Mrs. Lois Davis Tyus

Mrs. Tyus had memories that were close to my heart, like that of my mother's wedding.

"I remember Mrs. Viola's wedding - at Reedy Chapel. Mrs. Martha Cort Jones, Mrs. Jessie McGuire Dent were in it. ... Mrs. Martha Jones was a Fisk graduate -- she taught us well. We were way ahead when we got to college. ...

I remember hearing you practice your music on the piano all the time." They lived across the street from us.

As for amusement in Galveston, she said, "Dr. Stone used to come down here, go to the beach with us." Her other social memories were based elsewhere, where she was in the cream of society, since her husband was very important to the national effort in education.

Dr. Rufus and Janice Stanton

The Stantons spoke briefly about what they did for fun here.

"We went to City Party Park on Avenue S, between 37th and 39th streets. For social life, we went to and had a lot of yard parties. Others who gave parties were Miss Annie Williams, Florence and Ruth Phelps, Mrs. Tillie Phelps, Ruth Stanton, Lollie and Uncle Buddy."

Reverend Handley Hickey

As he and his wife had dinner with me, Rev. Hickey spoke on the cultural life of Galveston in the early part of the 20th century. He participated in the music program at church and at school, and was a very talented man who participated in many activities in Galveston. So he told me more details about musicians and of the fun things they did here.

"John W. Coleman directed the Reedy [Chapel A.M.E. Church] Orchestra. He was a very excellent musician. Bernice James played the clarinet, Mildred Roman played the second violin; Mrs. Coleman played the flute. Williams -- don't remember his name. ... It grew from Reedy Chapel to Central High, the gymnasium. It grew to about 35 or 40 people when it moved out. I guess I was too young to really appreciate what we had. We had six violinists. I was first violinist ... remember Katie Pitts? She was second violin, as Smith was first violin. I've often wondered why we didn't have a cello. I don't remember a cello. We had about three cornets, about four or five sax ... I forgot who played the trombone. ..." Hickey played first violin himself.

"Louise Delaney, does that ring a bell? ... played the piano. [Mr. Coleman] could play up a clarinet, a sax. He was a first-class musician. It was unfortunate he didn't have the support of the people."

I asked him, "Where did he get his training?"

"Wilberforce. Gibson sent for a lot of people -- he came on request. He taught for a while, but he didn't have the patience. So [he] went to the post office. I remember the teachers only got a hundred dollars a month then."

Hickey also remembered the Petrees, close kin of my husband's mother.

"Mrs. Petree asked my mother if I could play the violin, while she was here. I'd go there and play the violin for Mrs. Petree. Her favorite song was *Jesus, Lover of My Soul*. "

Island of Color

I mentioned Ernestine and Hortense Douglas, sisters of my husband's mother. Ernestine had a reputation for playing the violin very well. And I still have the violin that Hortense gave me for my children. They called her Aunt Doodie, and she loved music too. She had a large record collection, and as she listened to music, she often recalled how well their sister Ernestine played.

Hickey went on, "Mrs. Petree would sit up in bed and I'd play for her."

"How old were you, then?" I asked.

"Fourteen," he answered. "My mother would send me over there to play for Mrs. Petree. From the West End to the East End wasn't that far. I'd walk over there. I'd play the violin for her, and she'd smile. Later on in my life, I got concerned about women, girls, and concerned about things other than the violin. ..."

This very normal comment about his adolescence, from a man who has a wonderful dedication to spiritual matters and great respect for the things in life that really matter, was refreshing. Not that I was seeking seamy things, although it often seems that is all anybody wants to know about these days. He recalls some lovely, fun memories, and that gives me hope.

Hickey also mentioned the Triple Dip ice cream parlor, which was my absolute favorite establishment in my childhood. It was up on Seawall Boulevard at 9th Street, and I was there as often as I had the money to buy a cone. I have trouble getting younger folk to believe me today when I tell them that one could buy three dips of the best ice cream available, for only one nickel -- 5 cents!

And they had several different flavors. Not the variety that there is today in specialty ice cream stores, but we loved having about 10 flavors then. Hickey said that his favorite flavor had rum in it; it sounded like the rum-raisin flavor of today. I loved the banana nut and the tutti fruity. In the summer time, I'd obey and do extra chores all day for the promise of getting an ice cream cone in the evening, and the chance at licking three flavors from a cone.

Just to be in the store was exciting enough, because it was bright and pretty, with shining tile floors, and smelled of the flavors you wanted. You never minded waiting your turn, and hated to leave when the cone was in your hand. Since there were no stools to sit on in there, we knew no discrimination. No bad memories from the place. You would just come and go, smile at people you knew, and keep on out the door.

Maud Cuney Hare

Maud Cuney was born in Galveston on February 16, 1874 to famed politician Norris Wright Cuney and Adelina Dowdy Cuney. She left the island to study piano at Boston's New England Conservatory, under Emil Ludwig and Edwin Klahre.

There she faced racial prejudice, struggling to remain in the dormitory as one of only two black female students. Although the other student left at the end of the first freshman term, Maud Cuney completed her studies. During her struggle to remain, she met influential members of the Colored National League and became close friends with W.E.B. Du Bois, who later helped found the National Association for the Advancement of Colored People (NAACP), and William Monroe Trotter, then students at Harvard. She also received a marriage proposal from Du Bois.

She returned to Texas to teach music, and in 1893 had persuaded her father to start three free night schools. In 1897-98, she taught music at the Texas Deaf, Dumb and Blind Institute for Colored Youths in Austin. In 1903-04, she taught at the State Normal and Industrial College for Negroes at Prairie View, Texas.

In 1904, she returned to Boston as a concert pianist and piano teacher. She married William Parker Hare in August and the couple remained in Boston the rest of their lives.

Her summer home became a mecca for black intellectuals. Through her good friend Du Bois, she became music editor for the NAACP's magazine, Crisis. She also wrote for Musical Quarterly, Musical Observer, the Christian Science Monitor and Musical America, educating readers on black music as it emerged in mainstream American music over the next 25 years.

She traveled internationally, visiting Cuba, Puerto Rico, the Virgin Islands and Mexico to collect instruments and songs for ground-breaking research in musicology. She lectured and gave recitals on "Music of the Orient and Tropics" with baritone William Howard Richardson, explaining the history of black music. Her connections with upper class black Boston society aided her in funding these events and influencing a wider audience. She is also credited as the being first to popularize New Orleans Creole music and bring it into the concert hall.

In 1927, she opened the Allied Arts Centre and Musical Art Studio to expand her teaching into the national "little theatre" movement and create a school for children of all races.

In the last year of her life, she wrote Negro Musicians and Their Music, a book that combined her knowledge of black music history, rare

Music: Art, Recreation & Worship

songs from African and the Caribbean, and little-known black musicians as well as modern jazz, popular and concert musicians -- to illustrate the broad influence of black music up to 1936. Her volume continued to be mentioned in later texts as the definitive source of Negro music history. She died February 13, 1936.

Mrs. Theresa Mae Roberts Lewis

I continue with description of a grand lady of music who has recently passed on, who represented the finest in the spirit of dedicated church musicians. Mrs. Theresa Mae Roberts Lewis was a model of a real Christian musician.

Bay City's Linnie Roberts Elementary School is named in honor of her mother, who taught across the hall from me when I was beginning my own teaching career. And the Roberts Funeral Home was and is the largest funeral home that serves the African-Americans in that city; Eddie Roberts, Theresa Mae's brother, still owns that establishment today.

Theresa Mae Roberts' obituary stated: "Out of Matagorga County, in a small town known as Bay City, Texas came a giant of a personality.

Theresa Mae Roberts Lewis

An individual who never became too busy or too important to help anyone who needed a cheerful word, a smile, a pat on the back, or little encouragement.

Theresa is the second daughter of three children born to the late Ikeleys and Linnie McHenry Roberts. ...During her very young years of elementary school ...she loved music and though she was a member of Enterprise Baptist Church, gave her talent to many of the area churches. At one time, she was so small in stature, she had to prop herself on a stack of books, to adequately reach the piano keyboard to play.

Theresa graduated with honors from Hilliard High School. ... She received the Bachelor of Science Degree from Prairie View, and later a Master of Science from Texas Southern University, Houston, Texas. She began her first teaching experience at Dixon High School, Sheppard, Texas. There, along with her schoolwork, she served this community well. Each Sunday, she served as pianist for the local Black churches, alternating between churches each Sunday of the month.

In 1944, Theresa was united in marriage to the late Mr. Carol Lewis. They moved to Galveston, and in July of the same year, she united with the Live Oak Baptist Church. During these years, she served as church pianist, Sunday school teacher for the Junior Girls, Intermediate Girls, Women's Missionary Society, and the young adult class. Later, she became the church organist. She was involved in the inception of the Live Oak Day Care Center, serving as chairman of the Board of Directors, Director of Vacation Bible School, and worked with the Tiny Tots of the Junior Church Division.

Also during these years she taught in the Galveston School District, exhibiting the same Christian action on a day to day basis to the children who needed her guidance other than classroom instruction. Many times her home not only served her family, but she continued her Christian deeds, and opened her doors to many who needed a place to stay.

Sister Lewis served her church faithfully for fifty-five years. She served under the Rev. S.L. Rugeley, a father image for many years. She and Rev. George W. Barron worked as brother and sister for twenty four years, then the Lord sent her another son in the Rev. Byron Williams..."

Theresa Mae's daughter, Carol Lynne, named after her father and grandmother, had a real surprise for the persons attending her mother's funeral. The last guest soloist to sing for this service was the world-famous Gladys Knight, who was a special friend of Carol and her husband, Jesse. Theresa Mae had never bragged about that.

Mrs. Earnestine Poston Staton

Mrs. Staton was a grand lady -- small in physical stature, but very large in spiritual measurements. She remembered many of Reedy Chapel's golden days, because she and her family have been active in the church's life for a very long time. She kept up with Reedy's choirs and orchestra, and urged others to join in playing at the church. And even while continuing to serve as superintendent, and to serve any other Sunday school need, she has the distinction of being the only musician I know who has continued to play for Sunday school as a great-great-grandmother.

(My sister and I love it when she recalls our mother teaching her in her youth, and says, "I used to hold you two on my lap; I guess you don't want to hear that now." We both rush to assure her that it makes us feel wonderful, to hear someone in full possession of her mental faculties remember holding us senior citizens on her lap when we were children.

She has also been a role model for many, including my daughter, Cheryl, who taught and brought children to Sunday school.)

Margaret Bess

The Bess family has all passed on now, but they were very active in the East End, in community and church life. Margaret Bess taught piano; she taught my son, Roy Collins III, to play the piano when he was 5 years old, and gave him lessons until she passed, when he was in the second grade.

I would also have him play the trumpet when he was in the second grade -- with my Hitchcock band in parade, and in the stands at our Lorraine Crosby High School football games. Though he didn't continue in piano, he showed a very keenly developed musical sense, playing in high school band and writing music. He has a fine baritone voice and still loves to sing. Margaret gets credit for his musical development.

Mr. John Clouser

Mr. Clouser told me, "Your mother and Miss Jeanie Mabson came in the evening and taught us music. I liked music, but I wasn't very interested in playing, singing it..."

On the subject of music and bands, John Clouser named Sid Oliver's Band, which played in Houston for all the big Juneteenth celebrations, as well as in Galveston. He could not remember some entertainers' full names, but mentioned someone with the first name Roy who played in big hotels and was tops in ragtime. He remembered the nicknames of some who played at the Cottonjammer's Park: Crip John, and Lazy Daddy.

This reminded him of the fact that "Mr. McGuire, Jessie McGuire's father, owned the land where Menard Park is now, and his property was bought for a little of nothing."

Returning to music, he mentioned Callie Dickerson in much later years teaching choral music at Central High School. And he concluded, "Your mother was very active in music on an elementary school level." he concluded. I tend to forget that myself, because she taught English all her latter years in the schools. My mother, Mrs. Viola C. Scull Fedford, was my first piano teacher. After starting my musical career, she sent me to Mrs. Hattie Freeman for piano instruction.

Mr. Clouser was also responsible for the annual Health Parades that we had in Galveston. The parades were for the whole community, with floats, a band, marching groups, and decorated cars. I can still remember the large replica of a tooth on one of the floats, and the message urging children to brush their teeth after every meal to prevent tooth decay. The atmosphere was quite festive, but very wholesome for children; the parade was a teaching tool, with none of the lewdness now associated with parades. We have given up dignity for showmanship to please gaping, leering manipulators.

Gwendolyn Bridge Heard

Gwen was my bandmate in Central High School Band, and came home for our centennial celebration in 1987, which included a celebration for members of the famous Bearcat Band. Gwendolyn played alto sax, and sang in a trio with Joselyn Hunter and Lois Henry.

When Gwen and I talked at her home in Charlotte, we found that we shared a lot of high school band memories, with very high admiration of our band director, Fleming Smizer Huff, who was also my cousin. She also recalled singing with Henry and Hunter, who was her best friend in school and valedictorian of my class, and who played saxophone in the band. Their trio harmonized well and was requested to sing at various functions.

And Gwen's father, Mr. Addison Bridge, as I have mentioned elsewhere, was the only violinist I knew as a child. He played beautifully for many occasions. An elementary school teacher, he was a man of dignity, poise and bearing as well as fine-tuned musical skills.

The Stinson Family

The Stinson family is known for superior voices, and is active in church music. As surely anyone would agree, I have never heard a Stinson who couldn't sing. And there are quite a few Stinsons in Galveston, as well as elsewhere. The Stinson men are frequently featured soloists.

Mrs. Ada Simmons Butler

Mrs. Butler is now my neighbor, in this same block. She used to live in the same block as First Union Baptist Church, where she was a longtime musician. She began playing for the church as a young girl, and has since married and raised a family, taught music at Sunshine Training Center and given scores of programs. She now oversees her grandchildren's musical educations -- Kalee Martin, a student of mine, should be a fine pianist one day herself. She is Mrs. Butler's legacy.

Music: Art, Recreation & Worship

Emile Fatha and Elisha Perkins

Fatha and Perkins are two men whose names must come to the attention of anyone who wants to learn about African Americans in Galveston's music scene for so many years.

Elisha Perkins was my cousin on my mother's side of my family. He lived with the matriarch of our family, Mrs. Annie Smizer McCullough, who we knew as Aunt Annie. He was so large that he had to be weighed on the hospital's freight scale, I was told. I believe he weighed around 350 pounds. But he was amazingly light on his feet when he danced, and was my very first dancing partner when I became a teen-ager and had my first real party.

We called him "Lish." And Lish was known all over Galveston for his friendly manner, and love of baseball. Lish could be found by the radio listening to every ball game of local interest. He would go to some football games -- but only to hear the band, I believe, since his cousin Fleming "Snooks" Smizer Huff, was Central High's band director. Climbing up in the bleachers was a little much for Lish. He walked a lot, though; this probably kept him alive.

Lish was known best for his superior tenor voice. I don't know how many years Lish sang in Reedy Chapel Church's choir, but they were many. He sang solos, ensemble parts, and balanced the whole choir without the help of any other tenor. Though Lish could really cook, too, and was known for his fabulous appetite, his voice was his claim to fame.

Emile Fatha had a gorgeous bass voice. He was very large also, built differently but huge. Fatha drove a truck for a local paper company, and we always wondered why he refused to leave Galveston. He had a chance to become very well-known as a performer, but would not agree to leave home. Fatha sang the bass parts in all of the Reedy Chapel Choir's music, and was also a soloist of no equal.

When these two men sang, the choir, which included 20 or so women, was well-balanced. They were both very dependable as well, lending our choir quite a fine reputation for performing, both at Reedy and elsewhere.

Mr. John W. Coleman was the choir's director for a long time, teaching music of concert quality. The choir sang anthems almost every Sunday, as well as hymns and other songs. After Mr. Coleman passed away, there was little choir activity at Reedy until Mrs. Barker, wife of the pastor, came to Galveston. Mrs. Barker was a trained musician who knew how to teach proper vocal production as well, rehearsing choir members whenever they were available – individually as well as together. The choir excelled and gave many concerts away from the church, often traveling to do so.

When I came back to Galveston as a married adult, I started playing for the choir and for Fatha's solo concerts. We became quite a team, and I used to wish that he could give concerts as a regular source of income, rather than drive a truck for a living. We did perform for several weddings, however.

After the passing of Lish and Fatha, Reedy unfortunately could not replace the talent of these two shining stars of their time.

John W. Coleman

Records on Mr. Coleman are limited because he was really God's servant -- an humble man who simply did great things quietly, without much fanfare or publicity. He was the driving force behind my continued love for elegant and reverent music. He is the reason I love the pipe organ today, and why I will remain devoted to improving my skills on the organ. To me, it is truly God's voice.

Mr. Coleman was never late, nor did he ever miss a service in all the time I attended Reedy Chapel Church. As I entered the sanctuary for morning services, it was he who set the mood for holy worship in a way I can never forget, and will always follow. His manner was very dignified -- quiet, reverent, but not haughty, never negative. He would look over his glasses to gauge the progress of the service, turn to his place on the organ bench, and set the environment for a divine experience, with the ease and serenity of a master at work.

We talk of role models today, and how our children need good ones so much. He certainly was mine. With him and my cousin band director, Fleming S. Huff, as examples, there was no other course but music that I would ever be happy following.

(I still don't understand how I ignored all this and started to major in mathematics in college, until my appreciation and understanding of math both came to a screeching halt and my college advisor gently led me to see what I had been prepared for all along -- music. We had next to no career counseling in my high school days, which is another chapter.)

Mr. Coleman was born in Xenia, Ohio, on Nov. 30, 1880. The Reverend Handley Hickey, a present resident of Xenia who was born and raised here in Galveston, told me about Mr. Coleman's early years during that dinner at my home several years ago (after Rev. Hickey had hosted me for a couple of days one summer in his lovely home in Xenia). He spoke of Mr. Coleman's work in music in Galveston at church and school.

Mr. Coleman graduated from Wilberforce University, which is located in Xenia, with a major in music. In 1904, he moved to Galveston and began teaching at Central, where J.R. Gibson, also a Wilberforce graduate, was principal. Other teachers at Central at the time were the late William C. Green, W.J. Mason, Theresa Smith, and Clara E. Scull, my mother's aunt. He left teaching to become a letter carrier, as No.22, in 1909, and retired 38 years later.

He married a young Reedy Chapel member named Bessie Eula Morgan on Dec. 14, 1904, with Rev. W. R. Beamer officiating. To this union was born a daughter, Gertrude Coleman Pierce. Bessie Coleman died May 16, 1916. In April 1921, he married Elizabeth O. Miller, a nursing graduate of Meharry Medical College in Tennessee, who began a music career with her husband.

At Reedy Chapel A.M.E. Church, which he joined in 1904, he served as choir director and organist for over 40 years -- in addition to serving as the superintendent of Sunday school from 1904-1907, as steward, and as secretary of the official board. Thanks to him, Reedy Chapel was known for its well-trained choir, and its fine organ.

The organ was built in 1872 by the E.& G. Hook and Hastings Company of Boston, Opus 647, with 866 wood and metal pipes. Originally made for the Trinity Episcopal Church of Galveston, it survived several major hurricanes and was later traded in by Trinity for a newer organ. Reedy bought it from Goggan Bros.

One of only two left in the nation, it was once water-powered, a tracker organ. It is the only one of its type still in service; the other is in the Smithsonian Institute. Ours was restored by Roy Redman of Fort Worth, who invited the Organ Builders, a worldwide organization, to see

Music: Art, Recreation & Worship

it in 1979; the renovation number is Opus 20. For the dedication of the restored organ on May 29, 1992, Henry McDowell Jr., an expert organist and African American native of Durham, N.C., gave a wonderful concert.

Small by today's standards, it has an unmatchable, beautiful, natural tone quality. Statistics of it now are:

Great: 16' Bourdon, 8" Open Diapason, 8" Dulciana, 8' Melodia, 4' Octave, 2 2/3 Twelfth, 2' Fifteenth, and 8' Trumpet. Swell: 8' Open Diapason, 8' Viola, 8' Stopped Diapason, 4' Harmonic Flute, 4' Violin, 8' Oboe, Bassoon, and Tremolo. Pedal: 16' Bourdon and 8' Flute.

The couplers are Swell-Great, Swell-Pedal, Great- Pedal. The gothic-style case is 18 feet tall and made of ash, with moldings and carvings of walnut. The stenciled pipes are duplicated accurately. Original mechanical action and wind system are preserved, including the hand-pumping feeders.

John Coleman knew this organ well, and played it with all devotion possible. Reedy purchased it while he was a member, so he was probably instrumental (no pun intended) in getting it for our church.

He organized the R. Nathaniel Dett Choral Club, whose memorable performances included a concert of spirituals at The First Methodist Church, Women's Circle, on March 1, 1932; and the operetta, *The Merry Milkmaids,* which *The Galveston Daily News* stated "attracted a large crowd" in 1934.

He also organized an orchestra with members of Reedy and other churches. This string orchestra, supplemented by woodwind and brass instruments, flourished for many years. Although instrumentalists played on occasion in other churches, I believe that it was the only full church orchestra in the African American churches, perhaps in local churches of any race.

Rev. Hickey remembers the orchestra well and gave Reedy a picture of the group. He played first-chair violin in it as a young lad, and was called upon to play for friends and relatives in the community when they were housebound. He remembers Mr. Coleman as an exacting musician who tolerated no foolishness, and demanded the best that the young musicians could give.

Mr. Coleman also served as first vice president of the Texas Association of Negro Musicians in 1939, and was later elected president of the association. He was president when the state convention met in Galveston, in October 1946. He was also a member of the national association.

He was active in the Wright Cuney Lodge No. 63, Knights of Pythias, where he served as worshipful master and organized the lodge's Knights of Pythian Band.

John W. Coleman died at his residence at 3520 Ave. M ½ at the age of 76, on July 11, 1957. Brief services were held at Reedy, and the musician of city, state and national prominence was buried at the Mainland Memorial Cemetery in Hitchcock. The next profile is that of Avenue L's best-known music director, who was married to an outstanding organist at Reedy.

Music: Art, Recreation & Worship

Mrs. Elizabeth Coleman

Elizabeth Onzella Miller Coleman

Elizabeth Coleman was born in MacBeth, Brazoria County, Texas, on Jan. 18, 1889. She was the second child of Manuel Miller and Lucy Johnson Miller. In the winter of 1899, she and her sisters moved to Galveston to live with their uncle and aunt, William M. and Lucy Wallace, at 3021 Ave. M. William Wallace was a drayman and an active member of Avenue L church. With his help, Elizabeth went to Walden University in Nashville, Tenn., to study nursing in the summer of 1915. Walden closed in 1916, and became Meharry Medical College, where she graduated on Aug. 30, 1918, in the college's second graduating class in nursing. (Hulda

M. Lyttle was director of Nurse Training and Dr. George W. Hubbard, former Dean, was president.) That fall, during World War I, she held her first registered nurse position at Muscle Shoals, Ala. She returned to Galveston and did private duty at John Sealy Hospital.

Elizabeth's love for music also grew. She became a choir member at Macedonia Baptist Church, where W.P. Anderson was choir director and organist. She later became Macedonia's choir director. In 1920, she met John W. Coleman; they married in April 1921.

In June 1928, she began the first summer session at Manet Harrison Fowler, in Fort Worth, studying music there each summer until graduation. Her course work included methods, public school music, notation, terminology, ear training, sight singing, conducting, practical church music, and melody way of piano. She also took an active role with R. Nathaniel Dett Choral Club, which was organized by her husband.

In 1937, she organized the Onzella Girls Glee Club; Onzella was her middle name. She later organized another group, originally called the Mwalimu Chorus, as the Onzella Singers. The Singers gave a musical each year at the old George W. Carver School auditorium, performed at Christmastime for the sick in the community, and for Memorial Day presented songs of our nation.

Elizabeth and John Coleman were staunch supporters of the National Association of Negro Musicians Inc. (Founded in 1919, it grew in less than four years to a membership of over 1,000 with 34 branches.) The association encouraged the development of musical talent through scholarships for needy students, promoted professionalism through workshops and conferences, and served as a showcase for Black music and musicians. The association gave famous contralto Marian Anderson her first scholarship.

The 14th convention of the Texas Association of Negro Musicians (an affiliate of the national association) was held March 3-5, 1939, at Avenue L Baptist Church in Galveston with the Galveston Music Clubs as host. (I am not sure whether this was the Galveston Musical Club, or a group of clubs organized for this purpose.) Elizabeth headed State and National Scholarships, and served as convention chairman. John served as South Texas conference director. Concerts, mass choral groups, plays and recitals were presented. The late Thelma T. Bailey, a teacher at West District School in Galveston, served as state organizer.

The association also performed at Carnegie Hall in New York, with Elizabeth as a vocalist.

In 1939, she was elected to the National Board of Directors of the National Association of Negro Musicians. She later served as vice president, attending sessions in Chicago, Pittsburgh, and elsewhere.

In October 1946, Elizabeth served as chairman of the local convention committee when the Galveston Music Clubs hosted the 18th convention of the Texas Association of Negro Musicians, returning to Avenue L. Fleming S. Huff, Central High's band director, was director of State Bands and Orchestras. John W. Coleman served as president.

Dr. G.L. Prince was installed as pastor of Avenue L Church in March 1934. Later that year, Elizabeth and her niece, Bernita M. Bradley, who was like a daughter, joined Avenue L. Clarence Simpson served as choir director, and the late Addison Bridges, who taught at West District, accompanied the choir on violin, and also served as a leading chorister.

Dr. Prince organized Choir No. 2 and Elizabeth became the director, in 1935.

The late Mrs. Ruth Phelps Atkinson was organist for the Senior Choir. Mrs. Ethel Brown Bell and the late Mrs. Helen C. Lewis Perkins were organists with the late Mrs. Daisy Thomas, president, for the newly organized Choir No.2. Mrs. Ruth Thomas Hall began playing the organ in 1937. Both choirs were combined a few years later.

Dr. Prince was president of the National Baptist Convention of America from 1935 to 1956; in September 1938, the choir went to Fort Worth to attend the convention, and made annual trips to sing for the conventions until 1956. Elizabeth Coleman's training was reflected in the many anthems and hymns sung at the conventions.

Avenue L later purchased a bus, and David Davenport became the able driver who took the choir from coast to coast for 18 years.

The Avenue L Choir presented the Mary Allen College Chorus in concert on Dec. 15, 1944; Bernita M. Bradley's solo was the Twenty-third Psalm by Malotte. Bernita later received a scholarship to attend Mary Allen College, of which Dr. Prince was president.

Dr. Mary McLeod Bethune -- noted educator and president emeritus of Bethune-Cookman College, advisor to President Franklin D. Roosevelt, and founder/president of the National Council of Negro Women -- came to Avenue L on May 6, 1948. The choir presented Mrs. Bethune's favorite hymn, *Climbing Jacob's Ladder.*

Elizabeth's husband John W. Coleman died on July 11, 1957, after a lengthy illness. She continued to direct the choir and choral groups, and had a voice and music studio at her home at 3520 Ave. M1/2, where the Colemans had lived since 1930.

Mrs. Coleman was a charter member of the Avenue L Benevolent Society and was also active in the American Woodmen, Camp No.300; Mary Allen College Club; and Southern Beauty Court of Calanthe No.62.

During Rev. McKeen's pastorate, Mrs. Coleman's choir was heard on the radio every week, on radio station KGBC.

In 1960, Elizabeth Coleman retired and moved to Houston to be near relatives. She was honored with programs and receptions. After a stroke in 1973, she died peacefully on June 11, 1974, at Ben Taub Hospital in Houston. As she'd requested, services were held at her birthplace, MacBeth, Texas, at the Mt. Pisgah Baptist Church. Burial was in the family plot near the church. Many Galvestonians, including members of Avenue L, were present to give the final salute to a noted musician.

Fleming Smizer "Fess" Huff

Fleming 'Fess' Huff in uniform

Fleming Smizer Huff, known to his family as "Snooks," was both respectfully called Mr. Huff by his students and community admirers, and "Fess" by the fellows in the bands that he nourished so devotedly. "Fess" was short for "Professor," which the guys deemed him.

He was born on Nov. 1, 1909, and died on Feb. 27, 1966.

To quote a Houston newspaper article, written shortly after his death, "Without a doubt, this man was the top founding father of the instrumental music program for Negroes in the state of Texas."

Educated in the Galveston public schools, he received his bachelor's degree from Wiley College, and did graduate work years later at Wilberforce University and Northwestern University, and received his master's degree from Texas Southern University.

He returned to Galveston, where he was a substitute teacher for a time, offering his services free of charge to organize a band after school hours. After a year of free service, the district hired him as band director of the first high school for Negroes in Texas -- leading the famed Bearcat Band of Central High School of Galveston, Texas.

Mr. Huff produced more top award-winning bands than any other Negro high school in Texas. In many of the Prairie View-based Texas Interscholastic League contests, the Central High School Band received the first-place trophy as top band of the entire festival. At this time, the competition consisted of both marching and concert performance. After the concert contest (characterized by competition with Anderson High School of Austin, which used University string instrumentation; I.M. Terrell of Fort Worth; and Hebert High of Beaumont -- all music giants), the bands filed onto the college football field, and exhibited marching form that could put military presentations to shame.

Music: Art, Recreation & Worship

At the end of these festivals, all participating bands formed one massed band for a final selection and awarding of the winning trophies. Central High School Bearcat Band had an award-winning dynasty in this regard, and was highly respected and feared by competing schools for years.

With Mr. Huff's graduate training came his ability to arrange music, and the Bearcat Band was known throughout the Lone Star State as the fiery spirit behind the winning Central High School football team. Performing in all local parades, as well as in neighboring cities and at all appropriate civic affairs, the Navy Blue and White attired Bearcat Band usually had a huge following of adults and children of all nationalities who could not resist its rhythms and strong-toned harmonies.

Residents of Galveston from the latter 1930s to the end of the 1950s recall the broad smiles and bright eyes when someone would call out, "Here comes the Band!" Feet began tapping, and shoulders and heads were held high when Fess' Bearcat Band took the field or rounded the corner. The precise band seemed to sweep you right along in spite of yourself, as it moved forward.

More importantly, such a high percentage of his students were so filled with the love of music that they went on to become band directors themselves, or make a living by performing music in one capacity or another. In no other field can one boast of so many dedicated and devoted followers, who were able to earn a decent living while following a dream.

In addition to his school service in Galveston, Mr. Huff directed the Municipal Band at Wright Cuney Park for many seasons. He instilled in hundreds of admiring young musicians the ability to improvise, to feel and play jazz -- which has proven to be America's only continually developing art form, its own classical music, constantly evolving and recreating itself.

Mr. Huff also served as band director in his last years in the towns of Shepherd, Crockett, and Lovelady, Texas.

He was the son of Clara Smizer Huff and Edward Huff, a professional musician himself. His mother died shortly after his birth, and he was raised by his grandparents and a devoted cousin. His first marriage to Verna Newton was blessed with the birth of a daughter, Jacqueline Irma, who was a longtime employee of the Texas Employment Commission in Corpus Christi.

Huff will be remembered by hundreds for his honest, forthright manner; genuine personality; and love of family, but most of all for his genius in the field of music and his contagious passion for it -- contagious to anyone who has experienced music as communication, as a tuning fork to things eternal.

Music: Art, Recreation & Worship
Clyde Owen Jackson

Clyde Jackson

"Humanitarian, Music Director, Postmaster, and Author"

Mr. Jackson was born in Galveston in 1928. He has lived in Houston the last three decades. Mr. Jackson's career goal was increased management responsibility; he was regional postmaster general. He holds a B.S. from Tuskegee Institute, and a M.A. in music education from Texas

Southern University. His hobbies include music writing and composing. He is an avid reader with particular interest in international affairs.

Excerpts from *Galveston's First Black Postmaster: A Hometown Kid Who Made Good* by Jim Curran, Houston Chronicle Galveston Bureau:

"A skinny kid who grew up during the Depression in a small house on a barren alley has returned to his birthplace as the first Black postmaster in Galveston's history. Clyde Owen Jackson credits his three college degrees, his devotion to God and church, and his success primarily to his father, Earl Jackson, of 5406 Avenue M.

The father was a cotton warehouse worker for 45 years. Widowed at 24, he had two small sons, Clyde Owen, and Earl Jr, now assistant director of food services at the University of California at Santa Barbara. Jackson says, 'My father never remarried. Most men that age would have given the children to a grandmother or an aunt, but not my father. He insisted we go to school and church. I think it was the church that kept us out of trouble and under the influence of good people who cared about us.'

Jackson, is unmarried, for the girl he loved died of leukemia. Jackson graduated in 1945 from Central High School, all Black in the days of mandated segregation. After receiving his degree from Tuskegee, the army drafted him in 1950. He served three years, emerging as a first lieutenant.

Someone suggested he apply at the Houston post office for a night job when he was honorably discharged, and use his GI bill to go to school during the day, which he wanted to do, and study Music. So, in 1956, Jackson said, 'I'd get off at 7:00 a.m., get a bite of breakfast, and go to classes. Then, because the choirs I worked with didn't rehearse until afternoon, I did most of my sleeping in my car.'

After receiving both of his Music degrees, as well as serving as music and choir director for Wheeler Avenue Baptist Church, he felt that he had reached a crossroad in 1964. 'I really had no intention of staying with the postal service when I began,' Jackson said. 'But by then, I had eight years' service plus three years' army service, toward seniority, and the postal service kind of grows on you.'

He worked into management ranks, and in 1969, became supervisor at the Houston post office, with six promotions in nine years. While all this was taking place, he also was writing and publishing four books. They are a history of Negro folk music, a collection of his newspaper's editorials [the Informer] and essays, a novel about a spinster school teacher, and a study on motion pictures, which grew out of his love for the movies he attended for a nickel at the old Dixie Theater in Galveston.

Then-postmaster Jim Wortham of Galveston was promoted to postmaster of Irving, and Jackson applied for the job along with several others. Jackson won and was appointed, effective October 21, 1978. Did the fact that he was BOI (born on the island) have a part in his selection?

'I don't know, but it surely had a part in my wanting the job,' he said. 'My only hope is that I can be an inspiration to youngsters to work hard, sacrifice, and have faith in God.'

Clyde Owen Jackson has been Interim Music Director of Houston Ebony Opera Guild and a former student of William Dawson. He has served as conductor of the 63rd Infantry Regiment Chorus, Texas Southern University Men's Glee Club, Houston Post Ofiice Chorale, and for nineteen years, choirs at Wheeler Avenue Baptist Church. He was guest conductor for the National Baptist Convention in 1987. He was the conductor of the choral works when the Houston Symphony and Community Music Center of Houston presented a tribute to William Dawson in 1989. Most recently, he served four years as conductor of the Tuskegee Choir, touring throughout the country to critical acclaim. The Galveston Public Libraries last year honored him as one of twelve Black pioneers of the twentieth century. He is also a former army officer."

His nomination by E.C. Stevenson, postmaster in Houston, on Aug. 3, 1978, for Federal Employee of the Year, included the biographical information above, with further information that follows.

"A. On-the-job Narrative

Mr. Jackson is Manager, Stations and Branches, in the Houston, Texas Post Office. His outstanding performance through the years has been recognized by initial promotion to supervisor and later to Station Manager and his present position. He also served as Manager, Delivery and Collections, the number two Customs and Services position, for seven months this past year.

He is now responsible for nine stations in Houston which deliver mail to 243,000 delivery points and employ 850 people. The annual budget for his stations exceeds $14,000,000. His area is not only notable for its operating, safety, and service performance, but also for its continuing improvement as well. In his decisions, Mr. Jackson not only recognizes Postal Service requirements, but is also responsive to postal customer needs.

One of Mr. Jackson's foremost strengths is developing people. Both supervisory and craft employees in his area of responsibility have excellent promotion records. Several years ago he conducted voluntary

Music: Art, Recreation & Worship

Saturday training for supervisors in his stations. He was chairman of the Postal committee which developed the Postal Technology Degree Program at North Harris County College in 1976. He is still an instructor in that program. He has been instrumental in developing a week-long Basic Training for Station Supervisors that was given three times this Spring. He also headed a group which developed a financial training program for supervisors which begins in August.

B. Community Narrative

Mr. Jackson is an active member of the Wheeler Avenue Baptist Church, where he serves as Minister of Music and Director of the Young Peoples Workshop Choir. He is founder (and Chairman) of Citizens Against Drug Abuse, an organization dealing with publicizing the danger of misuse of drugs. He is a member of the Texas Junior College Teacher's Association. He also has membership in the Museum of Fine Arts, Houston Grand Opera Association, Young Mens' Christian Association Century Club, and other civic and professional organizations. He is a Presidential Associate of Tuskegee Institute, and has served on a planning committee for Texas Southern University. He has received numerous awards for outstanding community and church work. He is the author of four published books and was the subject of a television special reviewing his accomplishments and contributions on Channel 2, KPRC-TV, October 24, 1977. Mr. Jackson spends about 16 hours a week on community activities."

In the June 1982 issue of the Houston News, Earl T. Artis Jr. describes the very busy life of the multitalented Galveston native now living in Houston. The article is headlined, "The 24-hour man," with the statement, in display type: "Clyde Owen Jackson inspires others because he leads by example. His accomplishments as teacher, author, music director, and postal manager are conquests of dedication and self-discipline."

My personal association with Mr. Jackson has been one of mutual appreciation, a sort of mutual admiration society. Because we share a passion for the same kind of music, and realize that so many of our own people neither know nor seem to want to learn what their own music is all about, we support each other. We both cringe when so many supposed musicians have our children screaming and hollering in the supposition that they are singing music. We each value our heritage of Galveston teachers and fine education. And we both value the heritage that is most precious, that of the great spirituals of our people. No diluted forms, or jazzed-up gospels – spirituals!

Clyde Owen Jackson, who graduated from Central High School in 1945, also treasures my mother as one of his finer, caring teachers.

The many articles about him are hard to summarize, because he has accomplished so much in so many different fields. I will do my best to give the important facts.

Clyde Owen Jackson was born April 7, 1928, in Galveston. In 1949, he earned a bachelor's degree from the school of commercial industry at Tuskegee Institute in Alabama.

He spent one year as editor of the <u>Omaha Guild</u> newspaper, and another as city editor of the <u>Arkansas State Press</u> in Little Rock. He entered the U.S. Army in 1952. He was an army officer from 1952-1954. During those years, he was public information officer of the United Nations Command in Tokyo and for the Korea Civil Assistance.

Music: Art, Recreation & Worship

Jackson left the military to become managing editor of the Informer, where he remained until 1956. At that time, he joined the U.S. Postal Service as a distribution clerk.

He worked during the day and studied at night to achieve his second bachelor's degree, this time from Texas Southern University in music education in 1960. In 1964, he earned a master's degree in music education at the same school.

Jackson was promoted to letter sorting machine clerk in 1967. In March 1969, he was named acting supervisor of parcel post. Three months later, he was promoted to foreman of mails in the Houston Post Office, and to the next level foreman of mails in 1971.

In 1972, he became manager of the old South Park Station, now the Martin Luther King Station. A year later, he was named acting manager of stations and branches in Houston. In January 1972, this acting level became permanent. Jackson became area manager of area IV in September 1977, acting for a short period as manager of delivery and collections.

In October 1978, he became postmaster of Galveston, and in December 1981 became acting sectional center director of the 114 associate post offices around Houston; he has since retired from the post office.

Jackson has received numerous awards. In 1955, he won a merit award from the National Newspapers Publishers Association for a series of articles on Texas school desegregation. He was selected to Who's Who Among Students in American Universities and Colleges in 1960. In 1975, he received an award from the National Council of Negro Women for outstanding contributions to the community. In 1980, he was named outstanding Citizen of the Year by the Galveston County Chapter of the Alpha Phi Alpha Fraternity, Inc.

An Aug. 25, 1990, Galveston Daily News article by Robert Frelow Jr. is headlined "Former postmaster appointed director of Tuskegee Choir":

"Retired Galveston Postmaster Clyde Owen Jackson has been appointed acting director of the Tuskegee University Choir. Jackson, a native of Galveston who retired from the U.S. Postal Service in 1984, is a 1949 graduate of Tuskegee. The university is known world-wide as one of the country's most historical Black institutions of higher learning.

Jackson, who retired June 1st as minister of music at Wheeler Avenue Baptist Church in Houston, was appointed to the post by Tuskegee president Benjamin F. Payton. The appointment was made due to the illness of the choir's former director. Jackson is a former Army infantry officer and newspaper editor, the author of eight published books and also a composer.

His latest work -- 'Now This Trumpet Summons Us Again' -- is based on the inaugural address of late President John F. Kennedy. Jackson has received hundreds of awards for professional accomplishments and community service activities."

CHAPTER EIGHT
MUSIC: THE JAZZ GENERATION

While Galveston has a rich heritage in church and concert music, the real story of jazz in Galveston is one of the best-kept secrets there is. New Orleans may have more of a reputation for jazz, but the difference was not necessarily that of quality -- a good press agent or promotion company for Galveston could have changed the whole picture.

The New Orleans musicians actually learned a lot from the guys in Galveston, because Galveston's "homies" told me how these fellows came down here to jam, and went on to Houston to play official gigs. Blues celebrities like B.B. King, T Bone Walker, Lightning Hopkins, and a host of others were just guys "looking for a good gig when they, like my friends and co-workers, played in this area in the old days."

Jazz Musicians

Their names are: left to right, Clifford Duvall and Buddy Williams, saxes; Rip Bolden, drums and vocalist; William "Smitty" Smith, trumpet; A.D. Adams, bass, and Elbie Fleuellen, piano.

They played in small smoky bars in Houston, sometimes in the better lounges. And even in the early '30s and '40s, they were "no big thing."

When I toured with the Prairie View College Coed Orchestra in the '40s, I recall that these fellows were in Houston playing in small places then, while the Coeds were playing in the main place for our people in Houston: the El Dorado Ballroom, on the corner of Dowling and Elgin streets, across from what is now called Emancipation Park. We played there almost every week; it was like our home away from home while I was in school.

Galveston's musicians who had national reputations in jazz have been far too modest, and their stories have not been told, so I will attempt to name as many of these men and women as I can.

Buster Pope

Buster Pope mimicked Louis Armstrong's voice and manner so well that he could almost have passed for him, if you couldn't see him clearly. With his gravel-voiced imitation of Louis' voice, and his wide grin, he must have been around the master. Buster played trombone, though, and not trumpet, as Louis Armstrong did. His specialty, requested every night that I played with him, was <u>St. James' Infirmary</u>. He could actually make you cry with his sense of drama and pathos. And he'd play that trombone with a wail that outdid Louis Armstrong's on the trumpet.

Buster was very protective of me, as were all the guys I played with on these night jobs. I will never forget how kind he was, not letting the patrons talk to me when they were obviously inebriated or up to no good. He and all the other fellows were very protective; although they treated me as a professional and paid me right on time, they also treated me like a sister, or like their guest for the evening. He would laugh and joke with any drunk who tried to come over and talk to me, get him out of my way. Then he would strike up a lively tune, and clown to get the fellow's mind off what was going on. So there was never any violence, simply because he knew how to handle the situation.

Buster was such a character, though. He came in every night with his trombone in two parts, carrying it in a cloth bag, seldom in a case. The bag wasn't very protective, but it was what he had. The trombone had dents in the dents, from where he had bumped up against something, and it had lost its sheen; but he buffed it up when he had a chance, and held it close like a loved one. It might have been a beat-up silver-tone instrument, but he made it sound like gold.

Robert "Rip" Bolden

My classmate and jazz combo buddy, Robert "Rip" Bolden, and I played in the high school band together; he was an expert snare drummer then. He later got his own set of orchestra drums, and played around the Galveston and Houston scene for a very long time. I played with his combo on occasion when I could, and he played in my group when I got requests; whoever got the gig was the leader for that engagement, selecting other musicians to play. Rip has passed away now, but he was a very good vocalist and drummer, who sang as he played, with all ease.

John "Bubba" Tarver

Another member of our group was John "Bubba" Tarver. He has continued to play tenor sax with several bands over many years. He also played with the bands that Mr. Huff directed for the city at Wright Cuney Park in the days of segregated amusement activities. He is the only African American member of the city's Park Band today; the band requires a musician's union membership, and he is the only one who has bothered to keep his membership in force.

A.D. Adams

Tarver, Bolden, A.D. Adams (on bass) and I had an active combo for a while. A.D. Adams played bass horn in the high school band as well. He switched over to string bass for jazz purposes. He is one of the few men who did not play the electronic bass when it became popular, in deference to the string bass.

All of us were taught the rudiments in high school band under the direction of Mr. Huff. So we all had a good background, and appreciation for music played with class, skill and understanding. Long before I came back home, after college and my first teaching positions, they had traveled with some well-known bands, playing with different celebrities, so I tapped into their jazz experience when I had a chance to play with them.

Along with these fellows, I must mention the nationally known names of Charles Brown, writer of the hit song, Merry Christmas, Baby; and "King" Curtis, who was a brilliant composer as well as a sax artist.

King Curtis

Curtis typifies the plight of the jazz musician who is serious about his/her craft. It is next to impossible to make money from it, because the public wants to hear the watered-down version of real jazz. What most people call jazz is really rock and roll, rhythm and blues, or some other diluted form of syncopated rhythm. Not to give the impression that I don't like any of these other forms: I love quite a few selections that fall in this category. I also like hot dogs with potato chips, and other junk food that I try not to eat too much. But that doesn't compare with juicy vegetables well prepared, grilled seafood, or prime rib.

Curtis wrote music at the New England Conservatory, where he studied. Leonard Bernstein played some of his compositions with the symphony orchestra that he directed. But Curtis would have starved if he had waited for the next call requesting commissioned work. So he started playing a bluesy, rocking sax, and made a living playing what the public wanted to hear. Some other man used the name King Curtis, but the one from Galveston, now deceased, was champ.

His brother, Bernard Curtis, collected many of his manuscripts after his death; it is a shame that these have never been published.

(Their mother, Mrs. Amelia Curtis, frequently accompanied mine at the segregated Opera House in their youth, to take in music and other arts events of their day.)

Willard "Dick" Dickerson

Dickerson, recently deceased, was a real pleaser of audiences that crossed color lines. Playing an attractive, romantic style of piano and organ music, he employed the services of Edward Jones on bass violin,

Roy Merchant on drums and vocals, and sometimes added a sax player for melody enhancement. The Dick Dickerson Trio was very popular fare with both White and Black audiences for dancing or listening pleasure.

I have talked with several men who used to play the nightclub and lounge circuit, and the dance halls, in the days when they really brought in crowds. Two of these Galvestonians who played with famous groups are Clifford Duvall and Phillip "Buddy" Williams.

Clifford Duvall and Phillip "Buddy" Williams

Both of these men specialized in playing tenor sax. Clifford is older, didn't have the same start as we did, but has a lot of experience. Buddy, who was in high school band with me, was a teen-age idol, wowed the girls with his good looks and smooth sax playing in his youth. I spoke with both of them in 1994; Duvall was then 77, Williams was 64.

Asked how they first got started playing music, Buddy said that Mr. J.W. Coleman started him on alto saxophone. (This surprised me, because I knew Mr. Colemen as an organist; I would like to get much more information on him.) Buddy said that he learned to read music in those private lessons, but he changed to tenor saxophone at Central, studying with Mr. Huff.

Clifford said that when he wanted to start playing music, there was no band at Central or music teacher. He did yard work to earn money to buy a saxophone he had seen at Nevelow's in Galveston, advertised for $40.00. When he had the money needed, he went to Nevelow's and found that it was already sold. So he bought a trombone, and after Nevelow got in another saxophone, he begged Nevelow to let him trade in the trombone for the alto sax a week later. Then he bought a method book and taught himself to play from the instructions and illustrations.

"I had one lesson in my life, and guess who that was from? Huff! He was going to college then, and I knew he could play saxophone. So I went out to his house, so he said, 'You give me a dollar. It'll cost you a dollar a lesson, and I'll show you the scale on that horn.' So I gave him a dollar -- something I had worked all the week for, cause I made $3 a week. So he showed me from low C to high C, and that's the only lesson I had all of my life -- the only lesson.

But later years, Dickerson came along. By then I had taught myself to read, and I started hanging around Buster Pope, and Bubba Pope, and Russell [Lewis]. I wanted to go to the beer taverns where they were playing. They weren't that much older than me, but I couldn't go in the beer taverns where they were playing. So I'd go around the clubs, and I'd watch Russell's fingers. Like he [Buddy] was saying, in Louisiana, they had great jazz in New Orleans, but we also had bands around here -- like Old Man Sparks, bass player. You used to see him on the street. He used to play at Oddfellow's, on 27th and M.

Most of these fellows were self-taught musicians like me. Charles could play trumpet, and he didn't talk much -- ooh, he could play! What would come out of that horn would surprise you! Tone! Technique!"

"How about Buster?" Buddy asked, referring to Buster Pope. "Buster would sit down, that cigar in his mouth, go to sleep, wake up, come in right on time for his solo.

"He'd be snoring," Buddy said, demonstrating, "and when it was time to come in, he – shoop," Buddy said, imitating him moving the slide on the trombone. "Ah, man."

"And he'd be smoking a cigarette," Clifford said, "and never burn his fingers."

I was laughing heartily, also recalling how Buster would bring his trombone to the job in two sections, as casually as one would carry a loaf of bread. Then after horsing around with the people in the place, he would pull it together just in time to play, blow a few little riffs on it, and then say to the rest of us, "OK, what you got?" to find out what we wanted to start off the night playing.

Clifford continued, recalling others: "Roy Brown was a singer. He's the one who wrote <u>Rock Around the Clock,</u>" the '50s hit attributed to Bill Haley and the Comets.

We talked about how white performers such as Elvis Presley had taken credit for so much African American music. "Elvis copy-catted off everybody who wasn't well known, all of our folk," I said. Buddy agreed. "Elvis Presley couldn't do nothing. Couldn't sing, couldn't dance, just shake a leg. Well, they sold him." Clifford added, "Had a good press agent." I said, "Well, this is one of the main things I'd like for you all to address. I get tired of telling my folk. They [the youngsters] don't know. He didn't start a thing. He copied off everybody."

Buddy added, "He come on way late in the day. Like <u>You Ain't Nothin' But A Hounddog</u>. Big Mama Thornton had been singing that for the longest."

'That was one of her hits!" Buddy and Clifford both said, almost in chorus.

Buddy continued, "And Elvis made a million dollars from it. Big Mama had been going around the Chittlin' Circuit with that for the longest.

You'd get paid sometime, and sometime you wouldn't. I've been on that [the circuit] and I know."

This jogged Clifford's memory. "Sometimes when the dance was closed, and the man didn't want to give you the money -- didn't want to pay off, or couldn't pay off. I played many a gig like that where you didn't get paid. That's why we went over to Houston, had the union going strong."

Buddy said, "And what's-his-name -- Conrad Johnson -- well, he was the president. If you didn't get paid, you'd go to his house, even on Sunday, ring the bell, say 'I didn't get my money.' "

Turning the talk to novelty bands, Clifford said, "We had a band around here, called the Tuneville Tooters. It played on tin tubs, washboards, boxes, and played public dances. Took that name after the Tuneville Trolley. We'd play at the Cottonjammer's Park out west. Well, anyway, they had tubs and buckets -- used to make more music. They used to play all kinds of music. I was just a little kid then, but they had more people dancing -- the Tuneville Tooters."

We spoke about my grandfather's journal entries about the bands that played here not long after slavery was over, and the variety of instruments they played.

"Violins -- they called those who played violin or piano sissies, see, but my mother played piano for church for years," Buddy said.

He added, "If Joe heard something and couldn't [play] it like he wanted it, he'd go to the piano and get the chords right, then pick up his horn and try it."

Clifford added, "Well, my daddy taught me the keyboard, then he sent me to Mrs. Freeman out here, to take music. Well, I started with her, my sister, Elizabeth Duvall -- they used to call her Lossie -- and I. We took from Mrs. Freeman, and we went through that red book. So that's how I learned the keyboard. ... So I played church songs at church. I said I didn't have a teacher, but she started me on the piano."

"Did you know where she went to school?" I asked. "I have often wondered where the people who taught me went to school."

"I don't know," Clifford mused, "but she was educated."

"During that time, nearly everybody went to Prairie View or Wiley," Buddy said. I added, "Or Wilberforce, Howard, Fisk, other schools away from Texas" if they could afford it.

On the tape of their interview, a shrill flute sounds. My 3-year-old grandson, Roy IV, had started playing with one of the instruments I have collected from around the world. I have always let my grandchildren play with these, under my supervision, to make them aware of the many cultures, interest them in creating music for themselves. One of the guys remarked, with a chuckle, "Oh, I see you've got a musician now."

Buddy asked, "Remember Charlie Shiro? Central graduating class of 1936?

"You know, when they started bringing the big bands, I wasn't much bigger than him," referring to my grandson, "and my mama would say, 'here's your little half tickets. They'd belong to me and Nat. He's my uncle [Nathaniel Dean, a powerful trumpet player at Central in our day]. I was about 8 or 9 years old. We'd go to the City Auditorium just a block away, see Count Basie all the big bands."

Charlie Shiro was mentioned because he was a promoter who brought many big bands to the City Auditorium, where we all saw them in our segregated society. Few of the other race came, but the African

Music: The Jazz Generation

Americans in Galveston went in large numbers. Buddy continued with personal memories of the trips to big-band dances.

Clifford remembers, "I came [to Galveston] with Claude Hopkins, outta New York. Huff came up there that night, and we let him blow on the theme song. He said, 'This is *my* cat, man,' " remembering how Huff claimed him that night as his protege. Buddy chimed in, echoing how he said it. "People don't think about that. Very few people came back here with big bands." True – only a few of those who started out playing small gigs in the Galveston area made it into the big bands; and those who did seldom made it into the top-profile big bands, those bands that would play in our area. Which is why I was so proud when I got the chance to return and play, during my freshman year with the Prairie View Coeds at a dance at the City Auditorium, to the surprise of most people.

Clifford continued, "I came back with Claude Hopkins; then I was with the Three Blazers and Una May Carlisle -- Johnny Moore, guitar player. I was with Raleigh Randolph; we were the band behind them." I recalled Una Mae Carlisle singing with the PV Coeds for a while.

"I was in Milwaukee for a while. Camille Howard was one of our great musicians. Roy Milton, Milton Larkin ..." I asked how Camille got hooked up with Roy. Clifford said, "Because she had a style that nobody else had. If you ever listened to Roy Milton's records, you heard her ... and she had a 'tinkering style.' ... She ran up and down the piano, constantly. Roy picked Camille up ... Barney Google, Paul Love -- Barney Google was Worthley Richards ..."

"Another self-taught musician," Buddy said.

Clifford said, "Albert Johnson, they sounded just like the Ink Spots. Clarence Ward played like Wes Montgomery *then*."

"That's right!" Buddy said.

Clifford said, "That's another one! Johnny Moore tried to get him [Ward] to leave. You know, he's Oscar Moore's brother. Oscar Moore played all that guitar with King Cole." Clarence Ward was a very excellent player, but many of these men did not want to leave the families, jobs, surroundings they knew for an unknown fate.

"Don't forget," Clifford said, "most of these fellows *had* to have talent because there was no one to teach them that." In their specialties, there were no professional artists of national standing here to train with, and they had to just listen and learn, figure out for themselves how to excel in their music. "You know, I even auditioned for Jimmie Lunceford."

The two men tried to remember other artists who wanted Galveston talent.

Buddy said, "What's- his-name took Rathel [Lee] with him." Rathel Lee was a great alto sax player who played in Central High's band, then at area nightspots. "That's before Count [Basie] got him. Charlie Parker -- no, Billy Eckstine -- what's his name?"

Clifford said, "Oh, you talking about Hines; he [Basie] had him [Lee] before Earl Hines ... went to the Army with us ... Erskine Hawkins, Lucky Miller, come outta New York! He had 'em before Hines got 'im -- Bird and Dexter and all those cats. Kansas City?

He had 'em all together -- Billy Eckstine and all of them, and Earl Hines -- 'cause Billy Eckstine started them after Hines. Let me start thinkin' -- you know when Count got started with Brownskinned Models? Got stuck up in Minneapolis! Boy, it was cold!

I used to tell him I was from Galveston. Mama lived in Texas City ... Charles Brown ... Barry White's from Galveston."

Then they talked about the differences, similarities between the black and white music unions. "Joe Hathaway, the last time I saw him, he was teaching in Austin. That was years ago. Joe and Marguerite were first cousins. Joe showed me how to disassemble a saxophone, put on pads, screws, everything -- he taught me. He was working at the Galveston Piano Company," Buddy said.

"They didn't emerge in Chicago until way late. Black dudes were on 38th and State. White dudes were down on Van Buren, up in the Loop, around from Washington Boulevard, for years. ... Raising so much sand, until we all just struck, stopped playing," Buddy said. "We all just merged."

Clifford said, "They tried to improve the union, man."

"That's what I'm sayin'. Houston union was a little bit tighter. In Detroit, the Black union was on Adams and Hastings. James Petrillo kept us in segregation. You know why? He set us in different prices. The White men got more than we did. I came up Minneapolis and New York. We were getting $150.00 a week, which was considered top money -- 'cause you got paid on Wednesday and Saturday -- half Wednesday and half Saturday. Real good money. 'Cause it came outta New York. Joe B. and Moe G. sent the money. They were Jews; they booked you."

"And see, what else would get you -- they'd call out your name.

If you could read [music], you'd get paid more. If you had a good ear, like most of us had, you'd get paid, but less than those who could read. That's how they kept you down, too. Most of the white boys could read. Buddy, I made a few recordings -- nobody knew I was on it, 'cause I could read.

I was with Wilbur Shakesnider. He was at the Peacock."

His is a name I well remember. Long after he left Galveston, he was considered an idol, a hero, a role model by most of Central's band members.

Remembering how well he wrote music, they compared him to our instructor, Mr. Huff – a high compliment. "When Fess couldn't do it, he [Shakesnider] could write ... could really write, too. He lived two houses from me, in Houston."

Clifford says, "Well, at the Right Spot in Chicago, Nat King Cole played in the early '40s. I got out of the service early. Before <u>Straighten Up and Fly Right</u>, he auditioned for me. I was getting a group together. "

Buddy added, "Big bands used to come to the El Dorado. Pluma Davis [was one band that played there.] I was taking up barbering right down the street. Pluma Davis had a big band at the El Dorado. There were 16 of us. He [Pluma] played trombone. But you know what, Izola? Illinois Jacquet [quite well-known nationally then] used to come down here [Galveston] and play in the summer. Because there was nothing going on in Houston -- Houston was nothing but a big country mud hole. Galveston has always been a resort town.

In the summertime, the musicians would come down here, and try to put us out of work. I was playing on one side of the street, Illinois Jacquet on the other." Both men played the tenor saxophone. "We kept our job; Buster knew everybody. Saturday night off -- cross the street, here come Cleanhead [Eddie Vinson]. They were playing in Galveston, Texas, because they didn't have nowhere else to play. Houston didn't have no place. They eliminated the Harrisburg. I used to go up there and play. Other musicians were glad to come down here to play, 'cause they knew they'd have a big crowd.

"Yeah, we'd go to Gus Allen's, too. Schoolkids held musicians up as role models, cause we always had money in our pockets, and we stayed clean. They'd hear us blow, and they wanted to blow like us."

Clifford said, " All the kids knew Buddy, they knew Joe Woods, they knew Charles Green, they tried to hang around the beer joints to hear us. We dressed ... now they look so bad."

Buddy: "Wrinkles are now in style -- for women -- that don't make sense."

Clifford: "T-Bone Walker, Gatemouth Brown, Lightnin' Hopkins ... Lightnin' Hopkins would play for 25 cents and still couldn't draw a crowd!"

Buddy: "Muddy Waters ... Johnny Harris ... Me [on sax], Rip [on drums and vocals] and A.D. [on bass] -- used to pay us with a bowl of chili!"

I felt like laughing and crying at this remark. These men also gave free service when I asked them to play, just to further the hearing of good jazz, the way it really is supposed to sound.

Buddy continued, "When we got off from work, Houston musicians would come over to learn from us."

Clifford: "B.B. King is famous now just because of good press agents; talked about 9:00 to 9:30 on the TV station."

The men discussed how Black cowboys used to do the real ranching things -- had rodeos that were tops, but ran into money problems. They discussed the SandCrabs baseball team. "You're talking a lot of things just in Galveston! The racetrack used to be here, at 61st and Broadway; they had a dog track ... Galveston had everything you could think of at one time here -- our own airport." Galveston also had Army, Navy and Coast Guard bases, and Marines.

Ships also sailed straight to and from Galveston from New York; the Seminole and Algonquin were ships that came to Galveston every week. And they paid off when they got here, they said. "Didn't have cruise ships, but people had plenty of money. Those all got paid when they got here -- really spent money here, too." Clifford said, smiling: "Prostitutes were glad to see them."

"Don't forget Frederick Tillis!" Buddy said. "Wasn't but 14 years old, and playing with us. Fess would show him one time, and he got it and gone! 'Go on, Cat!' " Buddy said, imitating Huff.

Clifford said, "Richard 'Torch' Williams taught, too, fast as Tillis.

"Those guys could play! ... Harold Lemelle on trombone ... I played one number, *Whoop-tee-do,* with him. He said, 'Man, I can't play nothin.' I said, 'Just sit there and slide. Every time I say 'whoop-tee-do,' you say 'oo-oo' " Clifford laughed. "He's teaching, too -- and I paid full price, didn't have many musicians that night.

Bubba: "Joe Lemelle played drums with me."

Clifford: "Bubba Eaton, Paul Love's drummer ... We used to get $7.00 in tips a night in those clubs. But they came up -- about eight of us on the bandstand. So, $8 to $10 a night was good pay. I could play Rosetta.".

Woody Dickerson's name was mentioned.

They mentioned Oma Galloway; they would chaperone Galloway and Tillis for their mothers, Clifford said. Girls who sang with them felt safe. I told them how Buster Pope would clown around with the white guys, using psychology to steer them away from me and any female vocalist who might be on the job. I hated seeing him sometimes demean himself for this purpose, but I understood the way things were, and was very grateful for his wisdom. This was one of my first lessons in knowing when to pick your battles, in order to win the war. Men like Buddy, Clifford and Buster were the unsung heroes in my day, who more than the uniformed officers kept us safe.

Buddy Williams and Clifford Duvall provided more history in their conversation than can be found in anyone's writings about the good ole days of Galveston. Trying to think of good bands that came to Galveston, they named Don Adams, Chick Webb. They recalled a band called the Carolina Cottonpickers; they said that Don Albert Adams looked so sharp, clean and neat, but these kids came along, and really blew.

They mentioned a place called GeorgeRandolph's, later called Rudolph. I think they were referring to a place owned by Rudolph Raven, whose brother George Raven lived across the street from my mother, at 815 Ave. K.

"Downstairs was Ned Rose ... upstairs was Rudolph's place. Lou Rawls was with John Ervin, the policeman. People didn't like him because he couldn't sing the blues," Clifford said. "And John said Rudolph gave him this big diamond ring, and sent him all around Texas cause he could sing -- but he couldn't sing like they wanted him to -- so he fired Lou Rawls."

I began to see what Clifford meant, because I have great admiration for Lou Rawls' voice, which is internationally recognized by now. But the local crowd, always hardest to please, wanted to hear someone yell, bellow out, or warble, instead of pretty, straight singing – real singing.

Island of Color

It is still this way in the field of religious music. The uneducated have persuaded the educated to believe that the louder you holler, and the more your voice wobbles up and down on each note, the more skilled you are. And the younger folk, exposed to this lack of appreciation for real quality of tone and clarity of words, still don't know what good music is supposed to sound like. Blame the educational system for not instructing them in quality music.

"Lou Rawls sang in Chicago at the Grand Terrace, off 47th and South Park," Buddy added.

We recalled the Copacabana Club at 26th and Market streets. It was a hot spot for good band sounds in the latter '40s and early '50s. I believe it was the club owned by T.D. Armstrong, that my husband and I attended while courting. (We had a picture taken there one Labor Day evening.)

Buddy said he paid Mr. Coleman 50 cents a lesson, for lessons from 5 to 6 p.m. on Mondays and Fridays. He went to lessons regardless of whether it rained, snowed or sleeted. "Then I got in the habit -- she [his mother] didn't have to ask me. I had to put in two to three hours every day. Just like you pray every day, you got to practice every day."

Amen. They spoke of the discipline of having to practice hard, long and consistently. And how it paid off.

"That's why I ran into these young musicians now, and they say, 'How'd you learn chords like that?' "

"Practice, practice, practice," both men say together.

Clifford: "Now when I got with [Earl 'Fatha'] Hines, that was a test. I had to really do it. He'd put that big book up, and he'd go" stomping his foot in time "1-2-3 ... that was the first time down." If Clifford repeated a mistake, "the second time...[Hines said,] 'See, if you'd made that mistake again, I couldn't use you.' They wanted you to sight-read."

Buddy said, "Fess knew exactly who missed a note, and when you missed it. 'You want to try it again?' he'd say. 'I was listening for that G sharp. Wait a minute. You want to put your horn up?' He meant, 'Don't miss it again.' "

Both men talked of how they once memorized so much music, but now can't always remember telephone numbers; we all laughed.

Clifford said, "I'll never forget a piece called the Jitterbug Shuffle. When it came down again," when the band played it through again, "I closed my eyes -- didn't miss a note."

Buddy said, "You anticipate. You think, automatically, it was a D. Next time it'll be a D sharp or E or something. It wasn't always as you pictured it. You're right in that range -- you can read the 32nd notes. You can't always read the 64th notes.

You know the greatest feeling you can have? You play together a long time, you both think the same thing, at the same time, and the chord changes, and it fits, blends in -- you're really inside each other. Ain't no woman make me feel like that!" I chuckle.

In the jazz field, we old-timers are not the last of Galveston's proponents of good jazz. Top in his field of jazz today is Pat Williams. If I alone added up all of the times that Pat has performed free to help me put on a program – just to get the pure satisfaction of knowing that somebody was left knowing more, feeling more, experiencing more music – the account would fill a lot more pages.

Patrick Michael Williams Sr.

Patrick Williams

Patrick was born to Joseph and Bennie Williams on May 25, 1942, in Dickinson. He attended Dunbar School there, and while he was in middle school, his great-uncle James King, a Pullman porter on the Southern Pacific line, found a bugle on the train and gave it to him. His father, Joseph, had been a trumpet player at Houston College for Negroes, now known as Texas Southern University, and helped him with his embouchure -- the way the lips and tongue are used to produce a sound in the trumpet mouthpiece.

Patrick played the trumpet in a band started at Dunbar School under the direction of Mr. Henry Hayes. His sister, Weaser, already a student of ballet and piano, soon joined the band as a clarinetist.

Upon graduation from Dunbar, he received a scholarship to Texas College in Tyler. Under direction of Clifford Hodge, he played in the brass choir and concert and marching band for two years. After two years at Texas College, he returned to the Galveston area and joined the Bobby Scott orchestra of Galveston.

This band included Doug McKindley on bass guitar, Malcolm Esther on valve trombone, Joe Louis Smith on guitar, and Tooney on drums. All of these men were from Galveston. The band played a variety of music, featuring vocalist Louis Jones at area clubs, such as The Downbeat, The Manhattan, The Jambalaya, Selena's Blue Room, The G&M Pleasure Spot, and The Palladium in Houston. During their tenure with Bobby Scott's band, they backed Bobby Vinton, Chuck Berry at Galveston's City Auditorium, Johnny "Guitar" Watson, and numerous recording artists that frequented the Galveston area.

Vocalist Maxine Brown of New York heard the band in La Marque, and hired them to tour with her and move to New York City.

After this big break, Patrick went on to the "big time," playing with many well-known professional jazz and rhythm and blues artists. These artists include Stevie Wonder, The Temptations, Gladys Knight, The Four Tops, Smoky Robinson, The Spinners, The Supremes, ventriloquist Willie Tyler and Lester, B.B. King, Nancy Wilson, The Houston Pops Orchestra, Mongo Santa Maria, The Scott Joplin Chamber Orchestra, Johnny Taylor, Milt Hinton, Lionel Hampton, Bobby Bland, Stan Getz, The O Jays, O.C. Smith, Sammy Davis Jr., Bobby Vinton, Arthur Prysock, Ruth Brown, Dakota Staton, Roberta Flack, Millie Jackson, Eddie "Cleanhead" Vinson, Al Green, J.C. Heard, and numerous other recording artists.

He performed as studio and traveling musician with Motown Records, and performed everywhere from the Apollo Theatre in New York City; to Bermuda; to the Jones Hall in Houston; to the 1894 Grand Opera House in Galveston.

Patrick Williams has also logged a vast amount of teaching experience, after receiving private trumpet instruction from Billy Horner of the Detroit Symphony; studying at Wayne University in Detroit, Mich.; receiving his management and supervision certificate from College of the Mainland in Texas City; and studying essential elements of fine arts at the University of Houston.

His music teaching record includes: brass workshop leader, in the Metro Arts Complex of Detroit, Mich.; music management instructor with Arnett Cobb and Summer Jazz Workshop in Houston; band director at Houston elementary and high schools; private trumpet and piano instructor at Grant and LeBlanc's Music World in Houston; adjudicator at Texas Southern University Jazz Festival in Houston; music instructor at Chinquapin School, Highland, Texas; band director at Our Lady of Fatima School in Texas City; band director at Salvation Army, Texas City; band director at Galveston Catholic School; music minister at Holy Rosary Catholic Church in Galveston; jazz lecturer/historian for Elderhostel, Continuing Education Division, University of Texas.

Now living in Galveston, Pat has put more than 200 percent into whatever he has promised to do. This long list of occupations and interests does not include the much longer list of his volunteer efforts to help people young and old to enjoy music.

Pat Williams has played his magic trumpet as an individual and as an accompanist for the Moody House Jubilee Choir (retired senior citizens); with various children's groups; with very amateur youth at Galveston College; with semi-professional choirs; instrumental combos; junior and senior high school ensembles, and even on rare occasions his own professionally trained jazz combos composed of Houston area musicians.

Music: The Jazz Generation

These combos lift my spirit and remind me that such great music really does still exist.

Dr. Frederick C. Tillis

Dr. Frederick Tillis

Dr. Tillis is the most successful musician that Galveston has to call its own. There is no one of any race born in Galveston who has matched his achievements. Does this mean that he is respected and lauded as such? Not by Galvestonians. Most of the reason is that his own people, African Americans in Galveston, show little fascination with serious scholars of music. "A prophet in his own town. ..." Also, his mother, Mrs. Bernice Gardner, believes in Christian humility, and seldom talked about the wonders he has done.

Frederick Tillis was born Jan. 5, 1930, in Galveston, an only child. He was educated in the Galveston public schools, receiving his music training from Mr. Fleming Smizer Huff as a trumpet player in Central High School Band, and as the leader of an instrumental group in his senior year, where he learned the fundamentals of playing jazz.

After high school graduation at the age of 16, he attended Wiley College in Marshall. After his college graduation at the age of 19, he taught in Wiley's School of Music as a graduate student. Tillis went on to the University of Iowa, where he earned his M.A. and Ph. D. in music composition.

Dr. Tillis has explored composition in the serial mode and has written in a variety of other music contexts. Since 1966 he has deliberately written in a style that is based upon elements that are natural outgrowths of his ethnic and cultural background. Rhythmic and some structural influences in his works reach back to Africa and include some elements of jazz. Melodic and harmonic structures reflect elements of various musics of the world, including Eastern and Western cultures. As a soprano and tenor saxophonist, his performances are devoted almost exclusively to music in the jazz tradition.

Dr. Tillis has been the recipient of a Rockefeller Foundation grant, a National Endowment for the Arts grant in composition, and two United Negro College Fund fellowships. He is a Danforth Associate and has written a published text, Jazz Theory and Improvisation.

A composer, performer, poet (he has written and published several books of poetry), educator, lecturer, and administrator, Dr. Tillis has a distinguished career, having been commissioned by several symphonic orchestras to write for their special occasions. I have had the pleasure of hearing the Atlanta Symphony play one of his works. I have also heard the Houston Symphony, combined with a community orchestra and choir composed of African Americans, perform a commissioned work by him. This year, the National Symphony Orchestra at Kennedy Center in Washington, D.C., performed Dr. Tillis' *Festival Journey.*

After a long career as a university administrator, Dr. Tillis has just retired as director of the Fine Arts Center, professor of music composition, and director of the Afro-American Music and Jazz Program at the University of Massachusetts at Amherst. He has a wife and two daughters, one a photographer and visual artist who has assisted him in publishing his poetry. He lives in Amherst still, and writes more frequently, and tries not to forget that he is supposed to be retired.

Dr. Tillis' music is performed nationally, and abroad. Among his commissioned compositions are *Festival Journey (1992)* and *Ring Shout Concerto (1974)*; *In the Spirit and the Flesh* (1985); *Three Symphonic Spirituals for Orchestra* (1978); *Concerto for Piano (Jazz Trio)* and *Symphony Orchestra* (1975); and *Spiritual Cycle for Soprano and Orchestra* (1978).

Other commissions include *Voices and Colors* (1989); *Inaugural Overture* (1988); *Two Pieces for Orchestra* (1990); *Freedom* (1967); *Spiritual Fantasy No.9 (Sympathy)* (1988); and a choral arrangement (S.A.T.B.) of a suite of Duke Ellington songs: *I let a Song Go Out of My Heart, Mood Indigo, and Take the A Train* (1979). Of course, Dr. Tillis has written many other works for instruments and voices, solo, ensembles, as well as full orchestra and band, and choir. He has written more than 100 compositions, and is still going strong.

He has informed me that his latest performed major work is *A Symphony of Songs for Chorus and Orchestra*, with poems by Wallace Stevens. It has four movements, and was commissioned by the Hartford (Connecticut) Symphony and Chorus. Henley Denmeade was the music director; copyright was in 1999.

Dr. Tillis comes home to Galveston at least once every year to visit his mother, no matter how busy his schedule.

As for recognition at home, I have presented a two-piano work of his in concert for our Galveston Musical Club, with Mrs. Bernice Hightower, and played a selection from a suite he has written for pipe organ, and would play more of his works if I were able. Tillis wrote a Spiritual Fantasy for Pipe Organ based on the hymn *It is Well With My Soul*, which I premiered in concert February 2000. He has already followed that with two more Pipe Organ Spiritual Fantasies which I have also premiered.

God Bless! One day, before we are both too old to do so, I hope to perform some jazz with him.

LADIES IN THEIR 80s

A 1993 Conversation

with Mrs. Edna Barrett McCullough, Mrs. Bernice James and Mrs. Alice Hunter,

assisted by Mrs. Florence Henderson

I had invited these ladies to have lunch with me. All three had grown up together and knew each other well. And all of them had some special connection to me and my family. At this time, each was living alone and still taking care of herself, with just occasional help from friends or family.

Music: The Jazz Generation

3 ladies posing

Aunt Edna was living in the Gulfbreeze retirement complex at her own request. She had been glad to see the building constructed, and while she was still in her own home, she told us, "I sure would like to live there; I'm tired of trying to keep up all that work in my house." The problems of repair and maintenance were also getting her down.

Mrs. James was trying to get over the recent loss of her sister, Lois, and had also just lost her husband of more than 50 years. Since they had had no children, she was now completely alone -- no relatives left. She was living in her own home still.

Mrs. Alice Hunter was the mother of my former classmate, Joselyn, who had been our valedictorian. Both her daughter, an only child, and husband had expired, but she had a couple of cousins who looked in on her from time to time. She was also very fond of her only granddaughter, and yearned for the girl, now grown, to visit more often.

I had come to really appreciate her consistently positive attitude. I transported her to my annual musical program for several years, and she was always grateful for the attention. She gave me much to remember about handling adversity, because she never complained about her situation, and always spoke of any small kindness extended to her by church folk, relatives, neighbors. She lived in her own world, one in which she had always just heard from her granddaughter, heard that she was doing so well. I remember her constant smile, and her pure joy over small things -- how she wanted to give me pecans from her tree, which she gathered from the ground and shelled herself, whenever I visited in the fall. She showed pleasure over whatever I brought her, whether it was flowers, food, or just a printed program from some event.

I turned the tape recorder on after I had seated Aunt Edna and Mrs. Hunter at my dining-room table. Aunt Edna, my mother's first cousin, spoke first.

"Dowling Street ... Aunt Lu ... Alice said to me, 'Come sit over here by me -and I'll have room for you -- from Houston -- they had a party that night at Mrs. Anderson's house -- Interurban -- Kermit came near marrying me. ...."

Mrs. James came in with my sister: "I thought I had the wrong day!" (My sister was evidently late in picking her up -- Mrs. James was always extremely punctual.)

Mrs. Hunter said, "I thought I had the wrong hour." (Because the others had arrived later.)

Aunt Edna said, "Lollie used to say all the time -- 'Old age is a bitch.'"

As my sister and I try to keep a straight face, Mrs. Hunter tried to set the record straight on their relative ages: "I'm a baby! ... Out of eight children, I'm the only one living!

"My closest relatives are William ... Joseph Sanders -- he brings food, brings dinner, anything else I need. ...Cousin, but he calls me Auntie."

I asked, "Mrs. James, how are you feeling?"

"Much better," she answered.

Mrs. Hunter said, "I just had surgery for this eye. Yes. I had cataracts. Yes, doing O.K. So hot earlier in the day."

After a little more talk, I said, "I'm going to ask one of you to say the blessing." After one of them obliged me, I started serving the food.

"My silver set is still in the box," Mrs. Hunter said. "I don't have anyone to serve it to."

"Anyone want crackers ... dressing?" I asked. "I have water and tea -- tell me what you want to drink. Is it cool enough?"

"I'm going to take mine with me, because my eating time is so weird," Florence said. "I'm eating breakfast now, and I eat dinner when doctors say you shouldn't -- it is so late."

"She'd always be at Ms. Laura Williams'," Aunt Edna said. "I stayed with her on weekends. She played organ and piano. She carried me over to San Augustine [Episcopal Church] to practice -- the keys -- wooden keys -- her father directing the choir. No, he didn't play -- he worked the organ; the pedals, I couldn't reach them."

On yet another subject now, Aunt Edna said, to Mrs. Hunter: "You talking about some classy sisters! I remember all of your sisters -- dressed so fine." Mrs. Hunter replied, "I'm wearing now what I had when I retired in '68. I haven't bought any clothes." Mrs. James says, "Styles repeat themselves anyway."

Mrs. Hunter said, "My blood pressure is something else. ..."

Aunt Edna asked, "Now didn't you have a sister -- very classy -- and sang like a mockingbird?" Mrs. Hunter answered, "My oldest sister -- yeah, she sang. After she moved to California, they formed a group. They were raising money for the needy. They were the only colored, rest were white."

Mrs. Hunter said, speaking of her daughter and granddaughter, "Joselyn has passed but Jo Claire is there. Can't find Mr. Right! She has two degrees -- one in merchandise buying; one in banking."

Mrs. James told me, "I want my salad to stay right here. I want to eat it with my dinner," trying to make sure I didn't move it.

I told the ladies, "I've got some sour cream and chives to go with the potatoes. Here are the baked crabs -- I have okra and tomatoes, but I'm not sure if you like that, so I have some peas, too." They seemed to enjoy it very much, but couldn't eat too much at a time.

Mrs. James told me twice more, "I want my salad with me." I'm sure that she had experienced waiters and others taking her salad before she could stop them; that has happened to me as well.

I told them, "I started not to make rolls, but I wanted some myself. And I have some homemade ice cream for you -- fresh peach ice cream." They seem pleased:

"Oooh!" "I want some of that!"

When asked by them why she wasn't eating anything, Florence explained again, "I just finished eating breakfast, messed up my timing."

Aunt Edna asked, "Alice, do you ever hear from L-- Barnes? She had so many boyfriends and all that."

Then she asked my sister, "Florence, you don't do much cooking?"

"Well, it's a hit-and-miss sort of thing," my sister explained.

Aunt Edna said she tried to make baked crabs when her husband Walter was alive, but they didn't taste like anything – little flavor. Florence told them how her grandchildren, little Florence and Jenny Grace, loved my gumbo, and still talked about it in letters.

Aunt Edna talked with Mrs. Hunter about someone who had lived in Houston, who had died about a year earlier.

Mrs. Hunter said, "Mr. Mason called me Sweet Alice," recalling a Central High School principal.

Florence said he called Bessie and Vietta, cousins of ours in our generation, by their mother's name, Ella Mae, because he sometimes couldn't decide which was which. Their mother was Aunt Edna's sister.

I ask if the ladies want seconds or dessert. Mrs. James said, "I don't know when I've had any baked crabs." She protested my waiting on her so much, and I said, "It's my turn to treat *you* all."

Mrs. James next remembered the ice man, who I think delivered ice they used in making ice cream in her younger days.

She said, "Ruthie married fellow -- said the other day, they live somewhere way out West. Said they offered her some nice fresh redfish -- it was a nice size. When I cut it, I could make two nice pieces. I ate one side, and saved the next side for the next day."

I told them about the glasses we were using, with a rose design -- a gift from Shirley Price. And how she was born without arms, and is dwarf-size, but was also born with an outstanding spirit and will to excel. She was then working on her doctorate degree at Texas Southern University, which she has since received, despite frequent injuries and auto accidents.

Aunt Edna then told us that Buster Pope had once offered to teach her to drive, when she was a door-to-door Avon saleswoman. "Lester Holmes said he would teach me, too. ..."

After more talk, I asked, "You all ready for your ice cream?"

They all laughed, said they were too full. I offered to give them take-home portions, with expressions of appreciation and delight from all of them.

Mrs. Hunter purred, "It was a pleasure to be with all of you. I haven't seen you in such a long time."

Mrs. James said, "It was at the last teacher's meeting, I believe." They had been retired from teaching for a long time, and it was very likely that they had seen each other on numerous occasions since then. Mrs. Hunter understood Mrs. James' confusion and didn't comment again.

"Alice Beautiful," Mrs. Hunter told us again that they called her in her youth. She said it with such a sweet voice and mild manner that it did not sound immodest.

Mrs. James says, "When you're by yourself, you just [don't remember] how to make [foods] that you don't make anymore." I agreed. My daughter, Cheryl, who was visiting from out of town, passed through the room shortly after, saying she smelled something she hadn't in a while -- my cooking. We laughed.

Music: The Jazz Generation

Mrs. Hunter said, "When my sister passed, she was the first one there, my godchild -- Venita Jones and Alice Jones. ... Course we could *dance*, people from Texas. ..."

I told her that Gwen Bridge Heard, her daughter's best friend in their youth, had asked about her the other day during a phone call, when we had discussed her lavish 40th wedding anniversary celebration in North Carolina. Gwen also said that the Clousers and Esther Bright-Davies attended.

Mrs. Hunter spoke of a missed trip to California with Gwen, and mentioned Edith Gooden, a very good friend of hers.

We talked of problems we all had in acquiring and keeping a good pair of glasses, and the eyesight conditions we each had. They were surprised to learn that a "youngster" like myself was already having cataract problems. Mrs. Hunter and Mrs. James both said they sometimes could see better without glasses. I told them that glasses were made of better material in their day, and they now break more easily. Florence said something about leaving her glasses on the piano until she needed them. I mentioned the small print in Mother's book of devotions. From there, we discussed various spiritual reading materials; then Billy Graham, Jimmy Swaggart, Oral Roberts and other religious folk on radio and TV. We talked of those we saw as sincere and insincere.

Mrs. Hunter said, "They changed the [TV schedule] times -- when it's time for us to go to church, then they're just coming on."

Aunt Edna talked of the "healers" who make money in person, and how people respond to them.

The tape ends there.

We weren't even thinking about it, but it records a lifestyle we just seldom have anymore. I am so grateful that three lonely older ladies had a great time, and it was an important chance for Florence and me to remember a time when Mother and people like her in her generation tended to the needs of young and old. We were renewed spiritually. The conversation was rambling but warm, and I felt well rewarded just having their wisdom and encouragement in my home.

CHAPTER NINE
MEDICINE & HEALTH CARE

Several of Galveston's African Americans also turned their energies to medicine and health care.

Ralph Horace Scull

1st. Lt. Ralph Scull in uniform

Ralph Horace Scull was born to Ralph Albert and Florence Ella Scull on Oct. 5, 1897, in Galveston. He attended the public schools of Galveston, graduating from Central High School about 1914, and attended Wilberforce University in Wilberforce, Ohio, until World War I, when he joined the United States Army and rose to the rank of first lieutenant.

After World War I was over, he returned to Wilberforce University, where he was a track star among other activities, receiving his bachelor of science degree on June 15, 1922. He earned a degree in medicine from Rusk Medical School, and studied dermatology at the University of Chicago, where he later also taught. Dr. Scull began his practice in Chicago, and became one of the nation's leading dermatologists.

Ralph Horace Scull

He married Florence Viola McNorton of Cincinnati, Ohio, and they made their home in Chicago, where his wife was a master teacher of home economics. They had no children.

An entrepreneur, he invested in many promising inventions, including motor cars with engines in the rear. He was a member of all medical professional organizations and the Snakes Social Club, a professional social club in Chicago.

Medicine & Health Care

He was awarded many honors, but cherished the Central High School Outstanding Alumnus Award received here in Galveston at the Central High graduating ceremonies in the City Auditorium in 1943.

Dr. Leroy Sterling

Dr. Sterling was a prominent African American dentist, whose wife, a soror of mine, is well-known in education. He and his parents were native Galvestonians. His mother was a homemaker and his father was probably the first clerk of color with the Corps of Engineers. He graduated from Central High School and Prairie View University, worked for the government in Washington, D.C., and then attended medical school at Meharry.

After graduating, he practiced privately in Galveston, in an office over T.D. Armstrong's drugstore for at least 10 years. He also worked for the school district as school dentist, hired by school board president Dr. Glenn. He took the post after seeking the opinion of Rufus Stanton, his friend and also a Galveston dentist, who encouraged him to take the job. He practiced in the junior high school where his brother, Randall, was a well-known principal.

Dr. Herman A. Barnett III

Melvin Williams' book, *From Africa To America: African Contributions To America's Healthcare System; A Celebration In Memory Of Herman A. Barnett III, M.D.*, provided a great deal of background information on Barnett. Williams, a quiet but dedicated man from the Midwest, came to Galveston in 1997. He jumped right into the battle fray, when he simply started to do his job as director of affirmative action at

University of Texas at Medical Branch -- contributing to the wellness of our community, addressing racial unrest. The media has used him to divide rather than unite, quoting him out of context in the local newspaper.

I learned in my first year on the Galveston school board that that is something the newspaper does a great deal of: seeking the public's attention by whatever means is necessary to sell its wares. Sensationalism is riding high in our nation at this time, and people in all facets of the community have been victims. Lives are being lost and whole communities destroyed by the media's frenzy to make money.

But Williams has written about African Americans and health care in a very solid effort to inform and unite. That was one major reason I was a contributor to his book. I also had a very personal reason to want to praise Dr. Herman Barnett, because he was a friend and fraternity brother of my husband. More than this, he operated on my son, Roy Lester Collins III, when he was a baby; it was the first time any of my children had undergone surgery.

My son became ill in 1957 when he was only 6 weeks old, and faced his first discrimination in the waiting room of a white private physician. After he was passed over for so long, my husband and I left the waiting room, and headed for the emergency room of John Sealy hospital, because our baby had a fever that was climbing. Once there, when he was finally examined, we were told he needed immediate surgery.

We were not supposed to be told who would do it, but I was able to locate Dr. Barnett. When he would not divulge any information, I kept pace with his brisk walk, and simply asked him outright, "Are you going to operate on my baby?" He could tell from my anguished voice not to be too secretive. Sensing my desperation, he told me that he might, and asked me, "What's your baby's name?" I smiled, recognizing it as an affirmative answer. He had already been a guest in our home a couple of times, and knew well who I was and that his friend Roy was the child's father. I just said softly, "God bless!" and left him to walk on. I went up to the segregated hospital ward room where the nurses said they would bring my son after surgery. They brought him in on a full-sized gurney; he took up only a tiny fraction of the space, at the head of the rolling bed. He was very pale, and his hair was damp on his tiny head. With his eyes still closed, he looked as frail as a baby could, covered with a big green sheet tucked in all around. Because he was sleeping so soundly, they decided to leave him on the gurney for the time being. I took up my sad vigil, really afraid.

I'm not sure how long I was there by his side, because time sort of stood still for me. I only know that I was eventually told that the doctor was coming around to check on him very soon.

When I saw Barnett again, I thrilled at the sight. As long as I live, I will not forget seeing this team of doctors coming down a long hall, white coats moving in the rush they made -- about 10 of them, I believe. They were led by this short, handsome, and very capable-looking, earnest Black man, Dr. Herman Barnett III. And he sho' looked good to me. He was the only African American doctor at UTMB, so he was the only one on that team, and for my people to be in charge of anything that was all-white was a shocker back in those days. Seeing Dr. Barnett in charge of the men in the most trusted profession, the doctors who healed our bodies, was a definite charge to my pride, a sort of wake-up call to continue to excel.

Dr. Barnett examined my baby boy carefully, talking to the men around him briefly, then smiled at me finally, and said, "Don't worry, he'll be fine. Looks good. He should heal without much of a scar." He winked at me, and turned, moved right out, with his team trailing purposely behind him. He had marked the baby's chart, and the nurses moved to do their duties. I just sat in a daze of gratefulness.

Not long after that, the news of his death in his airplane just left me shattered. The continuing question for those of us who seek spiritual truths is "Why did he have to die so young? Why would God take him when he had so much to still offer all of us, but particularly his own children?"

I can at least tell my story, and include the information that Melvin gleaned in his book. I also include my thanks to the persons who helped him, Janice and Billy Stanton, gather also firsthand knowledge of the pioneering Stanton family; the Mosley family, cousins to the Stantons; the Sterlings, and all those other local African American medical figures who came before.

Herman Aladdin Barnett III was born Jan. 22, 1926, in Austin, to Lula V. Searcy Barnett. His father passed away when he was 2 years old; his mother later married Rev. Sylvester Byars. At only 4 years old, little Herman was already said to be developing an interest in medicine and a passion for flying. Barnett's stepfather was very supportive, and thought his boy could do no wrong.

Herman attended Grant's Elementary School in San Antonio. He graduated from Anderson High School in Austin in 1942. When the family moved back to San Antonio, Herman decided that he needed further educational training. Small in stature and young-looking for his age, he enrolled in Phyllis Wheatley High School in San Antonio, emphasizing a business curriculum; he graduated again in 1943.

Herman then decided it was time for him to serve his country, and enlisted in the U.S. Army Air Corps. His mother often related how on the morning the young men were to report and catch the bus that would take them to the base, several people questioned his presence. "Whose little baby is that?" "Whose little child are they shipping off to war?" This very young man trained and was qualified as a fighter pilot at the Tuskegee Airfield.

He thus became a member of the famed Tuskegee Airmen.

He was commended for his proficiency in flying but was thought too independent to be a soldier. He was a leader, not a follower. He was said to be in front when a group of Tuskegee men buzzed the nearby campus of Spelman College, an all-girls college. He served with distinction, however, until he was honorably discharged in 1946. His passion for flying continued and he eventually became a member of the Air Force Medical Reserve. He was a founding member of the Bronze Eagles Flying Club in Houston.

After leaving the Air Corps, Herman enrolled in Samuel Huston College (now Huston-Tillotson College) in Austin, majoring in pre-medicine. Here he and my husband met; Roy also received his degree in pre-medicine, and they entered the same fraternity, Alpha Phi Alpha. He quickly became involved with research, serving as a laboratory assistant with the chemistry and biology departments. He also taught biology for two summers. His undergraduate accolades include: president of Student Council, member of Phi Kappa Theta, recipient of the C.A. Yearwood Prize (1948), and business manager of the choir.

His musical aptitude was also extraordinary. He was an accomplished musician in clarinet, piano and voice. He graduated with honors in 1948, as did my husband.

The musical prowess of Dr. Barnett points to what those in fine arts have been trying to tell the general public for so long: It is no coincidence that many people who excel in other fields also demonstrate musical ability. Music has now been proven to sharpen thinking skills, the deductive reasoning of the persons who utilize this training, especially on piano. Music has also been responsible for training persons to work both independently and as part of a team.

Barnett was accepted at Meharry and Howard medical schools. But his grades and personality also made him an excellent candidate for the NAACP's attack on segregation in education. The group persuaded Herman to apply to the University of Texas Medical Branch, School of Medicine.

To avoid the expense of creating a separate medical school, state officials were forced to violate Texas segregation statues in allowing Herman to attend UTMB. The Houston press tried to give the public the false impression that Barnett would attend UTMB only until facilities could be built at the Texas State University for Negroes in Houston (now Texas Southern University). Dr. T.S. Painter, president of University of Texas at Austin, was quoted as saying "as soon as the medical education can be provided at Houston, Barnett will be transferred there." In reality, there were no plans to build separate facilities. After admission, it was reported that Barnett met with Dr. Chauncey Leake and was told to be sure that he was always the first one in the classroom and that he always wore a tie. Years later, as long as I knew him, he always wore a bow tie.

When the other students reported to that first class, they sat around Barnett, and very quickly noticed his keen intellect. He adapted to medical school very easily. Dr. Armond Goldman, Department of Pediatrics, and a classmate of Barnett's, reports: "Herman was very mature, quick and intelligent. Learning came very easily for him. In fact, he was superior to us, and everyone soon became aware of it." Goldman also reported that the classes were integrated and that there never was a problem as he could recall. Barnett was warmly accepted by his classmates, his instructors, and the general public with whom he came in contact. Goldman said, "Herman never spoke of any trials, he never got angry, he just displayed his superiority and led by his actions. He never sank to the level of the bigot."

He rose above one such trial after going with Goldman and another student to a friend's house to watch a college football game. The friend's home was on the far west end of the island, near the causeway. The student who gave Goldman and Barnett a ride had to leave early, to go back to the lab. After the game, they boarded a bus to ride back to UTMB. This was in the days of segregated public accommodation. Goldman went to the back of the bus to sit with Barnett, who was required by law to ride there. The bus driver yelled at

Armond, "You can't go back there with that nigger!" Goldman told him, "I'm just going to sit with my friend." At the same time, Barnett leaned over and whispered to him, "Let's just leave." They both left the bus, and walked down Broadway, "enjoying their leisurely stroll back to the lab," Williams recounts. This leisurely stroll had to be all the way across the city -- about five or six miles.

All was not smooth at UTMB either. Williams said Barnett had to sit in the hall once to see a slide presentation, because he was told there were no facilities in the lecture hall for Negroes. He endured and "aced the course." Other students, evidently fearing rejection by their peers, did not select him for a lab partner. One man finally did, and years later, his widow surprised Barnett's family by sending them a clipping of the man's obituary, proudly proclaiming that he was Barnett's first white lab partner, and that they had gone on to be friends and respected colleagues.

Then there was the time that Dr. Barnett was attacked and beaten by highway patrolmen. In 1953, Barnett was driving back to Galveston from Houston. He loved speed in cars and airplanes. Stopped by the highway patrol for speeding, he was ridiculed for telling them his name was Dr. Barnett. When asked where he had gotten his UTMB ring, he replied that it was his. They took it from him, saying that he must have stolen it, since "no niggers go to UTMB." And they beat him until he lost consciousness. They then took him to UTMB's emergency room, where he was immediately recognized, although very battered and bruised. The NAACP was called in, and the patrolmen lied, saying that Herman had a knife and they had to defend themselves. Dr. Barnett filed a report to get his ring back, and never received it, but a new one was ordered for him, which his family has today.

Another African American at UTMB, two years behind Barnett, was Dr. Robert Hilliard. They both suffered indignities that he related. Separate staff restrooms were created to satisfy the segregation requirements. Barnett was not allowed to eat in the cafeteria. Not knowing this, Hilliard did eat there with another African American student. Dr. Hilliard said that whenever they went to eat, the ladies serving them were always ready to give extra helpings, even without asking. After two weeks, they were called into the president's office, and told that it was all right to eat in the cafeteria. Barnett continued to stay away.

There was also the problem of student housing for Dr. Barnett. Fraternities provided UTMB's only campus housing; Theta Kappa Psi attempted to admit him, but one of their benefactors said that he would not tolerate it. And the apartment complexes surrounding the campus also would not let him in. As Williams relates, Mr. Leon Morgan, principal of Central High School, and his wife Olivette, a social worker, had a large home on 31st Street, with a servant's entrance to private quarters upstairs. Barnett moved in and paid them $25.00 a month for rent. Williams said they assumed guardianship of his social life, much to his amusement.

Williams said Barnett was "quite the ladies' man" until his time in surgical residency at UTMB. He was very handsome, and had a great personality, and so attracted the ladies' attention regardless of his professional status. I remember his attending a party or two at our home as my husband's guest, before he met his wife-to-be. He was a lot of fun, and was very nice, enjoying the company of our friends.

Williams said it was during his surgical residency that he met Wylma Lynn White of Beaumont. Herman knew immediately that this was the woman he was going to marry and proceeded to announce it to everyone on the very same evening. Wylma and her family found this to be quite amusing, but he did marry her the following May 29, 1955.

Barney, as his friends called him, and Wylma were married for 18 years and had five children. At the time of his death on May 26, 1973, Dr. Barnett was a very prominent surgeon and anesthesiologist in Houston. He was just 47 years old when his plane went down in high winds as he attempted to land during the Negro Airmen International Convention Air Show in Wichita, Kansas. The air show was canceled due to tornado warnings.

Dr. Herman Barnett graduated from UTMB in 1953. He received the Charles A. Phizer award for the outstanding sophomore student. Not only was Barnett the first Black graduate of medical school in Texas, he was also the first African American to serve on the Texas Board of Medical Examiners. He completed his four-year residency in general surgery at UTMB, as the first Black to receive and complete a residency at a UTMB hospital. Later, he completed training in anesthesiology at St. Joseph's Hospital in Houston. His academic interests centered on emergency room trauma and the psychological changes associated with post surgery.

I remember how pleased my husband was when Barnett was appointed a member of the board of trustees of Huston-Tillotson College. Barnett was also invited to participate in the White House Conference on health costs in 1967. In 1966 he participated in the American Red Cross Convention as the National Medical Association's representative, and in 1968, he was a member of the National Health Forum. The list of his civic involvements and memberships is so long that it would make this information burdensome to read.

Dr. Barnett held many professional positions, and received many awards and fellowships throughout his career and his life. He received a fellowship from the American Cancer Society for 1955-56, and another fellowship from the National Medical Fellowships for 1955-1958. In 1978, he was posthumously named an Ashbel Smith Distinguished Alumnus, one of UTMB's highest honors. Most recently, Dr. Thomas James, then UTMB president, created the Herman A. Barnett Distinguished Professorship in Microbiology and Immunology. Dr. Clifford Houston was the first faculty member to hold the professorship, which is funded at $250,000 to enhance UTMB's educational research and patient care endeavors.

Dr. Barnett also ran for the Houston Independent School District Board of Trustees under the 'Citizens for Good Schools' ticket. He won and was shortly elected president, another first for African Americans. He was interested in improving education because of his own experiences, but also because of his mother's experiences with injustice as a teacher in Lockhart. Dr. Barnett said then, "There is no liberal way to teach chemistry or conservative way to teach math. There are only children with problems and promise, children who enter our schools excited about learning and in a few years, in too many cases become turned off to the learning process." How true this still rings for our school districts today, Williams says, and I agree.

Dr. Barnett indeed was a visionary. He was a short man in stature, but is thought by many to have been large and tall because of his many accomplishments and his influence. Truly, he is a legend, and his spirit pervades the halls of UTMB.

(Dr. Barnett's widow, Wylma, is a professor in the Education Department at Texas Southern University in Houston. Their eldest son, Herman Barnett IV, lives in Houston. Another son, Marcus Duane, is in private practice in Northwest Houston, in obstetrics and gynecology. He and his wife, Gail, have three sons, Marcus II, Brandon, and Trenton. The youngest of Herman's sons, Keith, is with American Airlines in Oklahoma City. His daughter, Lynn-Etta Kay, lives in Chicago, is a flight attendant for United Airlines, and is completing her degree in airway science. Their youngest daughter, April Michelle, is an aspiring actress in Los Angeles.)

Island Health

In his book, Williams also talks of hospitals and African Americans on Galveston Island from 1890 to 1998.

"In the late 1800s, when African-Americans in Galveston needed hospital care, the old City Hospital along with St. Mary's Sisters of Charity Hospital served this purpose. John Sealy Hospital, which opened January

10, 1890, was maintained as the city hospital until the establishment of the University of Texas Medical Department (School), when the city, which owned the hospital and its grounds, transferred it to the State as an adjunct to the Department. During this transition period, the original City Hospital became the Negro Hospital and the Nurses' Home. The nurses who lived there were not African-American, but some of the white nurses who worked at the Galveston Medical College and the Texas Medical College, both of which were originally housed in the old City Hospital.

After January 1890, the first floor of this building became the 'Negro Hospital,' and the nurses occupied the second. Before this historic event, for the most part, African Americans received medical care in their homes. Upon the arrival of African American physicians, care was also delivered to the patients in the physicians' office.

The storm of 1900 made the Negro Hospital less inhabitable than it had been previously, and a philanthropist from New York donated money for the construction of a new hospital for the African American community. He stated the money should be used for erecting a new building and not repairing the old one. African Americans were without a hospital for many months during the construction of the new facility.

John Sealy Hospital was constructed in front of the City Hospital and when funds were given to build the new Negro Hospital, it would be built on the space occupied by the old hospital. The old hospital was a large wood frame, mid-Victorian, gingerbread building. It was moved to the eastern half of the rear yard of the new John Sealy Hospital. It was felt that this building was too valuable to be demolished and it was decided to thoroughly repair it and make it serve as the nurses' home.

The gift to the city for construction of the new hospital was in the amount of $15,000. It was believed by some that $15,000 was not enough to build a suitable facility, so $3000 was added."

He also includes the Galveston Daily News' statement that it would "be one of the best buildings of its kind in the south ... nowhere in Texas will the sick black man, woman, or child be offered such comfort ... will have all the conveniences ... of the white departments."

Williams continues, "This was the first hospital built for African Americans in the state of Texas, and it would serve the African American community until a new hospital is built in 1937.

The $18,000 spent for the new 'Negro Hospital' did not cover the cost for any equipment, therefore the Board of Managers of John Sealy Hospital solicited monies from the African American community to help furnish the new hospital. The campaign went forward and was a success.

J.R. Gibson (longtime principal of Central High School), is quoted as saying, 'The liberality, readiness, and cheerfulness with which the people and societies responded to our appeal is creditable alike to them and to the colored people of Galveston. We asked for $450, but are glad to enclose a check to your order for $574.85.' When presenting the check, Mr. Gibson also presented a petition to the board ... 'signed by many of the best colored citizens, requesting you to establish in connection with the new hospital, a training school for colored nurses.'

Additionally, controversy was put forth when the city was asked to adopt a new ordinance that would permit hospitals to be placed in residential areas. The original ordinance, which was called the hospital ordinance, restricted the building of hospitals and sanitariums to the east side of Ninth Street. The drive to repeal this ordinance resulted in a very intense debate back in 1907. An African American physician who was very vocal, and was one of the strongest advocates for the repeal of the ordinance was Dr. J.T. Moore.

Dr. Moore's arguments for repeal of the ordinance were quite strong, and his motives were not necessarily only altruistic. Dr. Moore, along with his wife, Dr. Mary Susan Moore, had petitioned the city a few months after the opening of the new hospital for African Americans, to allow them to open a private sanitarium at 4015 Avenue N. The request was denied and the reasons given to the Moores included things such as the area was unsanitary, lacked sewer connections and the fact that a city ordinance prohibited it. Eventually in 1903, the Moores defied the city and opened the Hubbard Sanitarium. This was a 40-bed unit that went into operation without a license.

The city ignored the fact the sanitarium was in existence. The only time it investigated the operations of the facility was when complaints were lodged by neighbors of the facility. But in 1907 the city did repeal the ordinance prohibiting hospitals west of Ninth Street. Even so, the city refused to grant an operating license to the Moores because, at least according to records, the Moores had not obtained sewer connections for the facility. The Moores continued to operate the hospital until about 1925.

Also, during this time, St. Mary's Infirmary accepted African American patients. St. Mary's had a ward designated for Black patients and those Blacks who could afford to pay would go to St. Mary's for their care. Many Blacks believed they would receive better care if they went to St. Mary's because the care was essentially given in the same facility, using the same equipment and supplies used for the white patients.

Medicine & Health Care

The Moore's Sanitarium, the Negro Hospital and the St. Mary's Infirmary were all in operation at the same time, but after World War I, the city was growing so rapidly that the number of patients admitted to the Negro Hospital were often in excess of capacity. This was especially true of the pediatric patients. In fact, it was not uncommon for pediatric patients who were African American to be placed in the John Sealy Hospital because of overcrowding in the Negro Hospital. This disturbed Dr. William Boyd Reading, who at that time was chairman of the pediatric department at John Sealy Hospital. He...'complained about mixing the two races on the wards and the lack of hospital beds for African American patients.' African American children had only six beds in his department. The problem continued until 1936 when a $112,000 grant was received from the Public Works Administration for the construction of a new three story Negro Hospital. This money was eventually matched with grants from the Sealy and Smith Foundation, the University of Texas Board of Regents and the City of Galveston provided $5000. Upon receipt of the money from the Public Works Administration, the Galveston Daily News editorialized:

'Texas has been remiss in the provisions of medical care for negroes, and the hospital for members of that race. Providing 90 to 100 beds and modern surgical facilities will go a long way toward meeting [the] state's obligation.'

This editorial appeared in the January 23, 1936 edition of the Galveston Daily News. The hospital was built at a cost of $285,000, and on August 31, 1937, two floors of the facility opened. The third floor would open two weeks later. The two floors that opened were the men's medical and surgical wards.

Island of Color

The Negro Hospital remained in operation until the new John Sealy Hospital opened in December 1953, at which time segregated Negro wards became the avenue for treating the African American population.

It should be noted that Dr. Barnett was permitted to perform all duties associated with his residency in general surgery, and he was allowed access to all the various wards in John Sealy Hospital. The students that followed Dr. Barnett were afforded this same type of treatment.

The new John Sealy became fully integrated in the 1960s with the elimination of the Negro ward. This was accomplished without fanfare and without incident.

The latest edition of John Sealy is the current tower, which was built in 1978. Currently there are eight hospitals on the UTMB campus. This complex of hospitals can provide any type of care a patient might require. Additionally, this comprehensive system of hospitals makes Galveston an attractive location for persons who may be considering vacation homes and/or retirement.

Up until 1970, African American physicians did not have privileges at John Sealy Hospital. If a patient of an African American physician had to be hospitalized or needed surgery, that person was referred and the surgery performed by a white physician or the person would be cared for by a white physician while hospitalized. The first African American to have privileges at John Sealy was Lafayette Williams, M.D. Dr. Williams was also the first African American faculty member of the Medical School."

Access To Health Care

I am not sure of all of the facts as written, especially the timeline. But most of Williams' dates came from the newspapers. I can also add my experiences as a young person with the hospitals; I had my first surgery at John Sealy, and my father was treated there before he passed away.

My tonsils were removed when I was 6 years old, in the summer of 1936. I remember how I craved ice cream, which I received to soothe the painful burning and dryness in my throat. There was no air conditioning in my ward; the air was circulated with large fans. And I know that I was on the ground floor, because my mother slept on the ground outside of my window all night after my surgery, because she was not allowed to stay in the hospital with me.

So I know that there was no new place for African American children that year, because I remember my surroundings. They were not bad, but they were not good, either, and I was really put off by the hospital smell and bland atmosphere. I was very anxious to get back to my cozy, comfortable and loving home. I don't recall being a patient again until the birth of my first child, in St. Mary's Hospital, on Sept. 28, 1954.

After my father fell in an accident on his job in August 1950, he survived on sheer will power until my mother and I arrived by train from Chicago, where we were when the accident happened. He passed one hour later, after letting Mother know that he knew who we were. And he was in a ward in the *old* segregated area of John Sealy Hospital; the new hospital was built and occupied at least three years later.

According to Williams, the African American population after the Civil War in Galveston was about 13,818 persons. It is not clear how they received their medical care, but home remedies and informally trained persons were probably the main sources of help until African American physicians came along.

"Documents indicate that the first African American physician, who had received a medical degree from a medical school, to practice in Galveston, was Dr. John H. Wilkins. Wilkins was born a slave in 1833 in Georgia ... records do indicate that he graduated from Meharry Medical College in 1880. One can surmise that because of the role that Galveston played, at the time, in the economic life of not only the South, but the nation generally, was probably the reason he decided to practice medicine in Galveston. Dr. Wilkins also had a brother who came to Galveston, Lewis M. Wilkins, who was also a physician and graduated from Meharry.

Being denied membership in the Galveston County Medical Association, in August 1886, the brothers called a meeting to form an African American state medical society. At their initial meeting, twelve African American physicians and a Galveston druggist, a Dr. Cameron, formed the Lone Star State Medical, Dental, and Pharmaceutical Association. This meeting was held at the Wilkins' office at 2128 Post Office Street and Dr. John Wilkins was elected as the Association's first president.

After 1900, presumably the result of the effort to control the many diseases and problems caused by the unsanitary conditions in Galveston after the huge 1900 Storm, several African American physicians came to practice in Galveston. These included the Stantons.

Mack J. Mosely Sr. and later -- Mack Joe Mosely Jr. (who was my doctor until he passed) were very capable additions, kin to the Stantons. Also, the Wilkins brothers, T. Adolph Jones, E.D. Chase, and the Moores -- James T. Moore, and Mary Susan Moore. Most of these physicians had offices located on Post Office or Market Streets between 25th and 28th streets, except for the Moores, who opened a hospital farther West.

These doctors did not have hospital privileges, not even in the Negro Hospital. This meant that they could not admit patients, nor care for them there. The patient went to their offices or they went to the patient's home to provide care.

Being shut out from the cycle of privilege, the doctors of this segregated group petitioned the Galveston County Medical Society for membership, stating very clearly that they had no desire to socialize with this group, but only wanted the ability to improve their professional status by attending the professional growth meetings. They were given a reply which stated that they could not be members, because of the Society's constitution, but that the African American men were invited to 'our scientific meetings.' The Galveston County Medical Society remained segregated until 1955.

With the opening of the new John Sealy Hospital in 1953, the Negro Hospital was essentially closed. It became the Randall Pavilion and was used for other patient care needs...It was also during this time that Herman A. Barnett, M.D. graduated from the University of Texas Medical School - Galveston and began a general surgery residency. In addition to being the first African American to be admitted to and graduate from UTMB's School of Medicine, Dr. Barnett became the first African American to serve a residency at UTMB and the first African American to perform surgery on patients, regardless of color, at John Sealy Hospital.

It appears the last community physician to practice in Galveston retired in the late 1960s. Because of the way the healthcare industry has changed, we will probably never see the classic community physician again. Those persons who want to serve their communities will do so through some type of group practice or in association with a University hospital.

UTMB Hospitals serve as the primary health care facility in the county. The institution graduates more minority medical students than any other majority college in the nation. The African American faculty members are very much a part of the community and provide health care to many in the community."

The above paragraph is true, despite its promotional tone. But the very use of the words "minority" and "majority" is already outdated, as the next major census of our nation will soon show if it is at all dependable and accurate. It should show Hispanic community members in the majority, and the African American members a very close second. The Anglo population, dwindling all over the South by comparison, will be more transient; some will move farther north in Galveston County, and others, recognizing what others have, will claim the inner city.

People are soon going to realize that we are all very interdependent, and work harder to respond to the now-famous Rodney King question: "Why can't we all just get along?"

Medicine & Health Care

Hospital Aid

Hospital Aid Society

Just as women's organizations had significant impact on Galveston's health in the years after the Civil War, they also took on much of the responsibility of making improvements in the post-storm and post-war years.

Mrs. V.C. Fedford

Mrs. V.C. Fedford

Though she served the community in many organizations, none was dearer to her heart than the local Hospital Aid Society, which her mother had helped found and affiliate with the National Federation of Colored Women's Clubs. (The Federation later became the National Association because of a conflict with the Federation of Women's Clubs, an all-white national women's club.)

Mrs. Fedford spent long hours shopping for and delivering supplies to the African American children treated in the segregated wards of John

Medicine & Health Care

Sealy Hospital, who often did not have daily necessities; those confined for long periods also lacked toys and activities. Many times she used her own funds, and it was common in all kinds of weather for her to walk from the downtown stores to the hospital on the eastern end of the island.

The following material is quoted verbatim from printed copy for a program by the Hospital Aid Society, presented in honor of my mother, Mrs. V.C. Fedford, at our church after she had suffered a crippling stroke in 1963.

From Victory To Victory, The National Association of Colored Women's Clubs Inc.

"Motto: 'Lifting as We Climb'

Song: Join The Federation

Colors: Purple and White

1905   The Women's Hospital Aid Society joined the National Association of Colored Women's Clubs, Inc.

In the year 1905, a special planning session was held at Prairie View College.

1915   The purpose: A National effort to federate the great state of Texas for membership into the national group, as like efforts were programmed to federate many other states not yet federated as members of the national organization

1925   During this period of twenty years, much was accomplished through the Prairie View College Committee. At this time, three young students and roommates, became interested in these sessions and was given permission to sit in on the programs. Back home: Galveston, Fort Worth and San Antonio, three young students claimed memberships in well-organized charity clubs and described their club activities. The three became obsessed with the idea and on returning home continued to work with the Prairie View College Committee, which resulted in a triangular basis for the development and expansion of Texas as a Federated Sate.

1935 The Viola Scull and Rev. Scull's home became "The Hostess House" for all National officers and famous representatives on business in Texas for the National Federation.

1942-1946 Elected State President -- Amarillo, Texas. Program platform was directed toward greater and more intense interest in federating clubs throughout Texas. Her campaign was a great and varied success. At the end of her duties as State President, she was appointed by the National office to represent Texas as one of the organizers of the New Regional Association in the formative period.

1945 As Texas Representative, she served as a resource person and member at large. Each Region had a supervisor. Texas was a part of the Southwest Region. Texas delegation to the Arizona Session elected a Texas State President to the office of President of the Southwest Region.

1955 The year of the Golden Anniversary or the year of Jubilee. The Women's Hospital Aid Society opened this period with a Thanksgiving Sermon at Reedy Chapel A.M.E. Church. Honoree, Mrs. V. C. Fedford, who was celebrating more than fifty years as Secretary and President of the Society, hostessed a 'This is Your Life' Reception. Madam President, no charity has ever been so small that you did not take note of and directed some relief to it.' In the course of more than seventy years, Mrs. V.C. Fedford has won countless honors for civic and humanitarian activities. So very many, only the most outstanding ones are recorded herein. The Medical Branch, Sealy Hospital Galveston award, Mrs. V.C. Fedford, a medal representing 10,000 hours of volunteer service, the first Black woman to be so honored --

Medicine & Health Care

1969-70 State Assembly, Church Women United in session at Trinity Episcopal Church, Galveston in their "As Hand Touches Hand" celebration honored Mrs. Fedford for her outreaching missionary activities as President of Reedy's Missionary Society.

1965 A program "This Is Your Mission" paid tribute to Mrs. Fedford for developing and inspiring 'Christian Home and Family Life'.

1967 A beautiful plaque for meritorious service was awarded Mrs. V.C. Fedford in recognition of her varied activities for the Southwest Region. President Myrtle Ollison of the National, awarded Mrs. Fedford one of the special certificates as a member of the National. Two copies were placed in the Senior Citizen's Department at the Rosenberg Library by the Youth Group in honor of Mrs. Fedford. Title: 'A Vibrant Autobiography' by the founder of the National Association is a moving drama of a great race. Passing Parade by T. Mac L — Note Friends of Mrs. V.C. Fedford gather round her today to help her blow out the 77 candles.. The accompanying picture shows her crocheting slippers for the Children's Hospital patients. She explained that a long time before integration was discussed, Women's Hospital Aid Society shared their needed gifts with any sick child and also assisted some adult patients regardless of race, creed or faith.

Obsequies for Mrs. V.C. Fedford, President Emeritus — May, 1974. In memory of 'A life that's been lived with others in mind; touches many hearts and goes on Forever'. It is hard to believe that the Hospital Aid Society exists without you. Yet, as we look among us, we see reflections of your grace in our activities for 'Lifting A We Climb'.

Thank you for being our Mrs. Fedford, with services unlimited."

CHAPTER TEN
THE 1900 STORM

Extinction of Families, Professionals, Property

African American boys on pipe watching the fill of the grade raising after the 1900 Storm. *Courtesy of the Rosenberg Library, Galveston, Texas*

Although the 1900 Storm has always been of interest and concern to native Galvestonians, a recent resurgence of interest across the country surprised even us natives.

We do want to celebrate our existence – we are still here after more than 100 years. Galveston executed its own huge, yearlong celebration of our recovery. (I regretted having to leave the planning committee and shift time from other groups when this book became my main goal.)

The 1900 Storm

With the centennial anniversary, the whole nation received a glimpse of what the 1900 Storm was like for those living here at that time. Yet no one has delved into how African Americans as a whole were affected.

My great-aunt, Aunt Annie, spoke on tape about her experiences as a grown woman in the storm. Joseph Banks shared what his grandfather had related to him. I also have a vivid memory of what my mother, who was 12 when the storm hit, told me.

Homes after grade raising following the 1900 storm.
Courtesy of the Rosenberg Library, Galveston, Texas

And, thank God, I have my grandfather's written account of some of the damage, loss of life, etc.

I believe that those who experienced the storm and didn't talk to us about it were too horrified to want to even think about it all again. However, the truth must be told.

Papa wrote about how the 1900 Storm changed everything:

"In 1890, W.D. Donnell returned from the Kansas schools and taught in the High School, then located at Avenue N - 15th Street. At the death of Mr. Webb, about 1896, Donnell became principal of West District School where he served until September 8, 1900, when he was drowned in the great storm. ...

"In the 1900 Storm, East District School was destroyed, and [educators] Misses Ada Rowe, Florence Holmes, E.W. McDade, Hattie Rowe, Mr. W.D. Donnell and wife, Mrs. Evelyn Whittesy Donnell were drowned.

There being no East D[istrict] School, and Donnell of the W[est] District drowned, Cummings was sent to W. District, and there remained till ... he resigned and went to New York, where he lived with his wife and son, until 1934, when he died.

The Storm of 1900 drowned W.D. Donnell and damaged Central School, so both Gibson of the high school and Cummings of the East District doubled up at West District the Fall of 1900.

In the Fall of 1901, a house at Avenue M ½ and 13th St. was rented for [Central], and East District school and three teachers and four grades placed there. Misses Sims, Huff, and R.A. Scull remained there one year till the East District school of four rooms was built, when H.T. Davis was principal with Misses Harris, Huff, and R.A. Scull as teachers."

Farther along, in his section on churches, Papa writes: "From the Broadway church [Reedy Chapel], there went out persons that formed the St. Paul M.E. Church, of which Rev. Osborne was the first pastor. They built on Avenue H, near 8th street, where they remained until the 1900 Storm destroyed the building, when under Rev. Frank Gary the[y] built on Broadway and 15th Street."

The 1900 Storm

He described the building of the Little Susie Railroad, and stated, "... then came the storm of 1900 that destroyed much of the road, as well as the amusement places -- the road was finally abandoned."

These are the facts of how it affected the African American community.

At the time of the storm, my mother's family lived right down on the beach, just a few hundred feet from the water's edge. The address was 816 Ave. K, and that was the front street in that section of the East End until the grade-raising after the storm; the city widens as you go westward.

(A census in the Clayton Library in Houston gives the address in those days as 816 Ave. M, but there never has been an 800 block on Avenue M; that street begins further west. The census also lists the Banks family and others as residents on that street whom I know did not live on Avenue M in those days. Checking with Joe Banks, whose memory was like a steel trap, he confirmed that even though he lived on that street, that his family did not then. The library itself offers a disclaimer, stating that many of the census takers were rather irresponsible, sometimes inebriated, and didn't record accurately.)

Most of the area around my mother's neighborhood was destroyed in the storm. My mother's family members all survived. My grandfather had either heard from a friend that something big was brewing, or had a message from God directly to get out. Whatever the case, Mother said that Papa came to her and called out, "Let's go, Viola. Right now!" They quickly evacuated to the courthouse, without time to gather up anything.

She told me, emphatically, that as Papa called to her to go, she looked up and saw a huge wave, bigger than she had ever seen, rolling toward them. She said that the sky was not even all that cloudy, making the wave even more alarming.

Beyond that, she remembered being holed up in the courthouse for a good while, and being glad when they could leave. Their house had washed away, and I believe they stayed with family for a while until they could rebuild. It sure was a blessing for her family that her father not only knew how to build, but had friends who had helped build houses for the ex-slaves.

I recall most how she said she longed for toys. She said that at the age of 12, she was in that stage between childhood and adulthood, and very lonesome for a doll to play with. The storm had washed away all of her playthings, and replacing them was the least of the adults' worries, I am sure.

Mother said she saw a doll advertised in a catalog, and thought it was a china doll, with at least a ceramic head. She was allowed to order it, and when it arrived, it was only a piece of cloth with the doll's features and clothing printed on. It had to be cut out and stuffed -- as she put it, an ordinary rag doll. She was so disappointed that she seldom played with it, and kept it more or less on a shelf for many years. Although my oldest child once entered it in a school contest in which several dolls were found to be older, it has always seemed a special antique to me, much more than a collector's item.

Mother never shared any other memories of the storm. She was rather protective of my sister and me, and routinely sheltered us from what might sadden or frighten us. We never even went to funerals until we were grown. And we lived in a city that might have another bad storm at any time.

For storm recollections, I start with Joe Banks' remarks.

Joseph Banks

He had been a modest, friendly man all of his life. He always had a ready smile, a helpful manner, and wouldn't complain about any aches or pains. And he remembers almost everything. He and my husband were about the same age, friends as well as neighbors and god-brothers. About the 1900 Storm, he relates:

"My grandfather told me, 'Joe, they will never know how many drowned in that storm.' I asked him why; he told me (this is a logical and interesting story): 'When the storm came ashore, and the storm surge came by, it was so great, it uncovered the local cemeteries.' " A storm surge is the strong wall of water pushed in by the unnatural wave motion, and currents caused by extremely high winds.

This is something I have not seen mentioned, in accounting somewhat for the huge numbers of dead. If the storm caused the caskets, made simply in those times, to split open and give up the recent bodies buried there, who would know the difference between storm victims and bodies buried earlier? No one had time or opportunity to do an autopsy, even if methods had yet been developed for such an autopsy.

Joe continued, recalling his grandfather's account: "The day after the storm was a bright, sunny day, just like summer -- September the 9th. There in the recent debris with the recently drowned, were the recently buried. You could not tell if they were white or black or what, whether they were just drowned or already buried. And this was the age of the horse and buggy; they had all these animals -- chickens, pigs, goats -- in their yards to contend with, along with the human victims.

"They had to bury the humans first, to keep down pestilence. 'Cause it had gotten *hot* the next day. So they put the victims of the storm in canvas bags with weights. They took them 4.5 miles off on barges, to bury them at sea. The offshore undercurrents were so strong, just like aftershocks of an earthquake, they broke them aloose from those bags, and here they came floating back on shore, making a confused count, because they were still counting.

So what they had to do was burn them on the spot, to keep down the typhoid and all of that. They will never know how many people lost their lives. ..."

"And," I suggested, "there must have been people who came to Galveston who were never registered or anything, came on ships. ..."

"He told me that the night before the storm was a beautiful night, a moonlit night. His family, the Smizers [my family], and others were all sitting on the beach at 10th Street, on logs." At that time, Joe's family lived right across from my family on Avenue K.

"My grandmother says that while she was waiting for my grandfather to come and get them, she saw the tides -- water rising -- and she saw Mr. Davis' father [Bernice James' grandfather] go down. He was an old man, and he slipped or something. She saw him drown."

His families' memories of a storm surge echoes Mother's memory of the tidal wave, perhaps caused by an underground eruption, as a volcano erupts. I have only read of natural disasters like this in areas like Japan. This was very similar, right here on the Gulf Coast, and should be recorded as such. As we try to unravel this history, let us pray that it is not repeated, and by understanding this storm prepare ourselves for any similar disasters that could cause devastating effects even today.

Joe says, "Papa [his maternal grandfather] said they went to the East District School first." Aunt Annie had also originally sought shelter there.

There was a man named Taylor, who was a real doctor, from Kilgore or somewhere, but never practiced much. He never had to worry about money. He was bald-headed, a brown-skinned guy. Mrs. Taylor taught music after she retired; she had many scholars. She lived across from Emancipation Park. Her daddy was a postman.

She got separated from her family. They lived in the house next to Micheletti on [Avenue] K. She was 12 then, so Papa took her along with his family.

When they got to East District School, Papa said he had this big two-wheeled wagon they called a dray. It had a big wheel on each side, a flat bed, and a mule got between them, and they had a stake on each side of the mule. When they got to East District, that wooden frame building was doing like this," Joe makes a rocking motion, "and so he said, 'Oh, we can't stay here.' And when they got ready to leave, they had this baby, and a little girl about 2 or 3, and my mother was in my grandfather's arms, and my mother's godfather was this huge, strapping Black man with huge muscles.

While in this wagon, they went along swimming, and saw this White woman hanging, clinging on. By this time, the water had gotten like this," he held his hand up to his waist, "in some places. But in the wagon, you could go up to where Rosenberg school was, and the water receded a little, but it was steadily coming in. During the height of the storm, traveling in the water, this White woman was clinging to something in the water. The godfather reached to rescue this White woman. The woman pulled back, and said, 'Nigger, take your black hands off of me.'

"Proud of his physique, the man let her go, pushed her down. She came back up, waited for a white person to rescue her, clinging to this thing."

Joe told of how people tried to take this man's wagon, and how they saw East District collapse. They then headed to Rosenberg School. A big piece of concrete, cornice work, came off Rosenberg School. A deputy sheriff came up on a horse, and said to them, 'If you don't want to stay here, go on to the courthouse,' and when they got to the courthouse, they let the wagon drift away. He tied the mule to the drainpipe. The mule was there the next day.

Joe was told that Maco Stewart was at the courthouse, among the dignitaries. There was no prejudice, because of the disaster. There were babies crying, the smell of urine and feces. During the night, one of the officials would announce how the water was going down, by so many feet. The next morning, they looked out and saw nothing but destruction. The currents had crashed things together. There was no standing structure. Everybody was on the sidewalk, standing, praising God.

The Black citizens got together and made up a song on the spot. The white folks said, "Go ahead and sing; we don't know how." Joe's face showed his own excitement as he recalled, "This was one of those impromptu songs.

'My mother was lost in that storm;

Somebody got lost in that storm

My sister got lost ... '

"It was never published, no evidence of it. They made it up on the spot. Then they sang,

'Thank God we were saved...'

And were hugging and crying. I want my children to hear this -- my first lesson in faith without any evidence. ...

"My grandfather said, in 1900, they preferred a wooden building that would bend and sway to a brick building that could break up into pieces."

Later in the interview, drawing a parallel to the Bible's description of the Earth's last days and of how hard it would be to have children, Joe said his grandfather recalled how the 1900 Storm survivors saw the body of a pregnant woman whose baby had perished -- it was half in and half out. I remained silent, imagining the horror of those sights.

Other persons interviewed had little to say about the storm. Some had heard little from their elders, and many families now in Galveston moved to the city just after the storm, searching for employment opportunities in the city's rebuilding.

So Aunt Annie's description of the Great 1900 Storm, recorded when she was 95 years old, is a rarity. My cousin, Corinne Scull Williams, was visiting from Chicago in 1972, and trying to verify what she had recalled hearing as a child, had asked her to describe the storm. Though I had not yet begun to think of writing our history, I taped her memories. She passed away two years later, on Feb. 14, 1974.

Mrs. Annie Smizer McCullough

We spoke in the home of her daughter, Aunt Irma, at 1202 Ave. M, where she was now living. Corinne asked, "You remember how I sang in the storm?" When Aunt Annie did not reply, she said, "You know, Aunt Annie, we want you to tell us about the storm."

As Aunt Irma, Aunt Edna (Irma's sister), Cousin Corinne and I waited, Aunt Annie began, addressing her remarks to me:

"Well, Izola, it's so much to tell you about it, till I don't know what to start telling you. Honey -- I'll start on my home first. Where I lived was 8th and K. I used to own that corner there. I had a little flower garden on the side, and I had a cousin, Ed's (her husband's) cousin, that stayed with me -- 12 or 14 years old -- named Henry. We lived near level with the beach. Wasn't no seawall."

She said that when the weather started to change, "They -- people called it fun, going to the beach, watching those big waves come breaking over. Lived next to Nan Lawton's mother. She was hurrying, saying she was going down there, [to] have some fun. The storm was on Saturday. On Friday, [I] had bought me a new pair of shoes. He [Uncle Ed] went to exchange them. When he came back, I made Henry take all the rosebushes and put 'em in a tub." Uncle Ed told her, "Don't say nothin'! Get these children outta here. I don't want to hear nothin'!"

Aunt Annie continued: "He had a dray and a mule. Went by to get Mama -- she had a trunk and some clothes for her children -- well, I don't guess you want to hear all of ..."

We all said, "Yes!" "Yes, we do!"

"And they got on the dray. I wasn't scared; I hadn't got any sense. I was on 8th and K. The school was on 10th and Broadway. I said I'll walk across over to the school.

When I got to the corner of 9th and Broadway, on the south side -- Mama and 'n'em had got there -- the wind was so strong, and those

The 1900 Storm

waves comin', so I stopped. I didn't try to cross. Somebody picked me up, carried me across the street. When we got to the school, a lot of people were comin' in, cryin'.

[There was] a neighbor lived third door from Mrs. Calhoun's house, named Daniel[s], drove for Goggan Bros. Music store, had a great big wagon that delivered pianos. Leon, my brother, and Mr. Daniels said, 'I want to get to Rosenberg School soon as I can.' Leon told Mama, 'Come on!' Mrs. Daniels said, 'Wait! Let me get the children's clothes. I got on these clothes that got wet.' Leon said, 'Damn the clothes! Come on! Get on the dray!'

When we got to the school, water was comin' in so fast, the wagon was floatin' and the mules were swimmin.' Dray was in the water. We got on the dray, the wagon. The men lay flat on their stomach on each one, holding the little children.

When we got to 10th and I, water wasn't quite as deep as on Broadway [Avenue J]. When we [hit] Rosenberg School, water hadn't come on there, but the *wind*! Oooh. Those men that was in the school, all they could do was stand up against those doors, try to hold them closed, keep them from blowin' open.

My husband's people were over there, came in from 8th and H. They was so glad to see him come in. Upstairs, people was hollerin', and cryin', hunting their folk, couldn't find them. Oh, it was an awful thing! You want me to tell you. But no tongue can tell it!

We didn't go upstairs. We sit in the hall going east and west, sit in the hall. It was crowded. No -- first [we sat] in the hall going north and south. They was screamin' and hollerin.' It was so crowded. Men tryin' to hold the doors. My husband says come sit in the hall going east and west.

We got up there. When we left that place where we just come from, we [had] just got from under it [and] the lightning streak come, knocked the flue in. It killed 15 people from where we moved! Just did get away!

It was a white man lived there on 11th and H in a big two-story white house. He had a little boy, was going back for his wife, and he couldn't get back. Boy asked -- there he was hangin' onto us -- would you please peek out there and see if that house was standin'?

By 9:00 [p.m.], that flash of lightnin' come, everything had ceased. You wouldn't believe -- moon came out like nothing had ever happened. Everything was quiet. One or two men came, said, 'If you love your folk, come pick these people up.' Didn't know they were dead, thought they were just knocked out. My husband said, 'Come, let's go to the courthouse.' Moon shining, water running off, wires down. ...

We made it down to the courthouse, stayed for nearly a week. This white man was cryin', told my husband, said, 'If your house is gone, you bring your family, come live with us.' So my husband about a week later went over there. His wife was scraping mud and stuff up. He said, 'Let it alone, turn everything over to him'. My husband went and got his mother and two brothers, put them in the servant's room back there in the yard. You want to know all about it; they all lived back there. My mother's people were worried so -- tried to get in touch with them.

My father worked for the government in Sabine Pass. He was cryin' and nearly crazy. He got on a tugboat that was comin' back, found us. He was so happy. [We] stayed with these white people till we could go to her people in Halletsville, Texas. Went to stay for a while. These white people just turned their place over to us. Mama and all of us went to stay in Halletsville.

"The law would come to your house, go all through it, conscripting men who were hiding." Authorities were drafting men for the city's huge cleanup. "They saw Papa, conscripted Papa. He said, 'I'm a government man. I worked in the Custom House.'

Everything that they had that had a horse, was used to stack bodies. The engine firemen were just like this -- you'd see a tree, bush, shrubbery or something. Somebody always out hunting somebody. They'd kick it over, maybe find two, three dead people. They'd go in their bosoms and find their money." Corinne said her daddy, Uncle Ira, had told her that they'd cut off fingers to get their rings. Uncle Ira would have been about 14 or 15 years old at the time.

Ira Scull & Family

The 1900 Storm

"Put this place under martial law. They'd arrest every man they saw, make him work and clean up. [On] 14th and J, Catholic church, cleaned that out, had dead folk piled up there.

"[On] 15th and M, they had a milk dairy, some of the cows were dead, some alive." Aunt Annie imitated the sound of the trapped cows. "Buried under the timber. If the men couldn't get 'em out, they'd stab 'em in the throat, you know.

"I tell you all -- thank God -- I'm telling you the truth -- no tongue can tell.

On 11th and I, they had a Catholic school, high-raised wooden building. Storm blew that school down, full of people, and they buried them there. Five or six months, people buried there. They moved the timber, couldn't find places to put them. These barges come up to the wharf, carried them out to sea, dumped them over, come back to get another load. People piled up like wood.

On Postoffice, between 22nd and 23rd, north side of the street, [there was an] undertaker. His place was full. Dead people lying so close, you had to pick 'em out, identify your folk. First thing, when you got to the head of the steps, you saw a poor woman laying on the table, dead, pregnant. Got hit in the stomach, and the baby's head out.

I'm telling you the truth. My sight's bad, my hearing, but I got good sense. They asked the man to move the woman back. His -- there's no tongue.

The courthouse -- people just lived there, nowhere to go. Ball School on 21st and H -- it stood the storm. Colored school on 10th and J went down; 15 people got killed there. Mrs. Bland, Mrs. Piner -- lived across the street -- I know all those [people], Izola!! I'd -- you'd get tired of hearing me tell it. You're getting tired."

I encouraged her to keep on if she could. "Remember, I want to get your voice."

Aunt Annie, emotional from remembering all of the tragedy she had suppressed for so long, said, "The Lord knows, I'm telling the truth. They ain't nobody can dispute me, that went through it!"

"I know it!" I said.

CHAPTER ELEVEN
EMPLOYMENT AND BUSINESS: The Recovery Years

A City Raises Itself Up

The 1900 Storm could have devastated even an entire state's economy. But it did not manage to devastate even the city it struck. One would think it would have driven everyone from Galveston, never to return. Instead, because of the spirit of the inhabitants of this island, the way in which they believed in themselves and in each other, they survived.

Not only did they survive, they had such an infectious spirit of hope, sharing that confidence with others, that people of all kinds and persuasions came flocking to the isle to help in its new day.

One interviewee, Joe Banks, relates his grandfather's account of how men sang and rejoiced at being alive the next day after the storm. Although as African Americans they were not respected for their status in life, they had sense enough to know that a divine power had kept them alive when others of prestige and status had lost their lives. Certainly, here was a firm lesson that God is no respecter of human decision on who should go and who should stay on this Earth. That lesson continues to be taught to us every waking day.

There was no rhyme or reason to the destruction and loss of life that anyone can give today, but certainly those who did survive and praised God for mercy unearned had a story to tell that bears much repeating. In spite of lesser-quality housing, and poor access to transportation to get to safe shelter, African Americans did survive that great disaster.

Island of Color

Thank goodness for the testimony that was passed down by word of mouth about the generosity of spirit in these times. The story that needs to be told loudly and clearly is that of how many of these individuals rescued others -- those who allowed themselves to be rescued, both during the storm and in the years that followed. How many African Americans rebuilt housing, not only for themselves but also for others.

Although we may never know accurately how many people of all races helped each other overcome those first crucial days, weeks, and months, we do know that lumber and other building materials, food of all kinds, water and medical supplies were sent in to relieve the suffering. Galvestonians would not have survived had not kind people from across the water come in their boats, and brought all that they could to restore life as it had been, as well as possible.

As noted before, lumber from destroyed buildings was used to rebuild establishments and houses, and institutions started all over again, sometimes in new locations. Papa noted how the schools were rearranged and the administrators of these schools shifted to fill the vacancies caused by loss of life in the storm. But so many written records were lost. Thank goodness for those who not only remembered how they recovered, but were anxious to let others know about it.

The period after the 1900 Storm saw the entire community involved in the city's restoration by grade-raising. I consider our seawall, finished four years later, a marvel of construction just as the Astrodome in Houston once was. Even one of the wonders of the world, right up there next to the Great Wall of China.

This process of raising the whole city up was a tremendous undertaking, and the ensuing problems of filling in the whole city with

Employment and Business: The Recovery Years

dirt, mud, sediment, etc. was a huge health challenge as well. As stated, Galveston was like a lady of that period, lifting her skirts and petticoats high to step over a mud puddle in the street.

Mrs. Gertrude Siverand, born in 1899, told me, "I remember the grade raising. You had to walk across planks." Her family was one of those that moved to Galveston right after the 1900 Storm, when houses were raised and Galvestonians had to walk across planks to get from one place to another, often over water. "We would reach down and grab shrimp," she said.

So life went on after the 1900 storm. Though it was probably very painful getting back what was lost, there was an upsurge of will and good spirits, and the reconstruction of the city began in earnest. For many of our people, prosperity was just beginning. The horrible experience made them ready to do whatever was necessary to make a living for themselves. And the need to serve one's own people, to meet needs that went unserved by white establishments, was inspiring. African Americans built and provided for their own.

Social and Economic Emergence

It seems that the Galveston African Americans of the early part of the 20th century were very happy over their gains in prosperity. They were exuberant over their economic improvement, finding employment and going into business for themselves. Amidst the restraints of segregation, they counted the blessing of not to having to worry about competition from whites as they now do in an integrated economy. In addition to lucrative work on the wharves, in the early 1900s, there were thriving stores, hotels, restaurants, as well as doctors, lawyers, ministers and contractors; my grandfather's account also mentions such questionable fortune as gambling and saloons. The City Times said there were as many as 75 businesses representing 37 different services and professions. Is it any wonder that Galveston African Americans boast of the "good ole days" more than the other races here?

Few can succeed in business now, those of any race. The fat cats are the large corporations, which enjoy seeing us pitted against each other. Unless you learn to live in some outpost of civilization, permanently camping out with all of your resources in the outdoors, you will have to get along with your neighbor. We will not survive unless we put aside animosity and learn to exist amicably together in a new society all too dependent on the vast corporate world.

African American Galvestonians today do represent a range of businesses and employment. And I spoke with several who recall the variety of endeavors in our community's past as well:

Mrs. Gertrude Elizabeth Siverand

Mrs. Siverand, born in 1899, cited her father, William S. Johnson, who joined the force in 1913, as the first policeman of his race here. My grandfather cited his father as a policeman in 1873, but it is highly possible, though there are few good records of African American employees available, that there were no Black policemen in the interim, after segregation laws went into effect. Mr. Johnson began as a detective first, then was elected to be a patrolman, serving 45 years.

Her father mentored several other men of his race, who were well-known here early and late in the century. Policemen he influenced and supported included Buster Landrum; Goins; Leon Lewis; Thomas; Prince

Employment and Business: The Recovery Years

Edwards; Lacey; J.R. Johnson; Jack Lawson, and someone whose real name she could not recall, but knew by the nickname "Stoop and Glue."

Other businesses she named were the Havenette Beauty Salon; Martin's at 31st Street and Avenue M; and W.G. Lewis at 26th Street.

The first undertaker whom she remembered was J.C. Hall. And she mentioned Mr. Hebert. She said, "Mr. Hebert was my friend. He buried my little brother -- who died when he was 9 months old, of pneumonia." She described walking across planks to bury her baby brother out in Lakeview Cemetery.

Looking back, she recalled also that Galvestonians in these times didn't have cars; they used "hacks," which were horses and buggies. And she interrupted herself again to exclaim, "Oh, did I tell you that Jack Johnson was my cousin?" Jack Johnson, a native Galvestonian, was the world heavyweight champion in boxing. His father was her great-uncle -- the brother of William Johnson, her grandfather.

Mrs. Melinda Price

Interviewed Aug. 3, 1998, she said at the time that she was 101 years old. But her relatives say that when she passed in the summer of 1999, her papers showed her to be 112 years old.

She was always lucid and in good spirits, and really humbled me in her fondness for me. She would always ask, "Mrs. Collins, you came to see me?" and reach for a big hug.

Even as respect for elders was a given in our culture, so was respect for teachers and other professionals, and so she called me Mrs. Collins. Such gestures, once automatic, are not anymore. One of the things that make our people so disillusioned with integration is how our children have lost such values.

Two things that she told me about the working people in our culture really impressed me. I had asked how Hitchcock residents got to work in Galveston, before transportation was available for the laboring African American. She mentioned Mr. Smallwood, a large, strong man I knew well. "Yes," she replied, "Mr. Smallwood would get up and walk to work ... he worked on the wharf ... and walk back -- and it didn't make no difference to him. That's what he had to do!" Crossing the causeway and all the land in between on foot. And I thought of how I used to complain, when I was running late, of how long it took to drive to Hitchcock.

The other thing she said that surprised me was that her sister owned a restaurant and hotel near the Santa Fe train station on 25th Street in Galveston. "It was a two-story, where they could sleep ... Mrs. W.D. Lewis' restaurant, by the train station. All the people who came off the train knew they could eat there. This store, right on the corner, was the only Negro store in Galveston at the time."

This unfamiliar account again indicates that much information on our early days as owners has been lost, because it was not written down. Ownership was a changeable thing for our people in those days. The deed might have never even been recorded, as in the cases in which many African Americans lost their property.

Mr. John Clouser

I asked Mr. Clouser, born Jan.10, 1882, to share his experiences, shortly after deciding to write a book about the people who made a difference in our society. He had a lot to say in his own way. He was never afraid to say anything he believed in, whether it was popular or expedient to talk that way or not. Some of what Mr. Clouser said I did not agree with, but I certainly admired his fearless way of expressing himself, about beliefs that even his associates did not share at times. His son, Gerald, is my high school classmate, and Mr. Clouser, who taught with my mother and grandfather at West District, knew my father and all of my family.

He talked of the economic picture for Galveston's growth.

"Many African American people came from Brazoria County to Galveston to get jobs ... Will Christian, Joe Pope, George Brown, Jesse Johnson. These men had much to do in providing leadership for those coming into this county with them. They left the farm to make three dollars a day here. They could make 30 cents a day, which later went down to 20 cents a day on the Mallory Line." He mentioned another steamship line, the Morgan Line, and how Black people broke the union.

Speaking of religious leadership in African Americans' struggle for work, he said that in 1918, the bishop of the Galveston-Houston Diocese said that "the time had not come for Negro men to get white men's jobs." And yet African Americans in the diocese remained loyal to its leadership, Clouser said.

Other African American workers he mentioned:

Cochran was a paper hanger. Rene' Kibbe was a barber. A lot of men could do carpenter and brick work, but left "in the migration of the first World War."

Mrs. Ina Ivory Sibley Garner

She was 103 years young when interviewed in 1993, born April 18, 1891. Her daughter, Wilina Garner Gatson, my soror and neighbor, was the first African American to finish nursing studies at University of Texas Medical Branch.

Mrs. Garner said she came to Galveston not long after 1900, because her aunt had come here on an excursion from Many, La. She married Willie Lee Garner on June 25, 1919, living in Baytown at first. Baytown had its oil field and most of its residents were single men, she said, with only two families -- of our race, I think she meant – living there.

Her husband was the school principal and served as a first sergeant during World War I. They had two children: Wilina, born in 1925, and Melvin, born in 1928.

They had a woodyard here in Galveston, where the Sweatts later built a home. Mrs. Garner had been a seamstress and taught school, but was a homemaker after that.

Businesses and businesspeople she remembered that have not already been described here were the hamburger stand at 42nd and Winnie streets, as well as Dr. Etter, whose office was also between 25th and 26th streets on Market Street; Dr. Sellers, who worked with the Stantons; and the first African American doctor to practice here, Dr. Wilkinson, who was Iris and Honorine Wallace Harris' grandfather.

Mrs. Garner also remembered dentist Dr. Jones, whose daughter June Louise was about my sister's age, if I remember correctly; Daniel Carter, who delivered wood and ice; Mr. Jones, who sold oil, kerosene and vegetables; and owners Mr. Wheeler Taylor and his wife, Ethel, of the funeral home at 36th Street and Avenue H; the Hebert Funeral Home, Fields Funeral Home and Green's Funeral Home, now known as Wynne's.

Employment and Business: The Recovery Years

She also named the Strode funeral home, which became Lundy's -- after the strange disappearance of an airplane bearing Strode and other passengers.

Church musicians named were Mary Lee Canada Sweatt, St. Luke; and Mrs. Beulah Sheppard and Justine Allen Williams, First Union Baptist Church. Musicians who played for special occasions were Melissa Guinn, who lived on 11th Street; Mrs. Wallace, who lived on 35th Street near West District Elementary School; Mrs. Olga Lucas; and Mrs. Hattie Freeman.

Bands she remembered were the Knights of Pythias Band, and Russell Lewis' band, Joel Harris, pianist.

Mrs. Della Rivers Sims

I interviewed Mrs. Sims, born August 8, 1892, at the age of 101. (She was living then with her niece, whom I knew as Mrs. White, widow of Mr. Otis White, who had been an excellent mathematics teacher at Central High School.)

Mrs. Sims, a very sweet, intelligent woman, was extremely alert for her age, and was mixing a cake by hand as we talked. I marveled at how well she could function, her memories reaching back before 1900.

Mrs. Sims was the eighth child of 10 children. She revealed that nine of them made it to maturity, which certainly was not always the case in those days. (Mortality rates were very high. My own grandfather had written about the fact that his mother and father had twelve children, with only six surviving when he was young.) Her parents were George and Molly Rivers, both born as slaves; her father was born in Livingston, Texas, and her mother was born in Canton, Miss.

Many older people had told me about Mrs. Sims' Ice Cream Parlor. She and her husband, Will Sims, opened it with the Wyatts, with whom they lived; the parlor was in an addition on the Wyatts' house at 2827 Ave. K. They bought their ice cream from Model Dairy, Star Dairy and Purity Ice Cream factory, and also sold bread. Later, they heard of a house for sale at 3001 Ave. M, and relocated there.

They ran the business from 5:00 a.m. to 5:00 p.m. at first. Sometimes her husband was there even until midnight. She also worked elsewhere. After they had purchased a small house in the same area, the 3000 block of Avenue M, there was a lot of work to do on it as well.

Shortly after they bought their home, they also expanded their products in the store, adding a Coca-Cola vending machine. The company at first restricted them from selling any other soda water products, but they were able to add Dr Pepper later.

Mrs. Sims said that she and her husband had no children of their own, but they raised a little boy. When he was in kindergarten at Mrs. Ruth Hall's place in Bethel Hall, Mrs. Hall would line up the children, and let them march down to the parlor for ice cream after school

Mrs. Sims continued to run the store after Mr. Sims died. On nights when West Point had church services, members came over to the store to sit down and have ice cream sodas, etc. Although at one time she would keep the store open until 10:00 p.m., West Point's Rev. Sargent suggested she close earlier after a nearby grocery store owner was robbed and killed. She did usually close earlier after that, but sometimes her neighbor across the street, Pinkie Earles, would sit with her at night so she could serve the after-church customers.

Employment and Business: The Recovery Years

Though at one time she bought ice from Mr. Galloway, she later sold ice also, as well as kerosene and coal oil.

Other businesses that Mrs. Sims recalled, those not yet mentioned, were:

Fellman's store, with measured dry goods; Vanderpool, on 32nd Street; Mr. Collins' wood sales downstairs at his home on Tremont Street – he also drove a dray; and the store run by Mrs. Prince (Ray Don Dillon's mother), still in business at 29th Street and Avenue M.

CHAPTER TWELVE
EMPLOYMENT AND BUSINESS:
Prosperity

By 1910, not only had Galveston rebuilt after the 1900 storm, but African Americans had a lifestyle of their own, and they foresaw a bright future. Only by then, the nation was on a collision course politically, and Europe's problems soon intruded into their lives.

Gone to War

My husband's father, Roy L. Collins Sr., was in the Army during World War I, and met up with a man named James Ward, who later married my Aunt Irma. Uncle Jimmy and Mr. Collins were both medics in the war, and saw action over in Europe. Uncle Jimmy also said he used to blow the bugle. They were great friends, living in later years just a couple of blocks from each other.

Because my Uncle Ralph had attended college, when he was drafted into the Army in World War I he was made a first lieutenant. I have a picture of him standing with his uniform on. The hat resembled that that the Boy Scouts later wore, his pants were made like riding breeches -- they came just to the calves of his legs -- and he had high-laced boots on. When I was growing up, I was fascinated by the picture in Mother's album. She was very proud of her brother in his uniform, and told me that very few of our men made officer's rank for that war.

He was a colonel in the United States Army Reserves when he passed in 1959, and one of the nation's foremost dermatologists.

Employment and Business: Prosperity

(Ebony magazine later published an article on a man identified as the only African American officer during World War I. I sent information to correct that to three different Ebony offices in Chicago, with return receipt to confirm its arrival in the mail, but my letter was never answered.)

Flourishing After

As noted, an amazing number of businesses were owned and operated by African Americans in the early 20th century in the city of Galveston. The business climate only strengthened after World War I.

And when the whole country bounced back into prosperity, people changed habits, becoming more careless, more wasteful -- expecting too much, spending too much. I suppose it was only natural to be foolish after living under restrictions during the war. A free lifestyle flourished.

Galveston took on its Sin City reputation. Although things were not as extreme in Galveston as in other parts of the country, riotous living flourished. Prostitution was out of hand, and gambling in certain places had national notoriety. Most of this came with being a seaport town, and having so much money flowing in here from other countries. Just as Galveston had an undeniable tolerance for other lifestyles and other cultures, it was an open-arms port of entry for these activities as well.

One thing was true for our people of color: They learned to do many things for the white people who wanted service, and learned trades and skills by taking training and advice from those they served. And they learned much of the intrigue conducted by their employers, who thought it was safe to let them observe, since they had better not tell what they saw.

The 1920s were really wild in Galveston, and African Americans made money from these businesses and pursuits right along with whites.

Island of Color

In Harlem, Chicago, and other places that were not officially segregated, the creative spirit was also expressed without interruption among African Americans. Just as visual artists were depicting a life of parties, drinking bathtub gin, and dressing "to the nines," musicians were playing a new kind of jazz. The center of jazz left New Orleans and shifted to Chicago, with its original blues, ragtime, all the popular music of that period. In Galveston, musicians were coming to share and jam, coming into our port and then moving on to the Northeast. This is how musicians here started keeping up with the latest in jazz tastes.

Top actors and dancers, many whose names were unrecorded, performed in Galveston too. And Galveston was not without its own celebrities even then.

Employment and Business: Prosperity

Native Son

Jack Johnson

Island of Color

Jack Johnson, born and reared in Galveston, was world heavyweight boxing champion from 1908 to 1915. But he was known for his fighting in African American circles long before then, and remembered long after.

Mrs. Siverand, his cousin, was not the only Galvestonian to mention him. When I interviewed Mrs. Irma McCullough Ward, my own cousin whom I called Aunt Irma, she spoke of Jack Johnson also:

"In 1924, I was voted Queen of the Pythian Women." Showing me a photograph, she smilingly informed me, "That's the outfit I wore. They gave me a trip," paid for by the state organization of the Knights of Pythias, "and the prize was money -- I forget how much money -- to get my dress and all. I went to the Grand [Convention] -- big thing, all the states met in Chicago. They gave me money for that."

Aunt Irma's father was Ed McCullough, and he had been a friend of Jack Johnson's. "When Jack Johnson heard about it, he hadn't met Ira," my mother's brother, who then lived in Chicago, "but he found out that I was Ed's daughter. He came to see me and said he was so glad to see one of Ed's daughters; he talked about old times."

Joseph Banks, longtime family friend, also recalled his grandfather's comments:

"Now here's another impression. My grandfather used to often speak of the first black heavyweight champion of the world, Jack Johnson. His father was an invalid. His mother was a tall, raw-boned lady. The two of them were janitors of East District School. It was supposed to be his father's job, but his mother did all the work. All his father used to do was to brag, 'My son can lick anybody.' He had other children.

While my grandfather and the other boys were growing up -- this is before 1900, in the 1880s -- I know they used to congregate on the northwest corner of 11th and K -- across from what is now the First Union Baptist Church. And while they were congregated on the corner, Jack Johnson would challenge the boys of all sizes -- like he was 12 or 14, he'd challenge a boy 16 years old. And he took to carrying boxing gloves around with him. And he would come on the corner, and the boy who looked like he was the most stalwart boy of the bunch, he would throw these boxing gloves to him and say 'see what you can do.' And if the boy would say, 'I don't want to fight,' he would taunt him. He'd throw these gloves upside his head, and try to aggravate him into fighting -- he was just that bold. At the age of 14 or 15, he thought he could beat anybody.

He'd go all over town and challenge anybody in different sections. When he first became known and talked about by the local people, was when he whipped a Black man who knew how to fight real well, that they called 'The Deaf Bully.' Although he wasn't a bully, he was deaf man who knew how to fight. And he [Jack Johnson] whipped him. The word spread all over Galveston like wildfire.

And, in later years, when he became famous, he'd come to see my grandfather. When he fought in Cuba, my grandfather and some prominent fighters and a number of others had a silk American flag made. It was all silk. They mailed it to him. But, by this time, Jack had become so famous, although he had come to see them, he didn't acknowledge that he received the flag."

I am willing to bet that Jack Johnson never even saw the flag, that it was taken by someone else; often famous people don't get gifts that are temptingly expensive.

Whether or not Johnson forgot to acknowledge them, he was long remembered in his community. Although my Uncle Ira was closer to

Johnson's age, it was my Uncle Ralph, who had played with the boys who played with Jack, that I recall mentioning Johnson. They all grew up in the East End of Galveston.

Enterprises Remembered

Children in the East End were often around Aunt Rendy's store, a regular hangout as my Aunt Irma recalled it. Joe Banks remembered it too: "One of your relatives, a Smizer man who lived with his aunt, had a store on 16th and L."

I also heard my mother talk about Aunt Rendy's store long ago, but didn't know that she was kin to my family until Aunt Irma spoke of her. I wish in hindsight I had listened more closely as a child to so much information about our history, of African Americans in Galveston.

Joe continued: "When I went in, when I was old enough to roam around, she had the glass-covered cases, with cakes and pies, with counters.

Before you had cash registers, a man named Moore had a store. He had a drawer that you pulled out, with scoops in it. One had dimes, nickels, and pennies in it.

Aunt Rendy's store was as nice. I remember a big, handsome man with rosy cheeks."

I think he was talking about my Aunt Annie's brother, Uncle Leon; our family often spoke proudly of him, as the uncle "who sure could sing."

In another interview, I spoke with Mrs. Evelyn Sanders Jones, who was born Feb. 29, 1912, in Galveston. She mentioned her brother, Arthur Sanders, who lived on Ave. P, and I remember attending his school for typing and shorthand when I was quite young. I wish I had been old

Employment and Business: Prosperity

enough to appreciate what he tried to teach me, because I never did learn shorthand or to use the keyboard correctly -- again to my regret when writing this book.

Asked about other businesses or places of employment for Galveston African Americans, Mrs. Jones recalled working at the Galvez Hotel, helping her mother. Her husband sold vegetables, and her brother-in-law, Robert Jones, sold coal oil and had a wood yard.

She remembered Mitchell Thibodeaux's restaurant and described the Milk Dairy on 27th Street. She also spoke of sisters Ruth and Florence Phelps who played piano for churches (and were also my very active sorority sisters), and Beulah Sheppard, who sang for church celebrations.

And like many others interviewed, she mentioned the African American door-to-door insurance salespeople, who came to collect the premiums monthly or weekly – such as Mr. McCoy, who worked for Atlanta Life, and Fred Atkinson, who worked for Universal Life – from those who hoped to ease future troubles.

Tight Times

Galveston with the rest of the nation saw prosperity wane as the 1920s ended. Our city did not escape the grip of the Depression. But though money was tight in the years to come, truthfully our city was knit even tighter.

John Leltz, an Anglo American, called to share his memories. He had read in the newspaper about the book I was writing, and he wanted to tell me about his memories of my father from when Leltz was a child in our neighborhood. Our neighbors were Hispanic and mostly Anglo when I was growing up, and the Leltz family ran a florist shop close by.

Brister Marshall Fedford

He called our era of youth "the good ole days, and bad ole days":

"Your father was a carpenter. ... I was an acquaintance, and a friend of your family, the Fedfords. Our families were really friends -- and customers. My family had a little busines, Leltz Dutch Gardens, on 11th and Broadway. My mother had opened a florist on Sept. 16, 1932, ... in a nursery right after the Depression.

Employment and Business: Prosperity

My father had hurt his leg; [we] had family reverses about that time, too. That was in the days when there were no safety nets -- was truly a "do-it-yourself." Received help from churches and neighbors. You know, we didn't have a lock on the front door, kept the door open for breezes.

"We didn't really have much distinction along racial lines -- the Tresvilles, Pauline and George, had been living at 1109 Broadway, my family -- in 1918 or 1919. [We] were a thoroughly integrated neighborhood. Everybody depended on each other. We all played together. It was a better world when we had fewer of these so-called social programs. [They] alienated and isolated people from each other, diminished the value of the family, personal relations. Not just in Galveston -- a series of factions -- microcosm of the whole world is Galveston. ...

"Fedford was more or less the carpenter for the East End. I can remember seeing him with his strap over his shoulder. He had his saws neatly arranged inside of it, his plane -- knew how to sharpen so meticulously. I remember seeing him walking around town, going to other jobs. He always had a long, dignified step, seemed to be off in a dignity that was rare in many individuals -- composed, a serenity that was an admirable trait.

Many days he would work with a lot of used lumber. Banks were all failing ... He utilized [what we had] when my parents had no more money for repairs of their little flower shop. The idea of assuming debt – long- term money -- would have terrified anybody. [One] could not obligate money in the future. [It was] a wonderful world in that respect -- we had to do things to help each other. I can still visualize -- we had some old creosoted timbers, made a greenhouse extension foundation on the east side of my parents' [place].

He was a powerful man. Timbers, 3 by 12 and 25 feet long, he would pick 'em up and sight down 'em, turn 'em this way and that way, figure out the best way to use them. Most I ever heard out of him was a little low whistle, to himself. He calmly went about his work, very quiet man - very absorbed in his work. Put a dignity in his work you don't find now.

A lot of times we would trade flowers and sprays. The Fedfords were prominent people in their social circles. They would trade carpenter work for flowers.

I remember on the first of the month, when the bills went out, my parents had bought a bicycle for me. I would ride to E.S. Levy, on 21st and Broadway, with flowers on my bicycle; many times to the corner of 12th and L with flowers. I'd collect every time after school.

Every time I could come up to the Fedfords, I knew the Fedfords would always pay off promptly. I could come back home that night, we could buy food tonight! In a lot of turbulent times, your mother had a calming effect on me. I would feel warm and welcome in her presence. She always had a positive outlook, was a cheery person.

Back in the '30s -- impressions that people make on you as a child stick with you -- one of the greatest activities I had as a child was hearing 'Fedford's coming.' The steps would be replaced, screens would be taken care of, the flower shop would be extended.

We had used sash and all that; he knew how to turn and twist it, assemble it all. It was so fascinating to me how he did things, and the logic behind it. I'd watch him for hours. The most we had -- I'd bring him some

Employment and Business: Prosperity

ice water. He'd work meticulously, put his tools in his toolbox, and march home in a very punctual way. ...

It was good exposure, because when he was working around the flower shop, people who came as our customers used him. Hohn Gottlob, Reba Gottlob, their son Donald Gottlob was teaching, coaching, then went into administration. He was the first big [business] manager for the school board. Their other son, Junior, is a veterinarian in Dickinson.

It was a close-knit community, and one that I miss, the Galveston of old. I don't feel that way now. My wife said, "I feel like a foreigner in my own hometown." The children rarely come home to visit their parents ... It's like the story -- we are a nation of strangers.

When I saw this article in the paper, story about your family, it really ... fired up some old memories, because I could think back at the happier days. I'm getting old, too. If we don't learn, respect the past, how can we deal with the future?"

CHAPTER THIRTEEN
LIFE IN THE DEPRESSION

Though life for this nation whirled around the hub of the catastrophe that was the great Depression of 1929, the biggest moment in my life came within days of the Crash: my birth!

The world was in financial turmoil, and I felt none of it.

I was born Oct. 26, 1929, to two loving, caring parents; to a sister ready to play with me, convinced that I was the answer to her last Christmas request; and to a grandfather who lived in our home and was a very supportive role model. I probably was spoiled, although I don't really think it was a bad thing for a little girl of my hue in the days of segregation. I did not even know I was supposed to be depressed until the media and other sources tried to drive those points home.

We lived in an ordinary frame house, on an ordinary street. We had one of the few telephones in the area, two Ford cars in our two garages, and a playhouse in our yard. The playhouse could have served as a home for a single person, because it was tall enough for an adult to stand up in, with windows, doors and all the features of a regular house. All the neighborhood children were welcome to play with us in it, so we kept company.

I learned much later, with complete surprise, that my family was actually just barely at the top of the poverty level, financially speaking.

In my block were about three or four families of "colored" hue, and the rest were white. Later, when I was a preteen, a Hispanic family moved next door on our west side.

Life in the Depression

I was to learn that children of my skin color could not hunt Easter eggs with all the little children running past my house with empty baskets, and later that I could not ride the amusement rides just down the street from us at Stewart Beach Park.

When my mother took us children "in bathing" down on the beach just a couple of blocks from our house, I was told that I did not really want to play on the swings that were put down there for children of the other race. My father made and put up a swing in one of our backyard trees, so we would not feel deprived.

Although I well remember riding on the streetcars, holding onto the side rails, and jumping off when we got to our church, I heard the adults grumbling when the new, shiny buses rolled up on Broadway, a block from our home. I didn't understand what could be wrong with the buses; they looked so new, clean and interesting. Then I used my new ability to read, on the sign that the older children and adults pointed out to me. It said "Whites only" in the front of the bus. The sign near the last bench seat, on the back side of one of two side seats, just behind the bar people held when descending from the bus, read "Colored." Just one little neat sign, that could be moved forward if there were more colored passengers than white on the bus.

With such treatment, I was being brainwashed to think that I was not as good as the little white girls in my neighborhood that begged to play in my playhouse at home. To believe that when I saw those girls downtown, they did not have to speak to me, or even nod and smile at me.

And when we were back home, I was groomed by my family to be nice to them when they came over and asked to play with us. While my mother was trying to teach me to be a good Christian girl, she was also trying to teach me that life is often not fair. The two white girls who often came to play but seldom spoke downtown were victims too, and I felt sorry for them in adulthood.

I met one of them in recent years, one morning while riding my bicycle and she was looking for old cans. Though I had seen her before, I did not recognize her until she stopped and asked me about my mother and sister, and told me who she was. I was shocked. Though prejudice had hurt our friendship, she remembered our days together in the playhouse with such fondness. We had both been victims of ugliness.

Playhouse

On our block was also a house with a cement sidewalk, but our parents told us never to ask the owners to skate or bike there. Most of us had dirt sidewalks then, and so we went to the seawall to skate or ride bicycles. Sometimes, if we were lucky and the managers weren't around, we would skate on the paved parking lot of the apartment house at 8th Street and Avenue K.

Life in the Depression

Florence & Daisy in front of playhouse

I still think of my childhood best friend, Annie Pearl, when I ride my bicycle in that area today. After all these years, I can still sense the excitement we felt when our parents allowed us to skate on the Gulf side of Seawall Boulevard. We would race each other as far as Stewart Beach or just beyond, and as far as 14th Street. We were not allowed to go much farther.

Island of Color

All of this does not make me feel bitter today, just sort of sad. Restrictions were in place for a lot of reasons, and were just part of growing up for us. I am so proud of my parents for not teaching us to hate, nor to hurt.

In this community, we all should be grateful that no sustained ugliness ever broke out. We lived in such proximity with each other, and people of all kinds mingled together.

We paid our light bills at the "Light Company." We shopped together – on Church Street for furniture, at Plantowsky's; in Gengler Brothers Store; and around the waterfront for seafood, or chickens sold live from cages. At Galveston Piano Company, then later at Ginsberg's, and over on Market Street at Schreiber and Miller.

We shopped in the department stores and in five-and-ten-cent stores on Postoffice Street.

Our favorite place to shop for clothing was Eiband's and, if one could afford it, Levy's and Nathan's clothing and department stores.

Of course, we children spent a lot of time in Grant's, McCrory's, or Kress, buying with our coins our favorite cosmetics and fingernail polish, even candy and ice cream. We knew that we couldn't sit down on the stools at McCrory's, but we bought their wares anyway.

And I'll never forget the day they put in an escalator, the first one in Galveston to my knowledge. We "went to town" just to ride up and down the escalator. We also got to talk to Santa Claus at McCrory's, up on the second floor. I was a little past the age of belief in a real white-bearded gentleman who was supposed to bring me all of the wonderful things I received for Christmas. But it was always fun to play make-believe, and I was clinging to childhood.

Life in the Depression

Florence Fedford in her Blue and White Battalion uniform.

I never had distaste for the custom, as some of my peers and even my children had. I still love the mystery, the magic of the holidays, and think that anyone depriving children of these magical feelings should be whipped. Kids have it rough enough without having to give up belief that some power works things out for them, even if things don't seem to evidence that way. This is not to say that children don't need to learn responsibility for their own welfare, but they should feel that when things seem out of control in a bad way, there is hope. Call it God; I do. Call it whatever your religious beliefs tell you; that is your right. But whatever your belief, leave a helpless child with hope, please.

This is how life was for a Galveston African American girl in the years following 1929. No one had it easy. But, as John Leltz said, we all sort of pulled together in Galveston. There was more good than bad. For our people, inequity in pay and not receiving credit for the work they did were realities. Yet even with those memories come more amusing ones.

Island of Color

My friend Annie Pearl's mother worked at the old John Sealy hospital, now part of the University of Texas Medical Branch at Galveston. Mrs. Fry's job had very little description, if there was one; she did a variety of tasks, whatever the doctors asked her to do.

They left her in charge of putting body parts in jars to examine later. It seemed a gruesome task to me, but I was really intrigued when Annie Pearl promised to show the jars to me if I wouldn't tell anyone. The jars were kept in underground rooms, under the main hospital corridors. Annie Pearl went around so many corners as I followed that I couldn't be sure today where I was, but I'm willing to bet a goose that it was under the classrooms of Old Red. I remember the walkways as rounded, and it was cool and damp down there, adding to the mystery. I actually didn't even believe Annie Pearl when she told me that she could show me a hand all by itself down there, and a tiny baby, never born, in a jar. It sounded like some kind of hocus-pocus, a child's bragging.

Until I suddenly turned the corner, and saw that she had stopped, and was pointing. I was too frozen to run; I was afraid I wouldn't find my way back out anyway. In disbelief, I watched her look around furtively, bring the jar down from the shelf, and proudly prove she wasn't lying.

The things we tried to do in our day would be tame to kids now, but were quite daring then. She was exactly one year, two months, and seven days older than I, and felt it her duty to show me what made the world run. And I believed every word she said -- usually.

Sometimes I had an advantage over her: a mother with a car, who could take us places; a big sister who could chaperone us to some events; and a grandfather who did all kinds of good stuff, like caning chairs. But then she had a father who worked at the Phi Chi Fraternity house, and

Life in the Depression

brought home all kinds of edible treats and fancy things -- providing for our first try at alcohol when Annie Pearl announced, "Rum and Coke is really good. Want to try it?"

Ministers of the church, my father and grandfather did not believe in having any alcohol in the home. So I didn't touch the stuff again but once when I was in college, then not again until I was in graduate school, in my aunt and uncle's home in Chicago.

The 1930s were a period of recovery for all of us. Franklin Delano Roosevelt was viewed as a pretty good president, known as well as you could know a celebrity in those days. Most of his popularity with the people I knew was because of his outstanding wife, Mrs. Eleanor Roosevelt. A real eye-opener in the days of Roosevelts in the White House was the true friendship between Mrs. Eleanor Roosevelt and Mrs. Mary McLeod Bethune.

In my mother's Federation of Colored Women's Clubs meetings, a lot of reference was made to the fact that those two friends had done more good for the race relations situation than anything else in recent times. I believe that Mrs. Bethune, an intelligent leader, was the first woman of her race to be portrayed in the media to the public in a position of dignity. Much of the success that she had was because of her ability to speak frankly and strongly for her people through her friendship with the president's wife. And because neither woman was physically attractive, their pictures were also an early lesson that it isn't how you look that makes you great; it is what you know.

Sometimes the picture doesn't tell you what you need to know. A funny family story from the days of financial recovery was told about me. I had just learned to read at the tender age of three, without the help of phonics. My mother had taught me using pictures of items above their names, associating the picture with the word. I knew table, chair, baby, etc., and recognized my own name because it was placed under a picture of a little soft chick -- which I loved to hold in our yard -- taken from a Bon Ami cleaning powder can.

Well, my adult kin loved to hear me read, spelling out the words, but had caught me in one mistake that they loved to laugh over. Once when I was visiting my Aunt Irma, she called me over to demonstrate for her friends. There was a window display sticker for the National Recovery Act, I believe it was called, featuring an eagle, our national bird, in its design.

Pointing to the sign on her window, she ordered, "Izola! Read that sign for me!" Straightening up to my full height, I read proudly, "N-R-A ... eagle." I was devastated by the laughter.

The sting goes away with understanding, but you never forget the initial feel. We are so prone to forget how it feels to be laughed at, when we are older, more in control, and more able to shape our destinies.

In those childhood years, the 1930s, Galveston saw a lot of change. Many buildings were constructed, like the school in which I later taught the longest, Stephen F. Austin. But most of all it was a time of real change in our way of living.

We moved from a wood stove to gas stoves to heat the house. But I remember the little pot-bellied wood stove in the kitchen very well. It would roast you up good on one side, while you turned freezing cold on the other. So you warmed up like people fried foods: do one side really good, then the other. You learned to run to get your covers, warm them by the stove, and run back to bed while they were still warm and toasty.

Life in the Depression

And we still had ice boxes in the early part of the '30s. The ice box was kept on the back porch. I would sit on the back step for Mother, waiting for the ice man's delivery. It wasn't every day, but probably was more often than weekly, though, because the food didn't spoil.

When Mother told me to tell the man to leave 50 pounds of ice, I really got excited and happy. That meant that she was going to make ice cream that day, and I could help. I couldn't chip up the ice, or make the custard, but she would let me turn the handle, until I was ready to drop from exhaustion. It was well worth the wait, because nobody, not anyone, could beat the taste of Mother's homemade banana nut ice cream, nor her iced tea sherbet.

Idle Wyles picnic

The old ice box was replaced during the '30s by our brand new Servel gas refrigerator. We also got a new telephone number then -- instead of the old four numbers, we had five, with the number '2' as prefix. Galveston usage was growing.

Most of our buying for daily living was done in a two-block radius. Our groceries were bought at the corner store, Porretto's. There is a bar and grill there now. And on Broadway, at 10th Street, across from our elementary school was a drugstore. My father had constant stomach trouble and went to buy his Capudine there. He also occasionally brought home a quart of ice cream, in a round white carton, handpacked by the store owner, Arthur.

When my sister knew that Daddy was going to the drugstore for any reason, and thought he might be in a good mood, she would start singing, and signal me to join her: "I scream, you scream, we all scream for ice cream." We would sing it over and over until we thought it wise to shut up, or until Daddy, in pretended misery over the sound of our voices, set out for the store.

These were our simple pleasures. Mother's ice cream was much better than store-bought, but we couldn't beg her to make ice cream unless it was summertime. And this was before the beautiful Triple Dip Ice Cream Parlor came into being.

Toward the end of the Thirties, my mother was transferred to Central High, in the annex across the street from the high school first, teaching the high seventh grade.

We had a large amount of snow that last winter, in 1939, my first time to see real snow. I have pictures of it taken around our home, at the new school, Booker T. Washington, and elsewhere. It was the year I

Life in the Depression

entered the last grade of elementary school. I wasn't to see another snow in this area until I was grown and teaching, exactly 10 years later. Ten years seems such a short time now; then, it was almost forever.

(That winter in 1949 was really something: My little car was covered with the white stuff, and the ground was white from Bay City all the way to Galveston, where I visited my mother every week. The third snow in Galveston came again exactly 10 years later, during the winter of 1959. I was married and we were living out west in Galveston. With two other adults, we had a rare snowball fight – our silent home movie recorded all the fun – as our children, ages 3 and 5, watched, mystified.)

1939 was the year of my sister's graduation from high school, so I was like an only child that year, and had some real growing up to do. It wasn't fun for a while. I missed my big sister terribly, but didn't get any sympathy at school for that.

Then the Central High Band took all of my interest after I was in high school, and the time passed quickly. I grew quickly too. During those years, Rev. R.C. Walker was pastor at my church, and he once told me that every Sunday he saw me step through the church doors, I had grown an inch.

I do remember that Mother had Easter outfits made for my sister and me while she was in college. I was 13, in my junior year of high school. The outfits were just alike, and I was so proud that I not only could wear high heels, but stockings, just like she did. When I visited my sister at Prairie View that holiday, only months after seeing her during Christmas vacation, my sister and her friends swore that they thought I was my sister when I entered the dorm room. Florence said she nearly fainted. She said,

"I knew I wasn't coming through the door myself, but it sure looked like me!"

Going into 1940, I had turned a visible corner into teenage responsibility, and toward an adult approach to what was going on in my life.

CHAPTER FOURTEEN
WORLD WAR II AND SOCIAL CHANGE

Why is it that you can think times are hard, and that you are really not happy ... until you really face hard times? America was very gullible, very green, and totally unprepared when World War II started. No one even knew what battle was all about in the generations still alive in 1941.

Since I was only 12 years old, I was quite in the dark as well as to what was about to happen. I was in Central High School, had just finished a season of playing in band for football games, and was fully involved in activities. This day, the weather was mild, and it was the usual Sunday afternoon. I'd had dinner and was reading the Sunday funnies, about to stretch out for a nap -- when we heard the shocking announcement on the radio.

What? Bombed? Like by airplanes? Why? Where in the heck is Pearl Harbor? What. ... Then, as the news began to sink in, disbelief.

None of us could ever forget the afternoon (though it was morning in Hawaii) when a sleepy, quiet Sunday turned into a nightmare.

People ran to and fro, the telephones started ringing all over. Then, as we began assessing what had occurred, the newsboys came up and down the sidewalk in our residential areas. "EXTRA, EXTRA!! Read all about it! Japanese bomb Pearl Harbor!! President Roosevelt declares WAR!!"

Over and over we heard this, but the words had no real meaning to any of us. I couldn't understand. Why would some men way over in the country of Japan come all the way over to the United States to drop bombs on us? What did we do? And why did we do it?

Those questions were not really answered for me until January 1986, when I made my first trip to Honolulu with my daughter Cheryl. We went to view Pearl Harbor, see the memorial for ourselves, and read all about the conflict. We saw a movie there which explained, for me the first time, what precipitated such a drastic action on the part of Japan.

But in 1941, all of our lives came to a jerking halt in Galveston, and everywhere else in the world. We would never be the same.

"Declared WAR!!" I don't remember lying awake that night; I was too young. Mother and Daddy were around, and Florence was all right up in Prairie View. I had a full stomach, with clothes laid out for school as usual. But the next few days were sort of off-base. I know now that the adults purposely kept us calm until they had to admit that they didn't know either what was going to happen to us all.

Tides of War

Before too long, we were aware that fellows all around us -- with graduation plans, or recently out of school and working in some local job -- were packing up, leaving to join the army to do whatever they felt they had to do. My classmates were mostly 15 and 16, still too young to be drafted, but they became more grown-up; the conversations in classes and down the halls grew more serious. Our teachers tried to prepare us for more difficult days ahead; we were warned about how to conduct ourselves around public places, how not to get in trouble, how to be more accountable.

It wasn't too long before rationing of the products we used all the time, and had come to take for granted. No more could we go the store and buy butter as often as we needed or wanted it. The head of each household was issued a ration book for a series of things. One had to save stamps of credit until there were enough to buy meat, sugar, butter, rubber, gasoline for your car, etc.

Then we were told that saving the drippings from bacon fat and the like would count toward more stamps for butter and similar products. When you'd saved a pound of bacon drippings, kept in a can on the cooking stove, it could be exchanged at the local store for stamps.

Getting tires for a car was another whole problem. The war effort called for making every conceivable tire for trucks, airplanes, all military vehicles.

Meanwhile, at Central High School, things were slowly changing. The football games were the same for a while, with the mighty Bearcat Band and all the rest, as booster clubs and parents paid the expenses. But such activities were eventually cut back, as trip expenses became almost impossible to bear for each team. And as the boys in the draft age group went to the armed services, our attention went to wherever they were being trained.

Signs started going up in windows showing if a family had a son or relative in the U.S. Armed Services. A few fellows joined the Navy, but the Navy was rather notorious in denying promotions to Negroes who had given wonderful service for years. Most Navy sailors who were Negroes were cooks, or received any other menial position that was available. Some of our young men went into the Marine Corps, but they washed out most of the guys who tried to make it. The Air Force gave similar treatment.

Only the Army gave the guys a chance to make good. So, most of our young men were in the U.S. Army, glamorous or not.

There is always a silver lining behind every dark cloud. In the armed services, these men put up with a lot of pure ... well, I can't think of a nice way to say it. But many men would have had no money for college and no real job opportunities, if things had remained as they were. The GI Bill made higher education possible for our former servicemen and women, just as most of those in later generations have taken the risks of military life for guaranteed career training and possible employment upon leaving the military.

And in spite of what grown men of color had to listen to from their peers, and especially what they heard from persons inferior to them who were placed over them, these men soon learned to excel in some skill. They also learned to survive and actually made friends with those of other races who had to work with them at times. Most of these men came from the war much smarter than they went in, in many ways. So World War II, hell that it was, saw a surge of confidence and ability that would not go away in the following peacetime.

Ruthe Winegarten noted that Negro men were not alone in joining the services. The women had a definite purpose within the services as well as outside them. They suffered much more discrimination and indignity than the men did. But they served, nonetheless. Just as segregation kept the men from feeling like real soldiers, it made for a rotten life for the women, who were despised by white women and even their own men. But 39 volunteer African American women were sworn into the Women's Army Auxiliary Corps, or the WAAC, in 1943 at Fort Des Moines, Iowa.

They were separated from the white women in the barracks, and were trained by white men.

I remember the awful stories that were told about them, and knew some of them were just lies. These first WAACs did not earn the proper respect for what they did, even from their own people. Considering what some people have tolerated in modern times, just to leave a decent mark for their time spent on earth, I am so aware that not all martyrs existed long ago. Heroes come in all sizes, shapes and colors. Some never get recognized in any fashion.

The corps gave some women a chance to serve their country, whether they were appreciated for what they did or not. They replaced so many men who went on to battle or foreign posts in many other capacities. Although the Army controlled and managed the WAAC, these women received none of the Army benefits, and had lesser salary and rank than the men they recalled. WAAC women did the same jobs that men had done, except combat.

A Houston woman added to the discrimination -- the WAAC director, Oveta Culp Hobby. After Negro women protested her treatment, Mrs. Mary McLeod Bethune received an assistant's position with Mrs. Hobby, to help guide the destinies of the Negro WAACs. Because of Mrs. Bethune, some conditions improved, but the force never included more than 6 percent African Americans. And out of about 4,000 Negro women in the WAAC, about 120 were officers. Some of these were graduates of Prairie View: Annie Lee Brown Wright, Ruth L. Freemen, Geraldine Bright and Alice Marie Jones.

In short time, the term Auxiliary was dropped, and the organization became known simply as the WAC. The women did not fare better with the new title; the Army simply enforced its own rules of segregation. But

Island of Color

some earned the respect of having a career that they would not have had otherwise. Women also served in many other capacities, some not open to them before wartime. There was the small number of women in the Navy Nurse Corps, and quite a few in the Army Nurse Corps. The career boost from this service often carried over to civilian life.

My sister's age group was in college when the war broke out. Some fellows received deferments; some volunteered to go in then. Those who had already received ROTC training went into the service immediately as officers. ROTC had always been a requirement of the men at Prairie View.

There was a jazz band at the university known as the Prairie View Collegians. One after another man went into the services, until the group had to disband.

Prairie View Coeds – all girls jazz orchestra

The director of bands then decided to organize a group of talented young women into an all-girls' jazz orchestra, the Prairie View College Co-eds. Big bands were all the rage then, and the girls selected were about 15 of the prettiest girls who could play instruments for miles around. The girls were hits because of their uniqueness at first, but after a lot of publicity in the area, more real good talent was recruited, and they became known for their great musical ability as well. I joined later as a freshman in the fall of 1944.

The Sweethearts of Rhythm was another famous jazz orchestra, organized nationally for the same reason: few men available. But the interest in women playing good jazz was really just growing; there was the Darlings of Rhythm after that. Both organizations were primarily African American, although those of other races played occasionally as needed or desired.

My sister's roommate, Margaret Grigsby, was one of the first members of the Prairie View College Coeds, and a very capable trombone player. Our mothers were civic partners, working in the same organizations, and personal friends as well. Margo, as she was known to her friends, graduated with my sister in 1943, but she returned to campus to play for some engagements in the fall of 1944 because a player of her quality was so hard to find. She later attended and taught at Howard University Medical School, known as a powerhouse on the medical faculty until her recent retirement. Such was the quality of girls in the Coeds.

Galveston could also boast of another charter member, Melvia Wrenn. Melvia had played at Central High under Mr. Huff also. She was a tenor saxophone ace of the orchestra, and my mentor of sorts when I joined. Most of all, she told me that I had better not embarrass her with anything stupid in my trumpet playing, or in my actions or attitude in the band. Well, she acted tough with those piercing gray eyes of hers, but she was there for me if I needed anything and couldn't find another source of help.

Her best friend in the orchestra was alto saxophonist Bert Etta Davis, who was our student leader and knew more about instructing the group musically than our faculty leader. So Melvia interceded for me if I made a real musical mistake, before Bert Etta lost her cool with me. However, after a couple of months, Bert Etta respected me for my own character and musicianship, and we became friends. I was a bit young for their interests after work, but neither of us minded going on about our own business.

Earlier in the war, in those years before I left home, Galveston war efforts included talk of building bomb shelters -- before it was realized that Galveston doesn't exactly lend itself to bomb shelter building. The money that it would take to build underwater would hardly be had by poor folk like us. The idea just didn't fit island living, so we decided that other plans had better work if an air raid did occur.

The possibility of an air raid was not too far-fetched. We were a potential target as a leading sea port, with the possibility of visiting tankers or other vessels needed for war purposes, and with Texas City's oil industry next door. So there were occasional air raid drills at night. We had to blacken all windows; pull-down canvas shades were the only ones in use in most homes then. The air raid siren would whine and wail for a few minutes, sending chills down my spine, and we would huddle in a center room together as a family. After too many newsreels at the movies depicting bombing raids on London or other cities, I half-expected every drill to be the real thing, and listened carefully for the drone of bombers coming over. It was a real relief after crouching for 20 minutes or more in silence, required by the raid's organizers, to hear the loud blast of the all-clear signal from the waterworks -- blap, blap, blap, blappp.

Most likely, some parents enjoyed this period of quiet from their kids -- the only time of day when they would be scared into complete silence. Our parents enforced similar silence for thunderstorms when we were small. Mother always said, "Close your mouth, Izola. Your teeth may draw lightning!" We didn't play the piano for the same reason, or use the telephone, or anything. Though I still see some wisdom in not using the telephone, I wonder if sometimes in the summer our parents didn't pray for rain for more than the reason of the heat.

Back to the air raids, it may have been disappointing for an adventure-loving teenager that the Japanese didn't decide to bomb Galveston or that the Germans did not think Galveston qualified for a submarine battle, but it was surely a relief for a city with rusting Civil War cannons on the east beachfront as its protection against submarines, and aging leaky-light window shades as protection in air raids.

That teenager did try to aid the war effort once, by making rubber. I nearly burned down Central High School in the process.

As a 14-year-old high school senior, I was the baby of my chemistry class, and tired of not being noticed most of the time. Mr. Hall Dansby -- who told us that his name was really Hell Dansby because he planned to give us hell unless we learned everything he could teach us about chemistry -- was my most able instructor. He had a very wry sense of humor and could tell you something funny every few minutes while you were working on a lab project. But he wasn't given to silliness and never joked about his work. He gave accurate and detailed but terse commands about how you were to proceed with an experiment in a clear, moderate-toned voice, told you to carefully read your assignments, and gave any test or exam that he promised. If a person was careless, forgetful, or just not properly self-motivated to study, that person failed the course. So he had a reputation that caused me to study at home for the first time in my life.

After a semester of devoted study of chemistry, I felt secure enough to join his Camera Club, where we learned to develop pictures, make enlargements, etc. I'd do any projects that gave extra credit, just as a challenge; I already had a top grade of 1 in his class (we received number grades from 1 to 5). I decided to take part when he asked if we would like to make any substance in a book of experiments that he had, from chemicals in the storeroom.

When I looked through this book, I was fascinated by the recipe for making rubber. Here we were in wartime, with everyone wishing he/she could buy new tires, and we did not have many other commonly used items that contained rubber (this was before plastics), such as curlers and toys. Well! After I received Mr. Dansby's approval and organized my supplies, I excitedly went to work.

Now, Mr. Dansby had a nickname for each of us. The more he liked you, the more he called you by this slightly degrading nickname. His way of showing affection was to keep a straight face and say something slightly derogatory while patrolling around the classroom.

As he wandered up and down the aisles between our stations and tables, softly whistling his little tunes, we all seemed to be in control. Knowing I didn't want to seem too juvenile before my classmates, he would nonetheless call me "Baby Fed-ford! How you doing, Baby Fedford? Fedford!" Knowing his style, my classmates didn't even look up from their work; he would get on their case immediately if they did, anyway. "What you looking at, Rockefeller, want to do a little extra work, huh?" he would have said if anyone had wanted to tease me, so they didn't. It was a warm family-type class environment, but we were definitely challenged.

For a minute, my mixture was just gently bubbling in the little beaker over the Bunsen burner. I stirred it again with my little glass rod slowly, and sighed. A loud yipe was heard just below the window near me; it came from some students on the grounds below who were on a break while we were in class. It was just enough to divert my attention for a moment. Others were looking out of the window too, when somebody inside yelled, "FIRE!"

I looked back inside just in time to see my mixture, which had boiled over, run down the side of the vessel and quickly along the table countertop, flames rising higher from it as it passed the Bunsen burner flame.

Two more seconds, as I stood transfixed, and the fire alarm sounded and people ran from the building, pushing me ahead of them. I was out on the sidewalk, wondering what had happened before I realized that I had caused all this. The feeling of absolute doom took over my body, and I began to tremble like a son-of-a-gun. With extreme difficulty, I made myself look up to the window in the room from which I had just come. I could just see Mr. Dansby's shoulders, leaning over, busy putting out the fire.

We returned to the room shortly. I don't know how my legs made it back there by themselves; I know I didn't direct them. And I saw Mr.

Dansby still raking the mess back into the sink, partly with his bare hands. The man was herculean, cool, superhuman.

I tried to melt into the wall, but it wouldn't happen.

"FED-FORD!! Come 'ere!"

"Yessir!" I mumbled. I was waiting for the ceiling to fall in any minute now. I went to his side.

"Feel this stuff. You got yourself some real rubber! Feel it!" he urged. I managed to get my fingers around some of the burned product. It was elastic! He meant it: I had made rubber! He said nothing else to me, just whistled his tune between his teeth, and told everybody else to shut up and get back to work.

Everyone was back to normal, while I just stood there gaping and waiting on him to dictate my punishment. He didn't even send me to the office, and no one from the office called over the loudspeaker to ask what had happened. I think they were told where the fire was, and knew he would take care of whatever the problem was.

That's one of the first times that I seriously knew for myself that there is a God. How else could you account for my going without punishment, and not even much teasing from my peers? I think they actually forgot all about me after class. But not Mr. Dansby. I was entering the room the next day, still very tremulous, when Mr. Dansby asked me where all my new materials were, and why I hadn't started my experiment.

"Sir?" I said, incredulously.

He replied, "I said get going, Fed-ford."

Since I could tell that he was definitely not kidding, I ventured a question of my own. "What should I do, Mr. Dansby?"

Speaking quickly, as though he were irritated with my question or indecisiveness, or both, he repeated, "I said, get your stuff together, and do it over, Fed-ford."

"Mr. Dansby! You really want me to ... "

"Do it again! Yeah! You bet! Now, get on it!"

And with that, he was through. He had every confidence that I not only could get my nerves together to do it, but that I would not dare make a mistake this time. And I didn't. The experiment went perfectly. I wrote it up correctly and everything. Only one problem: It wasn't elastic like the first batch -- the burned batch. The first stuff was really rubber. And I could have saved military lives. Or bought some good tires by exchanging my material for rubber tires, like the bacon grease for butter, or ... .

And then I stopped daydreaming immediately, for fear I was about to cause some other major catastrophe.

That's my war story. Or it almost was. There were other bright moments.

As for social life, you couldn't beat the wartime situation. Believe me, many a young woman of whatever color was glad to see the military installations come up around Galveston. We went to USO dances with some regularity. Funny thing was, my family had rather strict rules of conduct for young ladies. But I could attend the USO dances at age 13 even though my older classmates couldn't, because for a chaperone I had my sister, who had begun teaching in Galveston and was single.

The U.S. Air Force had a base outside of the city limits. And there was Camp Wallace, the soldiers stationed in near Hitchcock, and there was also a naval base in the area. The first guy I called my boyfriend was a sailor from that base. His name was Obie Harmon, and I still think he was the cutest fellow that ever wore a sailor suit. He had the warmest smile, the nicest manners, and boy, could he dance!

When he asked me if he could come see me sometimes, I excused myself, and went to ask my sister if she thought Mother would let me "have company." She said she would have to ask Mother, and to tell him to call me on the telephone. I was delighted, pleaded my case with Mother, and was the first in my little group of three friends to "take company" at home. It was too funny. Six months earlier, I had announced that I hated all boys; they were dirty, and I wanted nothing to do with any of them. Now I had brought home a beau.

Mother had told me that she never wanted me to hang out on the street corner as some of my peers did, giggling, to see fellows. But when the young man came, she was waiting, and welcomed him at the door herself; my father met him later. Obie sat in one corner of the room, I was in another corner, and my mother was somewhere in the middle of the room. Quite romantic.

We also had an S-shaped love seat: If you sat on one side, you could face your company, who sat on the other side. It was in the middle of the room. When we sat on it, Mother was in a convenient corner, same room. Or Florence sat out on the porch, in the swing, with the window open for easy listening.

What it was, was "courting." After all, in one more year, I would be away at college. So my parents must have reasoned I had better learn some skills in dealing with interested fellows.

Of course, Prairie View in those days wasn't much different in terms of protectiveness. All the dormitories for males were on one side of the campus, and those for females were on the other side. And never the twain would meet.

When we went to the college gymnasium-auditorium for moving picture shows, you could arrange to sit with your boyfriend, but after the movie was over, it was night. There were bright street lights on all corners, and our faithful night watchman, whom every P.V. student knew as "Buckmix," stood there with his flashlight and loud, loud whistle. And he yelled at intervals, as we left the gym and crossed the street heading toward him on the corner: "BOYS TO THE LEFT, GIRLS TO THE RIGHT!"

He would hitch up his belt a little, and start over. And if a fellow tried to sneak by with a girl, he would blow loud and long, long enough to be heard in three nearby counties, on his trusty whistle. Since we didn't want to hear that thing, peer pressure meant we would demand ourselves that the errant couple get their act together.

Besides, if they really wanted to get into real trouble, they usually knew how to slip off the campus and go somewhere in Hempstead or Waller. Then they could count on hearing campus chaplain Mr. Lee C. Phillip's sermon, which we all knew pretty much by heart too. It went something like this: "Oh, the folly of a one night's thrill (pause), then spend the rest of your life (pause) paying the bill!"

But we really loved Mr. Phillips. He was a dark-complexioned man, with a short haircut, a very serious expression, a cute little goatee on his v-shaped chin that he stroked periodically, and a set of eyes that seemed to always be searching into the distance. He also talked with a soft lisp. And he could say something amusing to you, walk away, and you would get the point after he had left and just want to double over with laughter. His marvelous sense of humor often demanded a pretty good vocabulary.

We attended chapel twice a week: regular nondenominational church services Sunday, and chapel on Thursdays. Some girls made a fine art out of hiding from the matron to keep from going to chapel. Some had the unmitigated gall to even cook while we were gone.

Cooking in the dormitory rooms was outlawed, but the dining-hall food quality had most of us owning hot plates, which we kept out of sight. Since anyone could smell it, there was always some ruse devised to keep the adults busy; sometimes they had gone to town. Some girls cooked sausage, greens, and had a fine old time on a hot plate, with a little bottle of Moroline, a very cheap petroleum-type product, to grease the skillet.

Then if an adult was on the way to the room, the signal was given, the air fanned, the hot plate stuck under the bed, the cook hidden in the closet, and the smell would permeate an otherwise empty room. I think it was one way the dorm matron got a little free food herself, depending on who it was.

My matrons never accepted payoffs. But just talking about those stunts, laughing at night, gave us real relief from troubles and work.

Life certainly was not fun and games for the average Galvestonian during the war years. They raised vegetables in their own victory gardens, as was done all over the nation. Savings stamps and bonds were promoted, bought and put aside for the proper time.

A lot of the help to our community came in the form of personal items donated to the USO centers in town. Our USO Center in Galveston was at the present Wright Cuney Park. The dances were not the only activity there; it was also common to see servicemen strolling around the area, playing games in the center, using the reading rooms and just enjoying a place to relax. Wartime industry also created jobs for many African American men and women, especially those who would not have had a decent income otherwise.

That last summer before the war ended, I was traveling all over the East Coast with the Prairie View College Coeds. I played 2nd trumpet and had a lot of styling to do, though 1st trumpet had most of the solos and the highest notes to play.

We borrowed a young man, Thomas Jones, who played a mean trumpet in Talledega College, to play lead trumpet. The regular lady lead trumpet, Clora Bryant, left for Los Angeles to seek her fortune in the Hollywood area, where she still lives today. Now that we have finally been recognized by Prairie View in a magnificent Coed Orchestra Reunion during their Honors Day in March, 2002, Clora and I keep in touch with each other. After 57 years, those of us left living have reconnected friendships, like in another lifetime. Clora Bryant has been recognized at Kennedy Center in Washington, D.C. as Jazz's "Woman of the Year" in May, 2002.

Our faculty leader planned an itinerary for us that not only gave us good exposure, but the security that women of color sure needed in those changing times. We played one-night stands, big dance engagements, military camp events (we loved those -- the guys just babied us!), some small-town celebrations and eventually the big-time nightclubs and theater stage shows.

Some of the worst days of this wartime travel experience were driving through the South, through the deep southern jungles of hatred, resentment, segregation and discrimination. All our travel had to be planned so that we could be lodged together. So if a small town couldn't put us up for the night safely, we kept driving on in our three station wagons. We were not allowed in the white hotels, so in our search for a good, clean place to stay, we had a small selection of colored hotels or private homes. That took immense planning, I am sure. But Will Henry Bennett did make sure that his charges were never left to work it out for themselves. I will always be grateful for that.

He also had to work to make sure we could be accommodated in a decent cafe. We made a lot of cold sandwiches, which is OK in the summertime, visiting grocery stores in the South. But we had to have a hot meal, hopefully at least once a day. Some of the food was lousy, but I will never forget the wonderful down-home cooking we really enjoyed.

Coming from wartime food in the college dining hall, almost anything looked good to us. There, we got powdered eggs, not too fresh milk in little cartons, and very little fruit. But I remember buying real milk, eggs and fruit at a stand near the El Dorado Ballroom in Houston. And were my roomies and dorm mates glad to see me, when I returned to the campus!

The food was really super in some places. I don't believe anyone can match those Kansas City steaks we ate in some restaurants. I also recall the Meatless Tuesday meals served in most cafes. Talk about creative -- since most people expected meat, and it was hard to come by for these owners, they featured the most unbelievable vegetable dishes, some as flavorful and innovative as could be, with little meat to speak of. My favorite memory of such a meal was pig ears.

Home cooking for me in Galveston did not include soul food. In the Depression years, Galveston African Americans raised and bought poultry, especially chickens and ducks, and enjoyed mostly seafood. (Later, refrigeration raised the price.) If you needed food on the table, you went out with your cane pole, and you caught it. My husband often said he didn't want to be around seafood much in his adult life, because he had had to go fishing with his dad when funds were low. I sure remember my grandfather going out regularly with the cane pole that stayed against our kitchen wall, and I still love to eat freshly caught crabs. No hog maws for most of us, so we were eating healthier than most and didn't know it. So I wasn't too acquainted with the various parts of the pig until that summer of 1945, when I soon learned to appreciate them -- especially the pig ears.

We played the Baltimore and Howard Theater in Washington, D.C., and ended the theater circuit at the famous Apollo Theater in New York. During our off-time in New York, we visited the Savoy Ballroom; their featured singing artist, Betty Mays, joined us at the Apollo when our singer became ill.

At that time, the Savoy Ballroom was in its heyday, and featured two full-sized bands every weekend. People came from everywhere just to dance; if I remember correctly, there were no tables set up or alcoholic beverages sold. Since I loved to dance, and couldn't when I was playing an engagement, this was a fine opportunity, in a safe place.

All of Harlem was a lot of fun, and we saw much of it since our quarters were there, but we also visited as many of the sights in Manhattan as time would allow. My brilliant teacher from high school, Miss Alice Antone, was studying at Columbia University at the time; she learned that the Coeds were in town, and offered to take her Galveston students sightseeing. I went with another orchestra friend of mine. We were so impressed with the Empire State Building; with vending machine food, invented shortly before we arrived; and Manhattan department stores' atmosphere. Since we played five shows every day and night that we were in New York, you can believe that finding time to go sightseeing wasn't easy. But youth is wonderful -- I didn't feel tired, really tired, until after we left.

We were also hard-driven in rehearsals when we first arrived in New York, to learn the music just handed to us by the famous stars we accompanied, names famous then: The Crackerjacks, The Aimmee Sisters, PegLeg Bates. Being backstage to see what they had to do just to get up for a performance and keep up such high energy was a real eye-opening experience for me. Just watching the stars make up their faces and bodies each day was something.

There were so many thrills. The first time I was asked to sign my autograph for admiring young fans outside the stage door was really nice. And there was the way the servicemen would yell, whistle, stomp, and clap when we played for them. Afterward, they would wait for us to come out, to escort us to get our meals -- hanging over us, waiting to see whatever they could do to make us comfortable.

The Men In Uniform

Two rare African American idols were used to recruit soldiers for the war. One was Dorie Miller, a household name in the '40s, though his name is hardly ever heard now during Black History Month. Miller, a member of the U.S. Navy when Pearl Harbor was attacked, singlehandedly rescued numbers of sailors and gave his own life in the battle at Pearl Harbor. The Black men who did go into the Navy were probably inspired by the story of his heroism. With the absence of recognized Negro men in the media during days of segregation, to see Dorie Miller's face on a service recruitment poster was gratifying, to say the least. The only other face seen by the general public with any dignity attached to it was that of Joe Louis, the world heavyweight champion called the Brown Bomber in the media, and also used in recruitment.

To represent what happened to African American Galveston men who served in the military during World War II, I am very grateful for my interview with "Brother" Bess.

Mr. Andrew "Brother" Bess

We spoke in 1981. He lived with his sister in the family home in the East End in the 1000 block of Avenue L. The Bess family, the Clark family, and others had lived in the East End for several generations, among many African American homeowners whose family members have mostly moved away as work opportunities became scarce here.

I was visiting his widowed sister, Mrs. Elizabeth Bess Harrell, an excellent seamstress and family friend. They had always been very close, and both of them remembered things about the past I could not. When I asked Elizabeth something, she asked her brother. "Brother, tell Izola about ... you know, Brother went overseas in World War II, didn't you, Brother?"

I urged him to share details. Always smiling, Brother Bess obliged. He said he was drafted.

"What years were you there?" I asked.

"Well, I left from Boston, got off the boat in Scotland, went by train to England, was in England for a while, right after D Day, went across the Channel to France, but I didn't get to see Paris till after the war was over, when I got a pass. We bypassed Paris going to Germany; then I went to Belgium."

"What branch of the Service were you in?" I asked.

"Army -- Quartermaster Service. When I went in, I was an MP (military policeman). Then when I went overseas, they changed all that. They didn't want any colored MPs. When we went over there, they broke our companies up. We were asked often, 'Did you see any action?' I saw plenty of action. There wasn't anything between us and the front lines. We were in just as much danger as the guys on the front lines. Our captain used to tell us all the time to be very careful. The first thing the enemy was going to do was to try to cut off the supplies. They'd find your dump, try to destroy your supplies.

It was after Easter. I didn't get to go to church Easter Sunday, the first Easter I was over there. I was in England. You're just as much in danger as if you're on the front line. We were alerted." He explained that that meant they were confined to camp, and couldn't attend church. "Used to be you could tell the changing of the seasons by the budding of the trees. Easter Sunday morning, the trees were all budded out, the birds were singing ... people were going to church with overcoats on, 'cause it was cold -- really cold."

He recalled an earlier alert. "And before we went over, in California, we were practicing. It was guys that had any talent, practicing for Christmas music. We were alerted just before Christmas. When you were alerted, you were confined to camp. And I was so outdone. The Navy, their music was so pretty. You don't have these [choral groups] in the Army, I don't know why. It would just be a handful that wanted to do that.

World War II and Social Change

In high school, I was in the Choral Club, and all like that. It was right down my alley. I wanted to do this."

Bess said he was in Germany on VJ Day, the day we in the United States celebrated victory over Japan. "We stayed over there several months after it was over. The war was over when I got a 24-hour pass to go to Canada. We got to stay three days and we enjoyed that. We were in the 66th truck, and it jumped the ditch. Well, the ditch wasn't very wide, but the bumper ... they had to requisition us another truck. It was snow and ice all on the ground. Our driver lost control.

I tried to see everything I could see. When we were traveling from place to place overseas there, you tried to see things you had read about, but by the time you realized you were passing through it, you didn't have the chance to observe many things.

But everything you sent back from overseas, you had to have the officer OK it. Well, everything I sent, my officer said, was something worthwhile. The other guys would send more junk back home. You couldn't buy anything you'd get over there.

You'd feel sorry for the German people. We were in war and everything, but I'd say, these people didn't want to be in any war any more than we did. They were good, the German people were really good. I didn't want to be over there, and they didn't, either. We'd feel sorry for them."

As for Hitler's propaganda about Black people being inferior, he said, "Hitler was doing all this stuff, but the [German] people were good. They were really good."

Asked how the men from his own unit treated him and the other African-American soldiers over there, he said, "I got to be an orderly when

I went there, for my officer. My captain said, 'There are 211 men in this company.' We had three officers. He said, 'It's enough men for each of us to have our own orderly. I got mine already.' But I was orderly for all three of them. In fact, there were four of them, and they were fixing to separate, go to different places. He said, 'You get [your own], 'cause Bess is my orderly.'

They stayed in German houses then. We went to dinner [in their homes]. They had family service, no servants. Maybe they'd have three meats, a different plate for each meat. They don't talk at the table. They used a lot of dishes in their serving. Captain sitting up there talking to me and those people, too. That was holding up the dinner, you see. The mother and daughter were waiting for you to get through eating, and you sitting up there, talking. So, they don't talk while they're eating." He laughed. "Oh, it was an experience."

I hadn't talked before to any African Americans serving in Europe during World War II. My brother-in-law was in the Pacific, and my husband, who was too young, went to Europe later, during the Korean War. So I wanted to know how the men were treated overseas by the people who lived there, and by the military who received their time, energy, and even lives.

"Well, the worst that the Black soldiers were treated overseas was from the white soldiers. See, that's why I was changed up to MP. So many of the white soldiers was getting killed up, they thought some of the Black soldiers were killing them. So they started sending colored MPs with the white MPs.

When I was in Paris, I met some people who been over there from World War I. Some would say they'd like to make the trip back here, but didn't know if they could raise enough money. I said I didn't know what it would cost," he laughed, " 'cause I didn't have to pay to get over there."

"As we neared Europe, they gave us lectures, like 'Don't be showing out with your money and all that.' Well, we weren't getting but $50 a month, see, but the European soldiers weren't getting that. See, you'd go in a pub, and they said, 'Don't be going in there, treating and all, because they would like to return [the kindness], and they're not able, see.

But all you could find was cider -- and they'd call it 'see-der,' like apple cider and stuff, 'cause they didn't have liquor in that pub. However, it *was* liquor over there, because -- and it's funny, we were over there, fighting this war -- I didn't do any drinking, but if you bought a drink, a bottle of Scotch, you paid a terrible price for a bottle of Scotch.

Our officers would get liquor rations from the United States. The enlisted men were the ones fighting this war. My captain was from Arkansas, but he was nice. I didn't know it was white people from Arkansas like that [nice]. My first sergeant was colored, from New York, and he was worse than the captain, who was white.

Those two colored officers, they didn't drink much, but you know what they'd do with their liquor rations? Now, it was against the law to send liquor through the mail, see, but I'd have to pack their liquor up, and send it home. I know they had enough liquor to start a liquor store when they got home. Nothing I ever sent got broken.

But Captain and the youngest officer were white. So, Captain would have his liquor ration. So Captain would tell me if any of those guys would come over to his quarters for a drink, to get it. So I would. I didn't want anything. Some of them would come over there, they'd be drinking with Captain in quarters there, I'd have to fix it. He'd say, 'Get you one.' I didn't want it. He'd insist. I'd say, 'Well, maybe if I had some fruit juice or something.' He'd say, 'Well, go on down to the kitchen and tell them to fix you any kind of fruit juice you want.' So, I'd get me some grapefruit juice, and put a little bourbon in it. I didn't smoke either.

You could always tell when the lines were getting away from us. We were supplying the lines, but you know lines were moving all the time. The closer you'd get to the lines, the better the rations were. We said they were fattening you up to kill or get killed. 'Cause we got cigarette rations.

I was in 3229 Quartermaster Service. We were guarding the fuel dumps in California. When they were fixing to send us overseas, they changed us to this Quartermaster Service. Being in headquarters with the officers, at first, I didn't have to go out in the fields.

I was trying to locate a friend's mother. They were in Kountze, Texas. Well, I don't know -- when Margaret [his sister] got sick, I was trying to correspond with people. I lost track of 'em. Since then, I've tried to locate them; I don't know whether they're living or dead.

He called me 'Homie.' We met up in Houston, and he asked me to write his mother. I said, 'If I write your mother for you, she'll think you're dead.' He said, 'If you don't, I can't write her, and she might think I'm dead.' See, he was out in the field, and it was blackout over there. It was dark when they left, and dark when they came back. They'd take food out there to them [the front line soldiers]. I had the advantage, because I was in headquarters, and I had the advantage of daylight, so I wrote his mother. His name was Willie Flowers. So I wrote, 'When you get this letter, Mrs. Flowers, don't get excited, 'cause Willie's all right.' I explained to her about the blackout. I got back the sweetest letter from her. She wrote back and we remained friends.

Some guys liked to gamble. It wasn't permissible to gamble on the post, you know. They'd go out in the woods and all to gamble, and he'd gamble. He was pretty lucky. During that time, the guys would steal money off you when you'd gamble. And we wore our money in money belts. Well, by me being able to sew, I made me a holster, like a shoulder holster, and my money belt was there. I wore a belt around here," he pointed to his waist, "and one across my shoulder. Then, I wasn't staying in a tent with all the other guys. I was staying in a tent with just guys from headquarters staying there. So nobody got a chance to cut no money belt off of me. And then I didn't gamble, so they didn't think I had money anyway.

I was laying down with four or five hundred dollars on me every night. Of course, it wasn't none of mine -- for this boy and one other fellow. But I told them, I said, 'You can't tell anybody I have any money.' Well, he got ready to come back, he had more points [toward honorable discharge] than I did, 'cause he had a little boy. One boy wanted to borrow some money from him. This boy was going, too, so he could let him know I had money. You got points on age, and dependents. I got mine on age; I was late being drafted. I left in the next draft, after he did. But when they left us, they didn't send him home, like they were supposed to. They went from camp to camp over there. Supposed to be on their way home. Finally, when they got to one camp, they told them that if they'd re-enlist, they'd get 90 days furlough, and send them home immediately.

So he jumps up and re-enlists, so he could get on home, and, uh, you know the day I got in the States, in Boston, he was just getting home in Kountze!" Bess said.

Island of Color

"Of course, after I got to Boston, we had to stay up there a week, before we came down to Camp Fannin. We had to stay there about a week. Anyhow, when we were fixing to leave, he came to me, he said, 'Well, homie, now I'm fixin' to leave, how much money do you have for me?' I said, 'Well, I have $450.00.'

He said, 'How much you gonna let me have?' "

Bess replied, " 'I'm not going to let you have but $150, 'cause you'll gamble it away before you get back. I'll give you the rest when you get over there. And if I don't make it home, then you can tell anybody a good friend made away with $300 for you. 'Cause I'm not going to let you lose it on that boat.' This boy followed him over to that tent.

So when I got to the States, I sent him a telegram. When I got to Boston, I phoned home. When I got to Camp Fannin in Tyler, I called him. I said, 'I'll be home in a few days, and you'll hear from me.' I got home Christmas morning at 2:00. Well, Christmas was on a weekend. I couldn't get in the postoffice till Tuesday. I don't think you could get more than $100 in a money order. I got three $100 money orders, put them in an envelope to Willie Flowers, c/o Mrs. Lillie Flowers. I got the sweetest letter from her again! She said, 'The only thing I hate about him re-enlisting in the service is I know he'll never find another friend like you.' She called me her son.

Yeah, that's why I say that war was a good experience for me. I said I didn't want to go, but I wouldn't give anything for the experience that I got."

I asked Bess, "You were already out and working when you were drafted?" He answered, "I was working at the dry dock, making good money. I got drafted and had to come off to make $50.00 a month. After

I left the States, I didn't sleep in a bed until I was in a hotel in Paris. We had those cots that fold up. Until then, I was on the ground before we got those cots. And I never had a cold, never had sore throat. No, it was those shots they were giving us. We were in a big open field. They said, 'We're not going to put up any tents.' One shelter head down, two duffel bags. ... As soon as I got back, I had colds like I did before I left."

He said the European merchandise he recalled, unusual then, were men's gloves with knit backs and leather palms, and artificial flowers that he brought back for the wedding of a friend, Gwendolyn Bridge. And the material he bought for a suit.

"In Germany, one of the fellows got some beautiful material. We were going to have suits made. We left there [home], they were wearing zoot suits." I remember these so well, because I was in Harlem when they were very fashionable among African American young men. They were even popularized in the cartoons shown everywhere. "We went over to this German tailor's, who fitted us, was going to make the suits for us. ... I didn't know what they were saying. When I went back to fit the suits, I was with this friend from San Antonio; he spoke Spanish. All those foreign people spoke Spanish, so he would communicate with them. ..."

His varied experiences show a glimpse of life for the African-American soldier who learned how to survive, to return from the Big War as we called it -- the war to end all wars.

The Home Front

As many other authors have noted, major changes lay ahead for the African American soldier after World War II. After fighting for his or her country, the soldier was unwilling to come back to a segregated society, and just go back to taking a back seat, a side-door entrance, a second-class citizenship – to scratch heads, and say, "Yassuh, boss, suh." World War II saw the end of submission to unworthy people.

When it became clear that the former colored boys were American men, not all folks could face those facts. But there were those who had learned to share foxholes, bleed and face death together, and say to each other, "Never again." The madness of the Nazis, the fascists, the Japanese consorts changed the hearts of some of the former oppressors. Some never change, but there were enough folk once happy to subdue their neighbors who had another look at what they thought they knew, and found themselves very ignorant.

African Americans were not alone in feeling new purpose; they had a long battle to fight, but it was no longer just their battle. The dignity of all mankind was really at stake. We had all seen clearly in Europe that one cannot look away when domination occurs. New laws had to be passed, but hearts at home had to change.

Just as the pharoah in biblical times hardened his heart over and over to the Israelites' plea to be freed from the Egyptians, people of color would make small gains just to have some hard-hearted person rip them away. After the war was won, and the emergency was over, the average white capitalist could see only one course of action – a return to old, failed ways, to segregated society. Without recognition that these men and women just wanted an opportunity to enjoy a decent living, an education, a finer way of life, like those who withheld these things, hearts were hardened.

Well, as the struggle grew, African Americans formed new alliances, found friends in strange places, and started shaping their lives as the world rebuilt. Industries were diverted from wartime manufacture to peacetime prosperity. The new wonder, the atom, was being harnessed in the laboratory for new peacetime power instead of destruction. Money was freed up for new businesses, and skills learned for fighting purposes were studied for new ventures. The challenge was to build new lives from the damaged ones.

My sister, Florence, and I recalled what we were doing when V J day was announced. She had just married as the war was coming to a close, and her husband, Theasel, had left for Guam. She was in Indiana that day -- she recalled riding around with her new brothers-in-law, shouting from the car as everyone else was doing. As for me, I was with the Coeds on the East Coast. When the war was declared officially over, we were playing an engagement in South Carolina; I don't even remember where. But we blew the horns on the station wagons, rode all up and down the streets, hung out of windows, watched fireworks. Some of the girls even kissed strangers. It was a giddy, funny time.

We came back to earth sooner than some -- so much remained to be done, playing the smaller towns on the way back. It was a let-down after the glitter of New York, and we were tired and just wanted to get home. But the end of the war gave us new life. We could begin to really think of having a future.

I was too young to plan very far ahead, but I think that was the night I decided to leave the orchestra to concentrate on my studies. I knew I couldn't keep up this pace and learn much. And I had sense enough to know the guys' return would soon end this opportunity.

Before I left, I had the thrill of playing with the Coeds in my hometown, at the City Auditorium. An old boyfriend who had played bass drum in the high school band was also there to cheer me on. On the same stage where I had heard Duke Ellington, Count Basie and other celebrities; where I had graduated from high school; where I had made my first public appearance, in first grade under Mrs. Mary Lee Canada Sweatt -- I was back with a famous jazz orchestra. Now that was a personal thrill.

And so the growing up began in earnest, as 1945 moved on. In Galveston, things went back to as normal as they could be. It was wonderful to go to civic affairs that had been canceled for safety's sake or limited resources during the war. Florence returned home. Because of school job restrictions that required teachers to remain single, to keep her teaching position she did not announce her marriage until 1946. But neither of us felt the same.

Campus life went on. At Prairie View, I changed my major from mathematics to music when a wise counselor made me see that I was burning out in math, and had done a lot more with music. And Coach Billy Nicks had football players returning from wartime and built a powerhouse of a football team. We were Southwestern Conference champions, and we dominated all the games. I remember the annual Prairie View-Wiley game, played at the State Fair in Dallas. I reported on the Mighty Panthers' victory over Wiley for the school newspaper in my senior year, the first time my writing was published. Wiley was a strong team; Southern University and Grambling were our strongest competition, but we won several times over them as well.

Yes, the men had returned. Dissatisfaction with the mores and customs meant more men were challenging institutions of all kinds, and unrest was sort of bubbling in the pot, not yet ready to boil over.

And in Galveston as well as elsewhere, women had learned the hard way that they could not only be self-sufficient and raise their children by themselves, but have meaningful careers in the process. Women of color, however, were not just now learning to think for themselves and stand on their own two feet. Although the idea of leaving the home to work in a factory might have been a new concept for white women, African American women had learned to manage by whatever means necessary from slavery times, when they were separated by force from their men. However, in terms of job choices, things were beginning to open up, and new fields formerly left for men were now being tried by women.

I recently watched a woman climb a light pole in Galveston to repair some electrical problem, and smiled at the fact that that's not news anymore. And I recalled that I was a pioneer of sorts myself.

Because of the orchestra experience and my love for music, I breezed through my music education courses, and before graduation I was asked to organize, teach and direct Bay City's first band for African American children. I knew only one other woman teaching school band then: Melvia Wrenn, my homie and former Coed mate, who taught band in Navasota. (Later Betty Bradley and Argie May Rayford taught also, but mostly choral music.) So, Melvia and I, two Galveston girls, were the only two women band directors in the segregated Texas high schools at the time.

I didn't consider myself a trailblazer, but I heard later I gave some girls a vision of what they could become, as a woman directing a top group in the formerly all-male ranks of band directors. Our band had just won the highest rating given that year in University Interscholastic League competition, when I was offered a band director job in a major city, Corpus Christi. It was just before I resigned from Hilliard High School in Bay

City. I made the hard decision to instead head back to Galveston because I had just married the past December.

In Galveston, organizations started taking hold, including the NAACP, YWCA, YMCA and Greek fraternities and sororities. On my wall is a photograph of the 1946 local chapter of Delta Sigma Theta Sorority, then called Gamma Delta Chapter -- a mixed chapter of college students and alumni who had studied at least two years at an accredited college.

Gamma Delta Chapter of Delta Sigma Theta Sorority Inc.

(Interestingly, the sorority was founded Jan. 13, 1913, and there are exactly 13 members in the photograph.) It shows Mrs. Jessie McGuire Dent, our national and chapter founder; my sister Florence, the chapter's first inductee; Mrs. Lucy Huff Jones; Mrs. Sallie Maxie; Mrs. Vivian Hightower Wiley; Ms. Marguerite Hathaway (Dykes, later); Mrs. Verna Newton Huff, wife of Fleming Smizer Huff; Mrs. Ruth Phelps Atkinson;

World War II and Social Change

Mrs. Ella Louise Sterling Carter; Mrs. Cornelia Kidd Dansby, wife of Hall Dansby; Victoria Jones Dezon, Mrs. Jones' daughter; Florence Phelps, Mrs. Atkinson's sister; and Miss Alice Antone.

Alpha Kappa Alpha Sorority, Sigma Gamma Rho Sorority, Zeta Phi Beta Sorority -- all eventually had Galveston chapters. The fraternities with local chapters included Alpha Phi Alpha (my husband and son's fraternity), Omega Psi Chi and Kappa Alpha Psi.

Benevolent organizations, such as the Daughters of Zion, were losing popularity because policies providing much more money were now available from insurance companies. But the Masonic Lodge, Order of the Eastern Star, American Legion, other veteran groups and their auxiliaries have long had a strong following among African Americans. And federated clubs, like the Women's Hospital Aid Society my mother helped organize and federate, still exist for similar purposes today.

Organized voices are still heard louder than individual ones. Trends and demands change, but the spirit of these groups still survives. The persons who carried the banner for integration in the '50s emerged scarred but still battling for equal rights in the '60s. Despite numerous weak points, Greek societies still offer a social outlet and a channel for college-educated professionals to band together to meet social needs. Today's professional African-Americans are facing issues we had just begun addressing after World War II.

In the midst of our war recovery, manmade disaster struck in Texas City, reshaping Galveston County. How does it happen that in this dynamic county, we have had both the nation's most destructive natural disaster, and what was then the nation's most destructive manmade disaster?

CHAPTER FIFTEEN
EMPLOYMENT AND BUSINESS: AFTER WORLD WAR II

After World War II, returning servicemen started higher education or new careers. Women who had worked as nurses, factory workers or military personnel began to seek to earn a living without the traditional roles. And businesses and employment for Galveston African Americans resumed in variety and quantity.

Stanford's Barber Shop

Rev. Hickey, a Galveston native, was a retired presiding elder of the A.M.E. Church and past president of Payne Theological Seminary in Ohio. He recalled working as a youth at the Galvez Hotel, and reflected on how the professionals of Galveston have had to work elsewhere to make ends meet: "I walk in the Galvez Hotel in all dignity now, but I remember the time ... our teachers served as waiters during the summer time."

He named two well-known gentlemen, one a principal, among those who had had to wait tables. Such work in times of segregation and discrimination surely shaped their attitudes, what some younger people criticized as silent subservience and lack of action -- "crawfishing," or skirting, certain issues. It was a case of survival: If the whites in our community who were employers and good tippers were displeased, they could not live in the style to which they were accustomed. Because of their moonlighting, they did own their own homes, send their children to college, and took some nice vacations.

Rev. Hickey, who began doing carpenter work at age 12, also recalled his extensive furniture work, which included making furniture for window displays for a leading merchant, Maison Myro. He learned woodworking from Charles Johnson, the shop teacher at Central High, who also helped him get a scholarship.

Courtney Murray

Mr. Murray was born on Oct. 1, 1902. All five of his children – two by his first wife, three by his second -- preceded him in death. Interviewed at 96 years old, he was very spry, very debonair still, and had to end our interview on his porch for only one reason: He was ready to drive off, having promised to pick up his granddaughter.

A gentleman from the old school, he would not allow me to move a table so I could place my tape recorder near an outlet -- no indeed. He moved the table over himself.

It was a pleasant morning, and even though it was summertime, he was very cool and collected. As he talked freely of his experiences in the world of entrepreneurship, I felt so grateful to God for the opportunity to speak with so many excellent resources, and find them quite responsive to me, willing to share whatever memories they had.

I remember the many fine and wonderful attractions that he brought to our old City Auditorium for our community to enjoy. He is one of the few men who have lived to tell about the "good ole days," when Galveston played host to the most popular attractions in the nation.

Mr. Murray was born in Grand Cane, La., 21 miles from Shreveport. After his family moved to Galveston, he attended school at West District and Central High, through the seventh grade. He worked in California, then relocated to Houston.

In Galveston from 1941 to 1967, he hosted many people at his cafe at 27th and Church Street, the Tip Top Cafe. Gus Allen's place was across the street. Lane Hotel was at 25th and Postoffice streets.

He spoke in support of the effort to rename 27th Street as McGuire Boulevard. He recalled that Joe Polk operated the McGuire Bathhouse. At the bathhouse, Rudolph Wiley had a cafe, and the Manhattan was upstairs, at 28th Street and Avenue R. (And as I well recall from my youth, the joint was jumpin'.)

He continued, telling me that Dan Lewis was a promoter who worked for the Santa Fe Railroad on weekends. And Mr. Murray helped promote groups for Don Robey, a friend of his. He would also contact agents to get groups for concerts in this area.

When I asked Mr. Murray to name some of the groups that he brought to Galveston's City Auditorium, he named these:

Louis Jordan, Lionel Hampton, Jay McShan, Buddy Johnson, with vocalist Ella Johnson, who set up her own band later; Arthur Prysock, Billy Eckstine, Benny Carter, and the Pabst Blue Ribbon Parade.

He said that the average group cost him about $300.00 to hire, but the Pabst Blue Ribbon Parade cost him $750.00. For this affair were included "Peg Leg" Bates, who I once played for in the touring Prairie View College Coeds Orchestra; Joe Louis, world heavyweight champion; and the Jimmie Lunceford Band.

When I asked him about other entertainers I had heard in the City Auditorium – Count Basie, Duke Ellington, Erskine Hawkins -- he told me that Charlie Schiro, another promoter, had brought them.

I was thrilled just to hear the names again of guys like Buddy Johnson, who played for my Junior-Senior prom at Prairie View University, to a very packed house, for he was really popular then. And no one else seemed to remember Peg Leg Bates around here, but he was the star on all of the East Coast at the time when the PV Coeds toured there.

He told me how kind some of the guys were. For example, when Jimmie Lunceford was to appear, there was a thunderstorm that night. To keep Murray from losing money, Jimmie Lunceford agreed to stay overnight, to play the next night.

And their kindnesses were returned; though their manager would find them places to stay, sometimes he fed the musicians.

Mr. Thomas James Green

He was born Jan. 3, 1912. His parents were also raised here; his mother told him all about the 1900 storm.

After attending Central to the 11th grade, Green worked with a prominent Galveston attorney, John Neethe, for over 10 years. (He later received his G.E.D.) And during the war, Green carried mail at home.

Island of Color

He spent about five years with the post office, then went into business for himself -- Green's Taxicab, for over 10 years. At that time, he was affiliated with W.K. Hebert, who had a funeral home. Green furnished cars for the funerals, and also attended the Commonwealth College of Mortuary Science. He also became a licensed real estate dealer.

Green said he worked again for attorney Neethe, for about 20 years while he also worked for Hebert. When Neethe's health was failing, a doctor recommended that Neethe take Green along with him at all times. Green became more like a valet, and traveled with him a lot.

In this role, he said, New Orleans accepted him without racial prejudice, but he encountered problems at Houston's Rice Hotel, and a hotel in Dallas. At these places, they wouldn't permit him to come in the front door or ride the front elevators; he had to take the freight elevator to reach Neethe's room. Nor was he permitted to go to the cafe or cafeteria. His breakfast and dinner were sent up to him on a tray.

After Mr. Hebert's health also failed, Green established his own funeral home. He also attended law school at Texas Southern University, in its first class, until his own health failed. Green told me that he had an understanding of contracts, and had nice dealings with the local banks.

He said several times, "Everybody was so nice." He experienced prejudice and had his own stories to tell, but these were the exception and not the rule for him.

Telling me about other businesses he recalled, he described:

Mr. Sanders, who had a popcorn wagon, which was glassed-in and drawn by a horse, and from which he sold popcorn between 34th and 35th streets and Avenue M ½; Mr. Tart, at 1128 Ave. L, who sold doughnuts carried in a clothes basket over his shoulder; and the baseball field used by "colored" folk, at 39th Street and Boulevard, once considered to be "way out," far down the island.

He also recalled his Aunt Lucy, at 2601 Ave. P ½, who was a midwife. A recent Women in Medicine conference at Galveston's Ashton Villa mentioned the abundance of lay midwives before "colored" people received full service at the hospitals, but no one kept a record of their names. (If medical costs keep increasing, there may be quite a return to such means.)

Dr. Leroy Sterling

Dr. Sterling, a prominent African American dentist in Galveston, and his wife, Luella, named African American businessmen they could recall: the Langham family, who had a Busy Bee taxicab; the Robinsons' drugstore and cafe on 25th Street, between Market and Postoffice streets; Mickey DeWare's cleaning and pressing shop; Dr. Jones who had a dentist's office over the Robinson drugstore, and hair stylists Hazel Phillips and Armide Mason, my husband's cousin and godmother.

They also recalled Lucas, who had a cleaning and pressing shop; Mr. Fisher's service station and car repair garage; another dentist, Dr. Hunter; doctors Rufus, Robert and Elbert Stanton; doctors Mack Joe Moseley, father and son; Honey Brown's barbecue place; Sabu's shoe repair stand; Mitchell and Gladys Thibodeaux's (my husband's cousin) restaurant, and cleaning and pressing shop; Mr. Palmer, a photographer; Victor Wallace and Mr. Harper, who had radio repair shops; Robert McGuire's horse stables, park and bath house; and musicians Miss Laura Williams, Mrs. Mamie Richardson, Mrs. Gamble, Miss Gaston, and Mrs. Hattie Freeman (my piano teacher).

Mrs. Elizabeth Bess Harrell

Mrs. Harrell was a native Galvestonian, one of five children. Her parents came to Galveston early in the century. Her father was a longshoreman, and her mother had taught in Columbus, Texas. Although Elizabeth had also worked at the children's hospital and substituted in the schools, she was primarily a seamstress; all of the Bess family members I knew were excellent in crafts, tailoring and seamstress work.

Her husband, Fred Harrell, who had passed just before our interview in 1993, was a cabinet maker-contractor.

Naming other African-American business owners, she cited :

Ice -- Mr. Kidd; lumber yard -- Nelson Bowden; Alex Thomas -- wood yard; Mickey D. Ware – tailor shop; W.D. Lewis – who sold groceries; Aunt Marendy Wilson ("Aunt Rendy")-- grocery store at 15th Street and Avenue K, well-known in early part of twentieth century and frequented by boxing champion Jack Johnson; Mrs. Mill E. Clay -- barber shop (an excellent businesswoman and one of Reedy Chapel's finest members).

Other barbers named were Herbert Thomas, Clem Emerson, Johnny Phipps, Lewis Thornton (a longtime friend of my Aunt Clara), and John Tarver, still in business today.

She noted printers Mrs. Ethel Terry Dent, the former wife of Attorney Thomas Dent, and Sam Sterling; as well as auto mechanic Dudley Webb, between 20th and 21st streets on Mechanic Street. Church pianists she recalled were Janice Felder of St. Luke, and Melvin Howard (my neighbor), and Claudell Williams of St. Paul (her church).

Employment and Business: After World War II

Dr. and Mrs. R.H. Stanton

(lifelong friends and Reedy Chapel church workers, known as Billy and Janice)

Dr. Rufus Stanton Jr. was my dentist for much of the time that he practiced, before ill health caused him to retire. He is a member of the most active family in medicine in our community – several relatives had practices in Galveston for many years – and is now the last member to remain a resident of Galveston.

They told me that their uncle, Dr. Robert "Bob" Stanton, also owned the Darraugh House apartments at 15th and Church streets, as recorded in the Library of Congress. The family later sold it.

Billy's Aunt Carrie McFadden managed a dairy, where Ball High School's practice football field is now. She delivered milk to prominent white residents, starting off at 4:30 in the morning. Bill Myers and Richard Haller worked for her. She rented out land to truck farmers, sold vegetables, and milked cows.

The Stantons mentioned many of the business owners named already, but added: John McGaffey, who owned a nightspot on 25th Street, and served after-hours liquor. McGaffey was also the editor of a newspaper called *The Voice*. (His wife, Nina McGaffey, used to commute between Galveston and Bay City with me when I taught there, from 1948 to 1953.)

The Stantons also ran the Island City drugstore on 28th and Postoffice streets. Reapher Stanton was a pharmacist there. The Stanton physicians' offices were in a building they owned between Market and Postoffice streets, at 501 25th Street. They had been previously located at 407 25th Street, in the Lane Hotel, which was owned by the Mosleys and

Drs. Bob and Rufus Stanton. After they split up, the Drs. Mosley went to 2523 Market.

After the older Stantons retired, Billy Stanton opened office next door to his home.

The Stantons offered details about businessman Gus Allen. He started at 27th and Church streets, selling fish sandwiches, later in a restaurant. He also later had a cafe and a hotel, with a bit of backroom entertainment for the military and merchant seamen, and with Rudolph Wiley, operated the Manhattan Club.

Allen was also involved in politics, supporting such candidates as McHaffey and Biaggne, endorsing Cartwright for mayor.

During the 1940s, Allen, Wiley and Ned Rose moved their business to the beach.

Employment and Business: After World War II

Roy Lester Collins Jr.

ROY LESTER COLLINS, JR. was born on December 7, 1926 to Marguerite Douglas Collins and Roy Lester Collins, Sr. at 1111-12th Street in Galveston, Texas. Dr. Reid Robinson delivered him in his parents' home, which was the traditional way in those days. (The same doctor delivered me on October 26, 1929, in my parents' home.) Attending his birth was his paternal aunt, Carrie Collins Jones. He was a breech birth, so the doctor used forceps to help the birth along, as was the custom then. For that reason, his head was slightly misshapen for life, giving him that distinction. Other than that, he was physically perfect.

Since no other children were born to this couple, or even to the siblings of his parents, his adopted cousins were raised with him like brothers. His early best friends remained closest to him throughout his life, including his mother's godchild, Joseph Banks.

His parents were of the Roman Catholic faith, and so his early school training was also Catholic. He attended Holy Rosary Elementary School until the fifth grade. His first public school teacher was Mrs. Viola Scull Fedford, in the Low Fifth Grade at East District School, located at 10th Street and Broadway. He later told me that my mother was one of his favorite teachers, and he never forgot her kitemaking and kiteflying contests, held every Spring. One of his first prizes, for his own achievements, was a kite he made while in her classroom.

Roy's early schooling included going to Mr. Sanders' clerical school for typing and shorthand. He was awarded a certificate, although not much was retained, since he (as I) was so young, and we were just left to our own resources to practice our newly learned skills. We sort of forgot every thing we were taught.

Royboy, as he was called by early friends and family, attended and graduated from Central High School in the Class of 1943 Since his father was a lifetime United States Postal employee, and his mother was an accomplished seamstress, he lived a comfortable, but not affluent lifestyle. His friends were primarily from the East End of Galveston, but he knew practically everyone in town, since his father had acquainted him with his own route, and Roy later substituted for every postman. Being an only child, he was hungry for acquaintances and friends, so he learned more about family connections and had practically memorized everyone's address.

Roy attended Prairie View College the first fall semester after his graduation from high school. Tiring of the school's restrictions, and the military requirements (all boys had to take ROTC training), he went home for the Christmas holidays and did not return. His parents said not a word to him about the matter until the day that he would have returned to school. That morning, he heard his father call "RoyBoy!!" as he was jostled unceremoniously out of bed, and told to get dressed. As he tried to get fully conscious, his father instructed him to go down to the waterfront, and report to the foremen of the longshoremen, who had already been told that he would have another worker that day.

After experiencing the hard labor of the working world all of that semester, and the summer, my husband later told me that he was <u>the very first one in line</u> for registration at Tillotson College in Austin the following Fall. Having learned a valuable lesson that many teenagers need today, Roy Jr. then pursued a course of his choosing - "Pre Med" as it was called, then. He majored in Chemistry, having been trained in high school by the best - Mr. Hall Dansby, and minored in Biology.

Roy Collins, Jr. graduated from Tillotson College in Austin in 1948, and returned to Galveston, where he did substitute teaching in the public schools for a time, trying to earn enough money to go to medical school. He had not been able to apply for a scholarship, since the avenues that are available now were not available then. There was no admission to our local medical school for African Americans in 1948. There was a very lengthy list of applicants for Meharry Medical School, the only undergraduate venue for our race at that time.

At this time, the U.S. Armed Forces were still drafting men who were not in school at the time, or had other reasons for deferment. Soon Roy found himself drafted into the Army, during the time of the Korean conflict. This was a bit ironical, since his distaste for Prairie View's ROTC life was what caused him to leave Prairie View. What the military life did not do for him then, it did for him the second time around, when he had matured some more. Roy Collins became a Staff Sergeant in a short time, and commanded a sizeable group of men, eventually.

During this time, he and I became engaged, while he was stationed at Fort Leonard Wood in Missouri. It was convenient for him to visit his mother's sister, his Aunt Doodie (Hortense), who lived in Chicago. I happened to be attending graduate school in Northwestern University, in a suburb of Chicago, and visited my uncle and aunt in Chicago on weekends. So we were both near Chicago when we discovered that we were feeling serious about each other, although we were from the same city. He looked so mature and handsome in his uniform, and I suppose I looked a bit more mature in this setting, also.

On a return to his home for a furlough, we saw each other, and he asked me to marry him. When I agreed, he wanted me to marry him before he was to be shipped overseas. This was my first knowledge of his going over there to Europe. In 1951, the troops did not fly over. They went by ship - a very long and arduous journey - which is why I had such a hard time convincing him later to take a cruise with me. In 1951, just as in 1945, I was truthfully afraid of both the trip and the step in life. So I agreed that we would marry, all right - after he returned and had done his time in the service.

Roy returned to the United States in August of 1952, and we started planning our wedding. I was teaching in Bay City at the time, directing the high school band, so had no time to take care of wedding preparations. My mother and Roy did all of the details, including addressing the invitations (which was a blessing since his handwriting was better than mine, also).

We were married in the Holy Rosary priest's residence (rectory), since the Catholic rules at that time did not allow persons of other denominations to wed Catholics in their church. But, to be acceptable with his church, Roy could not marry in MY church, either. I also had to take instructions in his faith, and promise that our children would be raised and christened Catholic. Roy's own attitude was much more liberal, and he assured me that those procedures were just to appease the present situation, then.

So, we were married on December 26, 1952, at high noon, as I had requested. After the wedding, witnessed by our closest Catholic friends and kin - his friend Joe Banks, his cousin Richard Jones, my mother's dear friend Alecia Urquhart (I later realized was also Roy's cousin), and her niece, my friend Georgia Pumphrey Cashin, but also my sister, who was/is Methodist, as I am, Florence Fedford Henderson., we went to my home for our reception. This was bittersweet, because my father had just died two years before, and I missed his being there so much. My mother had to do it all by herself.

After our honeymoon in San Antonio, we settled down in his parents' home. Roy began working at the Post office as a substitute carrier and clerk, which was quite different from the school system substitute teacher. As a postal substitute, he could work every day, with longer hours than the regular carrier or clerk. So he made decent wages. At the end of the school year, I went back to Northwestern University to do my last summer's work, and received my Master of Music degree. I also made the decision to leave my employ in Bay City, to avoid going back and forth on the road so much. This was a major decision for our marriage.

Our first child, June Viola, was born on September 28, 1954. Since I was not able to get a job in the Galveston school system at that time, it meant tight times for us. I started giving private piano lessons, and did some substitute teaching. Our second child, Roy L. Collins III, was born on the same day as our fourth anniversary - December 26, 1956.

My husband, Roy, started having difficulty with his health on the long routes of the mail carrier, and had to leave the postal service. He worked for a time as a waiter, in the employ of the Public Health hospital of Galveston, and as a census taker, then finally as an interviewer with the Texas Employment Commission. This was his first job which took advantage of his college training. The position required either former experience in that field or a college degree. Meanwhile, Roy was a member of several organizations active in the community. Since his college days, he had been a member of the Alpha Phi Alpha fraternity, serving in several leading capacities. He affiliated with the local chapter, here in Galveston- Gamma Pi Lambda. Associated with his church, Holy Rosary, was the organization called the Knights of Peter Claver. He was a member of it all of his adult life. This organization was patterned after its counterpart, the Knights of Columbus, which had not admitted persons of color.

Roy often talked about everything in our society being based on "timing". Several of us were on the "cutting edge" of many things which changed in our community. As he was promoted on the job, and his acumen was observed by his superiors in the local and state offices, he was invited to break down several barriers, some of which were not revealed publicly when it was not expedient to do so. He was selected to be the first of his race to become a member of the Knights of Columbus.

When the vote was taken, by the old "blackball" method, which allowed just one person to privately drop in a black ball into the ballot box to stop admittance, he received one black ball. Although it was later ascertained who dropped the ball, and why, he refused to try it again. He was assured that the vote would have a unanimous affirmative result, but he declined the invitation, understandably. At this same time, Sacred Heart Church decided to allow the persons of color in this parish to become full fledged members. Although one could attend all of the masses and services there, persons of color had to sit and worship in the rear only. Their names were not on the roll of the parish members. Roy also refused this offer, knowing this could have been done long ago, and kept his membership at Holy Rosary. Others did take advantage of this opportunity because of its proximity for their families.

Roy stood alone on more than one social issue, not feeling comfortable with the "status quo". He was innovative, and saw advantages in future plans that few could see. Like many of his day who became noteworthy, nationally, he had a strong vision. Being human, however, took its toll on his actions. He often told me of conversations he had with co-workers who seemed surprised that he had lofty goals for his children and family. He was sometimes discouraged by the very people who should have been supporting his position on issues. This is not news to many who may be reading this fact, but changes were occurring so quickly socially, until it was easy to question the validity of one's purposeful actions.

After I had been hired in this area as a band director, working in Hitchcock for seven and a half years, I became pregnant with our third child. Before she was born, I was asked to come to Galveston to teach music in one of the elementary schools. I was not anxious to leave the band programs that I had brought to top status there in Hitchcock, but integration was changing the face of what I would do there anyway. Agonizing over this decision, which Roy refused to influence directly, he encouraged me indirectly to take advantage of this career change, and come home to work while I had the chance. Because of family demands, I did decide to take the position here, which impacted all of our lives in the family.

Our third child, Cheryl Lynette Marguerite, was born on January 21, 1966. We had moved from our former home to our present location. Cheryl came into a more settled, but busy lifestyle. Roy had more time for his children, and thoroughly enjoyed becoming a "papa" again at his age (39). He worked his way up to Claims Manager, and was just retired from being State Adjudicator for the Commission when he passed away on June 26, 1984. He was celebrating over twenty-five years with the Texas Employment Commission.

A biography about Roy Lester Collins, Jr. would not be complete without talking about his sense of humor, which was his trademark. More than anything else about his life, his friends and close co-workers would remark, he was missed for this constant sense of humor. He knew jokes of all categories and delighted in teasing me by threatening to tell something off-color when our children were present. Since this was an assured way to get me to react, he would start singing something risque', and stop just

Employment and Business: After World War II

before the offensive term was used, when I would yell out, warning him—"ROY!" He would fall out laughing and go on with something "clean" and unobtrusive. He was such a great tease until few knew just how devout he really was, and how much he believed in a merciful God. His genius in organizing or managing anything often went unnoticed because of the way he kidded around, and kept people in a light mood. Roy was marvelous as a crowd pleaser and had scores of friends. But the private side of his personality was seldom seen.

His last portrait was taken in the uniform of Commander of the American Legion, Gus Allen Post 614. He designed many things, including

the present post on 53rd Street, made signs for all sorts of fund raisers and activities. Roy was a person who learned to do many things without official training, picking up ideas from friends and acquaintances. He was an avid gardener who loved plants and could make almost anything grow, even in the smallest space. He could fix anything that was broken, from plumbing to electricity, to furniture, but drew the line at trying to fix anything on a car. He should have studied architecture, since he was so fond of designing buildings. He actually drew up the plans for this house, when I noticed something else he was doing, and just commented, "If you can do that, why don't you design a house for us?" The last plans he made were for the den, which I added to the home after his death.

He always wanted his own business, and inspired our children to be entrepreneurs, if it were at all possible. The number of people whom he helped to get whatever was their rightful compensation became legend. I still have some gifts in the home that he received from those who were so grateful that they received what was unknown to them. He was an expert at concensus building, feeling what was most important to most people.

His happiest days were with his buddies in his hometown. One of the main reasons I had to write this book about Galveston and its people was the Passionate Love that this man, my husband, had for his hometown. He absolutely, unashamedly loved Galveston. He knew all about its weaknesses and what caused them, was a top analyst of many conditions. A lot of what he told me over two decades ago is just coming to pass now, or is happening all over again, just as he said it would.

I really miss you, Roy, but I know that you are watching over all of us and glorying with me in the maturing of our children, and the advances of our grandchildren. God be with you. I know you are with God.

Employment and Business: After World War II

Mr. Joseph Arnold Banks

Joe and I go "way back". He remembers me as a little girl, and I remember him as a little boy. Our families were close.

Among many things about Galveston that Joe recounts well is details about African Americans' work and their employment situation, including those things that happened before his time. Of the many accounts he heard from his grandfather, Mr. Shelton Banks, a staunch member of Reedy Chapel, Joe remembers almost every word.

Shelton Banks Sr. came to Galveston from Sealy, Texas, in 1888 at 12 years of age. He lived in the servants' quarters at 1703 Broadway, behind the Adriennes' home. (The Adriennes had four sons, who later entered the insurance business.) He also later worked for over 50 years in the Adrienne building, a historic building now, between Strand and Mechanic streets on 22nd Street, next to the old First National Bank of Galveston, the oldest national bank in Texas.

When Joe asked him how far he went in school, Mr. Shelton Banks replied, "I went to the fourth grade, and my teacher was Mr. Ralph Scull, at the old East District School, at 10th and Broadway. Mr. Scull was an amazing person. In addition to being an early educator, he later was a preacher. He preached at a church on Strand. And when he preached down there, he also brought education to the Blacks down there that hadn't gone to school."

Turning to the post-World War II years, Joe also spoke about my father and his work:

"Mr. Fedford was a gentle man. Everywhere you met him, you felt his presence. He was tall, gaunt, very articulate, but quiet, almost shy. But the thing that impressed you most about him was his gentleness. As large as his hands were, you felt as if he touched you, you would hardly feel it. That's my impression of him. ... Izola's father, Mr. Fedford, pursued the trade of our Saviour. He was a carpenter and a preacher. The last sermon he preached at Reedy Chapel Church, this was his subject: "Foxes have holes, birds have nests, but the Son of Man has not a place to lay His head."

This was Daddy's last sermon; he was standing in for the pastor, who was out of town. I didn't get to hear it; I was in school at Northwestern University. His death afterward was sudden, from a fall during repair work on a two-story house.

Joe turned then to other African Americans' work. "Let me give you a picture of the merchant seamen who came here. They were usually working their way through. ... [but] these men were so polished, until they were welcomed into a church home. Black or white ones, they conducted themselves so well, they were welcomed. Most people want to picture these men staggering out of some bar drunk and on drugs or something. But this wasn't the case then."

I agreed. Merchant seamen I had known were Arthur Victor, Rufus Woodard and a well-mannered friend of Woodard's I met in New York.

Joe went on, "During the war, a lot of these women married these men. They were very affluent. Not only that, these men said, 'As soon as I get a chance, I'm going to get an education. I'm going to Fisk or Hampton. I'm not going to sea all the time.' The girls liked the fact that these men were gentlemen. They had a vision of a successful future.

"These ships that these merchant seamen sailed on were named after Indians. The line was the Clyde Mallory Line. The ships were named

El Jonquin, Seminole, and Iroquois. They would go to Miami and back. I think it [the port] was on 25th and Pier, near the railroad station.

I used to ride [with] Papa along Broadway, and where there would be a service station, or convenience store, I would ask him what was here or what was there [in his grandfather's day]. One day, we passed 1302 Postoffice -- that big white house -- and when we passed by there, a lady named Rimershaufer still lived there. She was the daughter of the owner of the Texas Star Flour Mill, which was on 20th and Water [Avenue A, now called Harbor View Drive]. It was a tall, 10- or 11-story corrugated tin building, and many Black men worked there. Mattie's husband worked there. She sent me down there with a message for him, and he was covered with that flour. They would sack that flour.

And Papa said, when we passed that house, 'This is the Rhymershaufer home.' I said, 'Well, who was he?' He said, ' He operated the Texas Star Flour Mill.' I said -- this is all in the '40s -- 'Well, why didn't we eat any of that flour? He said, 'It was milled here in Galveston, and sent to New York and the East Coast to feed people on the East Coast.' "

I recalled how my husband had once noted that refrigeration had caused our inexpensive seafood to go up in price, because most of it was then shipped away to markets where it brought higher prices.

Going on, Joe related, "On 14th and Water, there used to be a pile of sulfur. At that time, Galveston was the leading sulfur port in the world. And when you think of it, most of it was used as medicine. Because they hadn't discovered penicillin, and Aureomycin, and all those drugs. And the sulfur was in a lot of those drugs. ..."

He also spoke of how Lykes Bros. and all the shipping groups just left Galveston. They used to occupy a whole floor in the banks. That was the lifeblood of Galveston, especially for Black men.

"Just meant a good way for earning a living was taken away from them."

JACK JOHNSON

Jack Johnson was born in Galveston on March 31, 1878, thirteen years after the end of the Civil War. As a young man, he worked on the Galveston docks as a stevedore.

He began his fighting career in Galveston and went on to win the heavyweight championship of the world in prize fighting in 1907 in Sydney, Australia. He held that championship for seven years.

Always a controversial figure, he has been the subject of numerous books, articles and stories, as well as a Broadway play and a Hollywood movie.

Johnson reveled in attention. A man of contradictions, Johnson was shrewd and talented outside the prize fighting ring: He played what was called the bass fiddle and was said to have been well read and an interesting conversationalist.

He died as the result of an automobile accident in July 1946 in North Carolina and is buried in Chicago.

LEROY C. "BUSTER" LANDRUM

Leroy C. "Buster" Landrum was born in Galveston on April 28, 1909. He attended Central High School and played on its first championship football team. He graduated from Central in 1927.

Employment and Business: After World War II

Landrum made his way to New York City and began earning his living as a boxer and sparring partner for fighters such as Tiger Flowers, Jack Dempsey and Max Baer. He also became a friend of Galveston's Jack Johnson.

Returning to Galveston in 1935, Landrum joined the police force, and rose from patrolman to detective. Landrum received many awards in recognition of his outstanding work. In 1970, he was named Outstanding Officer by the Fifty Club; in 1973, he received the Distinguished Service Award for his years of dedicated service to the citizens of Galveston and the city's police department. He retired in 1974.

GEORGE PRADER

George Prader gained prominence with his radio show, "The Harlem Express," broadcast on Galveston's KGBC radio station. He conducted this show for more than 12 years, from the late 1940s and throughout the 1950s.

Totally paralyzed by an automobile accident in 1930, Prader lived at the Little Shamrock Motel, owned by T.D. Armstrong. As Mr. Armstrong became acquainted with Prader, he began to urge him to "do something with his life" despite his handicap. Prader decided to become a broadcaster, and started with radio station KGBC as a disc jockey, in an apartment near 31st Street. Armstrong then built a studio for Prader in his own office, with a large plate-glass window that looked out from the drugstore, where Prader launched his show with the support of Armstrong and the cooperation of KGBC personnel. He became a local celebrity and something of an island institution. His cool, quiet voice seemed to send a warm smile across the airwaves, and he was a favorite of radio listeners of all ages. Prader became a community fixture who could be seen easily from the street, broadcasting from his bed, in the large window. The story of a paralyzed broadcaster conducting daily radio shows while lying on his back in his studio gained national attention, with articles and photographs of Prader appearing in *Jet* magazine.

George Prader died Dec. 30, 1961, and can be remembered as an inspiration for us all.

ALBERTINE HALL YEAGER

Albertine Hall Yeager was born in Palestine, Texas, in 1897. She and her husband Charlie began to take children into their Galveston home during World War II while mothers worked in the war industries. This soon progressed into taking in orphaned and abandoned children. Over the years, "Mama" Yeager provided a home to nearly 1,000 children in the Galveston community. Most of the time, the Yeagers funded the care of these children themselves. In the 1960s, the Galveston community recognized the importance of maintaining this refuge for children and began to contribute to the ever-increasing bills of the Yeager Children's Home.

Mama Yeager's death in 1969 at the age of 72 prompted the Texas Senate to recognize her selfless service to her community. The resolution passed by the Senate reads in part:

Whereas this warm and gracious lady operated the Yeager Children's Home for the last 30 years; she cared for, loved and furnished a home environment for children who were in need;

Employment and Business: After World War II

And, whereas, Mrs. Yeager gave hundreds of children the only home they ever knew and turned the despair of these little ones into hope;

And, whereas, this distinguished lady served her community with great love and devotion and was an inspiring example to the children that she loved and assisted and to all those who met her ...

Now therefore let it be resolved by the Senate of the 62nd Legislature, that this resolution stand in memory of Mrs. Albertine Hall Yeager, outstanding citizen and humanitarian. ...

RAY SHEPPARD

Ray "Tuck" Sheppard, born in Waco, was one of the most gifted baseball players in the country during the first part of the 20th century. He starred with the Negro National Baseball League for 20 years, earning a .304 lifetime batting average. Although baseball teams were segregated in the United States, blacks and whites did play each other outside the country, and Sheppard played against such Major League greats as Babe Ruth and Lou Gehrig. And Sheppard recalled getting only one hit off baseball great Satchel Paige in the 10 years that Sheppard batted against him.

Sheppard came to Galveston in 1931 and became well-known in the community because of the outstanding football and baseball teams that he coached at Central High School. He retired from coaching and teaching in 1959, but returned to work in 1963 when Central was in need of a baseball coach. Sheppard's second retirement from the school district in 1969 did not end his influence on the young people of Galveston. He continued to work as a child care worker at the Youth Service Center.

KELTON SAMS

As African American people were asserting their constitutional rights throughout the South in the early 1960s, Kelton Sams led a group of Central High School students in sit-down demonstrations against segregation of various downtown Galveston stores and restaurants. African Americans could buy merchandise and food from these establishments, but were not allowed to sit down at the lunch counters to order and eat. Sams' group of students walked in carrying copies of the United States Constitution and sat down at lunch counters to wait for service. In most instances, the store managers either closed the counters or removed the stools so no one could sit down. The demonstrations remained peaceful, spreading as more people heard about what was happening downtown, and had the intended effect of bringing inequalities to light. City leaders worked with the African American community and eventually desegregated lunch counters and other Galveston institutions.

THOMAS DEBOY ARMSTRONG

(Related by daughter Thelma Armstrong Hannah, supported by Hannah's mother and Armstrong's widow, Mrs. Marguerite Armstrong)

Thomas Deboy Armstrong was born in Meeker, La., on Nov. 11, 1907. His parents were Thomas Henry Armstrong, a longshoreman, and Mary Williams Armstrong. T. D. Armstrong was their only boy, and he had seven sisters; most of them became teachers.

He moved to Port Arthur with his family at about age 6. He graduated from Lincoln High School there, and attended Tuskegee Institute in Alabama. He taught cabinet making at Prairie View after leaving Tuskegee, and received his bachelor's degree in political science

Employment and Business: After World War II

from Prairie View in 1929. He then taught at Prairie View briefly, going on to teach government and political science at Lincoln High for several years until his marriage to Marguerite Goodwin in 1934. (She was born in Beaumont on Sept. 1, 1914, graduated from Charlton Pollard High School, and also attended Prairie View.) The Armstrongs lived in Port Arthur until 1938, when they moved to Galveston.

In Galveston, T.D. Armstrong worked with Bethel J. Strode in the Strode Funeral Home. While working at Strode's, Armstrong started the BA&P Realty Company with Frank Bell of La Marque, and T.W. Patrick in 1944. Frank Bell Jr. and Vera Bell Gary are the children surviving Mr. Bell. Patrick's wife was Mary Patrick, for whom the African American branch of the YWCA was named.

Armstrong worked at Strode's until 1946, when he opened his first retail business, a drugstore, which also became a meeting place for African American teenagers. In my day, it was the first time a decent, clean place was available for youth to enjoy; I can remember the joy I had in finally being allowed to sit at a counter, on a stool just like the kids we saw in the movies. And we really enjoyed the booths, with the selection cards that could operate the jukebox, which had all the popular tunes, from our booths. Armstrong's Drugstore was not only the talk of the town, it was a real morale booster for us as a people.

Site of Armstrong's drugstore

Armstrong also built a beautiful establishment on West Beach, down on the sand, named Palm Gardens Beach Pavilion in the late '50s. Unfortunately, Mother Nature was not kind to these efforts, because a hurricane destroyed it not long afterward. (African Americans were left with the Downbeat, an older-looking club, down on the West Beach sands.) Armstrong also owned Kenyon Auto Supply, next to the drugstore. The Shamrock Motel was built in 1952, and the Shamrock Coffee Shop and Lounge came next in 1956.

In 1957, Armstrong bought Strode Funeral Home from Mrs. Celestine Strode Cook. (Mr. Pendergraff had been manager of Strode Funeral Home when Strode mysteriously disappeared in 1948, piloting an airplane carrying his mother and Rev. Hightower, pastor of Wesley Tabernacle United Methodist Church, toward New Orleans on New Year's

Day. The airplane never made it, and was believed lost somewhere in the swamplands of Louisiana.) The funeral home closed in 1980.

Armstrong had a very important political career for all of Galveston and especially for African-Americans. He first ran for the Galveston school board in 1944. Failing in this difficult at-large effort, he ran for city finance commissioner in 1957, when Galveston had the city commission form of government. He was appointed to work with the first Citizens' Charter Committee, as well as the Galveston school district integration committee. He then ran for the City Council in 1961, after the council form of government began in Galveston, and won by a miraculous margin of three votes. This made him the first African American elected to a civic position since the Reconstruction-era election of Wright Cuney. He served for one two-year term.

Armstrong belonged to Avenue L Baptist Church when he first moved to Galveston, later joining Wesley Tabernacle Methodist Church, where his wife was a member. At Wesley, his love was the Men's Bible Class, which he taught for several years, and he co-chaired the Education Committee with Mrs. Martha Chase.

Armstrong was a member of many civic organizations, including the Galveston Board of Realtors, and the Chamber of Commerce after its integration. He was also a delegate to the Democratic National Convention in 1968. He was a member of the board of directors of Wiley College sometime in the latter '50s or early '60s, served on the board of directors at Texas Southern University, and was the first African American elected chairman of County Memorial Hospital Board, a board he served on until his death. The Boy Scouts honored him posthumously with its Silver Beaver Award.

Other businesses that this unusual entrepreneur owned were a washateria at 40th Street and Avenue H, in the latter '50s to early 60s; and

The Gold Bond Insurance Company in 1967. Gold Bond began as part of Strode Funeral Home but became part of the Tyler Life Insurance Co. of Texas. It merged in 1987 with Hannah Life Insurance Co. in Houston.

Thomas D. Armstrong Sr. passed away on December 28, 1972.

The Armstrongs had two children, Thelma D., born in 1935, and Thomas II, born in 1950. After their father's death, the two ran the insurance business in East Texas and on the Gulf Coast, managing 18 different agencies.

Thelma D. Armstrong earned a bachelor of arts degree in business administration from Howard University in 1956 and joined Delta Sigma Theta Sorority in 1957, the same year that her daughter, Marguerite "Keta" G. Hannah, was born on Oct. 5.

Hannah is a 1975 graduate of O'Connell High School in Galveston, and 1979 graduate of Howard University, where she majored in public relations with a minor in journalism. Hannah has worked in advertising and broadcast media, and is a professional actress working in theaters across the country as well as television. She appeared in a one-woman show on singer Billie Holliday, and in the opening show for the Olympic Committee in Atlanta at its last Olympics.

Thomas D. Armstrong II graduated in 1973 from Wilmington College in Ohio with a major in political science. In addition to insurance management, Tommy has worked in radio as well as in sales. He lives in Houston and has two children, Tamisha Dyan Armstrong, a graduate of Dillard University, and Thomas D. Armstrong III.

Employment and Business: After World War II

MRS. BERNICE HIGHTOWER

Born March 10, 1918, in Marlin, Texas, to Lela Phillips and William Thompson, Bernice Hightower attended Marlin public schools and graduated in 1938.

She received her bachelor of arts degree from Tillotson College in 1942, and taught in Rosenberg. She married Ernest Hightower in 1944 and then moved to Galveston. Her nephew, Theodore Polk, lived with them during his high school years.

Mrs. Hightower did further study at Texas Southern University, receiving her master of music education degree in 1953. In the summer of 1956, she also studied at Oberlin in Ohio.

After arriving in Galveston, Mrs. Hightower joined and played for West Point Baptist Church. She was a member for 12 years with Rev. Sargent as pastor, then joined her husband at Wesley Tabernacle Methodist Church with Rev. Holiday as pastor.

Mrs. Hightower taught at Booker T. Washington Elementary School in Galveston, then at Goliad Junior High School when it was opened for African American children in 1958. She was placed at Sam Houston Junior High when Goliad was designated as an elementary school, then moved to Lovenberg Junior High after integration; she retired there shortly before the school was demolished in 1980.

She has been a member of the Galveston chapter of Alpha Kappa Alpha Sorority since 1953, the local chapter of Phi Delta Kappa for eight years, the Galveston Bay Area Music Teachers, the Galveston Musical Club, the 1894 Grand Opera House Advisory Baord, the Galveston Historical Foundation, and the National Guild of Piano Teachers.

During her career in the Galveston public schools, she also gave private piano lessons. She credits her husband for being understanding as she devoted so much of her time to her private lessons. She was proud to watch three of her former piano students become music teachers as well: Mrs. Carol Jones Broussard, Sharon Barron and Courtney Dawn Deyon.

CHAPTER SIXTEEN
TEXAS CITY EXPLOSION & MAINLAND GROWTH

By 1947, my junior year in college, the country was busy. Galveston County was working to restart improvement begun before the war. On the Mainland, the port created at Texas City, built to accommodate the large industrial ships that carried chemicals and crude oil to and from various destinations, was booming. The Texas City oil refineries were smoking away, and causing more employment on the Mainland than on the island of Galveston, for African Americans as well as whites.

Although visits by some ships, like the nuclear submarine The Savannah, to the Port of Galveston were significant, there just weren't enough events of this kind to keep the port very viable. Todd Shipyards kept up ship repair and restoration business at the Galveston port, but most shipping was now going to Texas City. Chemicals made in the Texas City plants were in demand. Oil processing was a part of the national scene. Texas City was growing.

Then, disaster struck. As far away as Galveston, miles across the bay, a shudder of the earth was felt as the ship Grandcamp exploded, rocking the Texas City waterfront with first one blast, then another aboard the ships in dock at the time.

The port of Texas City was unprepared for the loss of lives, the fires that went out of control, the panic and pandemonium that ensued. Agencies like the Red Cross went right to work before the Fire Department was through, and all sorts of help came across the causeway from Galveston, then from as far away as Houston. My mother reported seeing wagons, open trucks coming down Broadway with bodies hanging from them, all rushing to the hospital here for immediate treatment. University of Texas Medical Branch was primarily John Sealy Hospital in those days, and they could hardly provide all the emergency care needed.

Up in Prairie View, we received delayed news reports over the radio, and I was full of fear for the safety of my family at home. As soon as I talked to my mother, I felt better, but was horrified at the reports coming from what was a sleepy little comfort zone for most of us. It was like the war had come to us all of a sudden, for the eyewitness reports were much like the wartime battle reports. It really did not seem real.

Mother also reported that people gave blood freely and pitched in, doing whatever they could, without asking the price of what they might be facing. Nurses went on duty at all hours; workers fought the flames, and replaced homes or buildings as soon as possible after that.

But federal funding came through eventually. Industries received compensation for lost lives, facilities and supplies. La Marque as well as Texas City began phenomenal growth.

An area in LaMarque called South Acre Manor sprouted up, with quality homes offered to African American working people at a fraction of the cost of property in Galveston. Soon everyone was talking about the fact that a family could buy a house and land for less than you could buy a lot in Galveston. Developers on the island were not eager to sell to our folk, and so there was really no room for expansion for the working-class African American. Men and women found employment in the Texas City-La Marque area, and then found homes to live and raise their families in, of which they could be proud.

Shopping centers seemed to pop out of the ground -- grassy fields one day, a thriving shopping area the next. So shoppers no longer made the trek to the island for their necessities.

Of course, some things demanded coming to the island, such as county business; the courthouse was and is still in Galveston. But the handwriting was on the wall. African Americans needed the new economy of the mainland more.

This was the economic flight from Galveston. Effects were felt in the schools as well. Extracurricular activities saw a decrease in enrollment and quality. The La Marque schools, closer to the South Acre Manor area and adjoining residential developments for African Americans, saw more enrollment. Although the racial makeup varied for several reasons, Texas City remained more white than black, percentage-wise; La Marque became more black than white.

Galveston's African-Americans have been an invisible people, resettling near and far, impacting other countries and outer space. For further study of such Galveston figures -- such as Eldrewey Stearns, an African American man just two years younger than I who devoted so much time to integrating Galveston -- I again recommend Winegarten's and Turner's books.

Talk about the growth of the Mainland must include Hitchcock, also in Galveston County. My dear friend, Vander Lee Caldwell Haynes, is a member of the Phelps family, which is probably the city's oldest African American family. In the days when everybody came to Galveston for everything except a place to sleep, Hitchcock African Americans shared in all of the history previously mentioned, even some schooling.

The first all-grades school to include high school grades for African Americans was named for one of the area's most noteworthy African American teachers, Mrs. Lorraine Crosby.

I taught the seventh grade there and organized the new band, which met when the school day was over. Having started the band in Bay City and instructed it for over five years, and done substitute teaching in Galveston for five years after marrying, teaching was old hat by this time. I also had new reasons for working again, my first two children.

Hitchcock was good for me, and good to me. The people were neither rural nor urban. The African American community was used to a slower pace, a laid-back lifestyle, but they weren't "country." The people of Hitchcock knew what life was like in the big city, and generally preferred the pace of their own town. Without a resident industry, the employment picture for Hitchcock was limited by how far residents were willing to travel, unless they worked for the city, the bank, other small businesses or the schools. Some had their own businesses, and some had church positions. But most worked out of town, and came back to the haven of their quiet town.

In Hitchcock, I taught many in Clarence and Katherine Price's family. Those I didn't teach saw me so much, they probably thought I taught them too.

Ida B. Price was the first drum major of my band. Carolyn, her sister, was a majorette. Her closest sister in age was Shirley. The oldest daughter, Loretta, taught at Ball High for a long time, and retired to do her own beautician business justice, with her sister, Reva Nell. Reva Nell and then Eunice were in my band class. There was Earnest, who played a great baritone horn in my band. There was Bertha, who was in my seventh-grade class when I first taught in Hitchcock, and came with Shirley to visit me most. There was -- well, there were 17 living Price siblings. Four had not survived after birth.

Mrs. Price has brought so many more children into her home to raise as her own, both as foster children and adopted children, that I have lost count. She just loved children. And she still looked "like a fox," better than her children, I often teased them. Her husband Clarence passed away after over 50 years of marriage. He taught them much and won't be forgotten. All the Prices are attractive, intelligent and useful in one capacity or another.

Shirley has always been my bosom buddy. We go way back. I first knew her as a little girl wearing plaits in her hair, who studied my face very seriously to see if I was for real or for show. Then when she had decided, she smiled at me. She smiles at me often now. We understand each other. She has been more of an inspiration to me than even she realizes. She has also been an inspiration to literally hundreds, maybe thousands of people. Shirley Price was born without arms, and is a dwarf in size. It never stopped her from doing anything she really wanted to do. Her high school graduation in Hitchcock was followed by two college degrees from Texas Southern University. After a career at National Aeronautics and Space Administration in an administrative counseling position, she completed her requirements for her doctorate at Texas Southern University. Amid cheers from a huge auditorium filled with well-wishers that lasted for some 15 minutes or so, she walked proudly to receive her hood, and became Dr. Shirley Catherine Price. She now is a full-time counselor, after many illnesses, surgeries and accidents, and she has no intention of slowing down.

Island of Color

Hitchcock has many other wonderful African American families. I can't name them all. There were the McIntoshs -- Clarice was one of the brightest motivators in Hitchcock, who worked as a secretary in La Marque for a long time. Mrs. Melinda Price, who just passed away at the age of 112, was one of my favorite people; she didn't have children of her own, but in addition to her nieces and nephews, she raised so many. There were the Wrights, whose older girls I taught in Bay City in the band, and the younger ones in the Hitchcock band; the middle ones taught with me in Hitchcock. And I will just add one more, the Huffs.

Valencia and Edward Huff had four children. Ed Huff was a first cousin to my cousin, Fleming Smizer Huff. They were kin through fathers, and I was kin to Fleming Huff through his mother. So I am not actually kin to these Huffs, but we might as well be.

I didn't get to know Valencia Huff well until she brought me her daughter, also named Valencia, to take private piano lessons in Galveston. After I had begun to teach her daughter successfully, she brought other Hitchcock students to study with me. But coming over with a station wagon full of children every Saturday got to be too difficult for Mrs. Huff, so I went over to her house in Hitchcock and taught them on her piano.

Piano Class of Izola Collins 1957

So I already knew the Huffs when I started teaching in Hitchcock. I taught all but the oldest Huff child. Samuel and Jean were both outstanding band members. Jean sang in a winning octette in competition as well. But my prize student of all time was Valencia. In addition to learning to play the piano better than any student I have had since, she played several instruments in the band.

Island of Color

Mrs. Valencia Huff Arceneaux

Lorraine Crosby Band went all the way from a little beginning group of a few "tooters", to an award-winning Superior-rated band in University Interscholastic League competition. The Huffs had a lot to do with that. Sam played a mean baritone horn, Jean played great flute, and Valencia played clarinet, bass clarinet and oboe, as well as baritone horn for football games when Sam had to play football. They were such spirit-filled students, and urged others to do their best. Having an interested mother and grandmother, Mrs. Smallwood, had a lot to do with it. And talent will always triumph.

Although Lorraine Crosby was a small school, its students also sing the praises today of Mrs. Backstrom, Mrs. Haynes, Mrs. Rose Archie, Mr. P.C. Burns, our principal Mr. Stovall, Mr. Mitchell, Mrs. Margie Edwards, Mrs. Dora Betty Porter, Ms. Wright, Ms. Alma Ruth Henley, Mrs. Ima Fay Kay and all of the elementary teachers who taught on the sister campus with me. The super lady who wrote their school song for them is still playing for her church and doing well: Mrs. Ollie Jewell Williams. Ether Ricks taught English. Lonnie Watkins was a longtime football coach; Charles Garcia was also a great coach.

Wherever they go, the students of Lorraine Crosby will remember what we taught them, because it got them into any door.

Several members of that Crosby band have passed on to another life. I would like to honor their memories here: William Subjects, percussion; R.C. Turner, alto sax; Jean Huff, flute; Thurman Harrison, trumpet; Mrs. Vander Haynes' oldest son, George Haynes Jr. or "Tootie" as he was known to us; Vivian Moore, clarinet; and Joseph Moore. We were all so close. Teaching them during the day, when school was out, and whenever I could get them to rehearse for some occasion or other; going on trips, bringing them to their doors on the bus when we got back late from football games or contests – I got to know these guys and girls pretty well. Several were so young when they left this world. To them I dedicate this part of my book.

Some families, like the Harrises, left Hitchcock, but their instrumental prowess remained in the record books. William Harris played trombone, and his brother Eric Harris played clarinet in the Crosby Band. After they went back to Galveston and played football there, they went on to fame, eventually playing football for professional teams; William sports a Super Bowl ring today. They both have also taught in the universities of Colorado.

State champions in music I trained were Valencia Huff, on piano; Lynette Randolph, female solo voice; and John Michael Lewis, male solo voice.

To be able to say that these persons are successful in all sorts of professions is not exaggerating. They are doctors, lawyers, bank executives, psychologists, counselors, school librarians, nurses, visual artists, actors and actresses, beauticians, train engineers, nursing home supervisors, ministers of the gospel, judges, elected office holders, and, yes, teachers! You can't name them all; they went everywhere.

So Hitchcock is probably the town I knew best in Galveston County, representing Mainland growth and its effect on Galveston.

The bastions of segregation went down reluctantly, but steadily during my time there. We lost one grade at a time to Hitchcock High School, and it was painful to the outgoing students to graduate from another school not of their choosing. It was just as painful to those of us on the faculty, who saw our teaching go to someone else to complete, and we were afraid that their education would be shortchanged, just because of prejudice against them.

We spent as much time as we could, officially and unofficially, telling them that they would have to grow up fast. We warned them that the speech patterns would be different, and they needed to sit as close to the front as possible just to understand what their new teachers would say. The white teachers had a different kind of drawl, for the most part, and our kids in the first wave of integration came back complaining loudly that they just didn't even know what the teachers were saying. It was like a foreign language that they were not having translated.

African American teachers were concerned that frustrations would be taken out on our innocent children, and we had read, heard of many injustices perpetuated in other communities -- some reported and some never reported to the authorities or the press, out of fear of retaliation.

Our former students also reported to us that they were seldom given a chance to make up missed assignments if they were ill, and their grades were dropping systematically, as if to prove that they were not competent enough to be integrated at the high school level. We faculty members at Lorraine Crosby took personal issue with the complaints and were very angry inside, but we tried to show the students the need to cooperate, learn the new ways.

Integration was a very desirable goal, but it did seem very unfair that all the transportation problems, all the discipline problems, all the academic problems had to be borne by the students of color, and never the other way around. Eventually, some of us did teach at the other school, especially when they recognized that we were better teachers, frankly, and wanted our expertise for the white students. But building needs meant that they never had to come to us and our culture, and learn our ways, which was the main fault in the process of integration all over the South. They could have profited so much from our way of life, and their false pride just did not allow it. Our students never did regain some of the ground lost, the pride in excelling and belonging to quality groups, especially in extracurricular activities.

My award-winning Lorraine Crosby Band (Superior rated in University Interscholastic League in 1963, the top rating) had been one of only two bands so awarded that day in concert competition at Texas Southern University. But very few of its former members wanted to be in the Hitchcock High Band. Most did not receive any more instrumental instruction, just because they did not feel welcome and the procedures were so out of touch with the reality that they knew.

The band director who taught over there when I was asked to teach with him was relatively new to teaching band. We were friendly with each other, gave each other assistance, but could not reach past the prejudice that existed. As a teacher, I was treated with respect by most of the white students, but there were some instrumental students who showed both covert and overt prejudice. I will never forget the reaction of the white band director when I told him of some of the race-tinged comments and reactions. He would hang his head in shame for a moment, then, thinking of his own treatment by offended students from Crosby, say to me: "If you won't blame me for all this Ku Klux Klan stuff, then I won't blame you for the Black Panthers."

It was a good point, and I accepted it. My highest praise later came not only from him, but from the acting principal of Hitchcock High, who happened to also be the superintendent that 1965-66 school year.

I hadn't mentioned it, but I was expecting my youngest child when school started, due in January. The African American citizens really were upset when they learned that I was to be assistant band director to the white band director, newly assigned, because they knew I had more experience and more success, and should have the position because of seniority alone. They did not understand why I did not take up the fight, but I knew I was pregnant and that I would be in no condition to fight anything. I also knew the demands of training a larger and more involved band. Though I was not ever one to run from a challenge, I was older and wiser, and knew that care of my mother, now a stroke victim in my home in Galveston, would also demand my time and attention.

So I took the better way out. As assistant band director, I had two hours off at midday. I spent restful lunches on Mrs. Smallwood's porch, after leaving the Crosby School and before going to Hitchcock High for the afternoon. Then on to Northside Elementary to teach an all-white sixth-grade language arts class, where the students that had taken me as a surrogate mother offered a restful transition to going home to my many family responsibilities: a husband, two active children, my mother -- then to bed with the baby kicking inside me as soon as I got comfortable. As I grew larger and slower-moving, I also received the understanding from adults and students I needed. It was a win-win situation, even if I didn't enjoy the preparing for three schools and traveling everyday.

One day at Hitchcock High, the band director noted that the band room was always a wreck after the choir class had left it, a period before I came. He said the choir instructor would have to have surgery and would be out at least three more weeks. The substitutes had had absolutely no control over the unruly, mixed racial group, which seemed to act out all the frustrations both racial groups had. They would fight for almost no reason, I was told, and leave paper everywhere.

Having heard that I had had great control with my band members before coming to Hitchcock High and that I had taught vocal music, Mr. Mooney, the superintendent and acting principal, came in one day to talk to me in the band room. Observing all of the litter, he got down on one knee beside my chair and begged me to take over the choir class, which was held during my lunch period. "Just until the regular teacher can return," he assured me. I didn't want to do it, naturally. My time wasn't going to be monetarily compensated, I was pretty sure. But I also had enjoyed a long carefree lunch for a long time without being threatened with other work assignments, such as lunch duty, or even told to report to campus. And my time would later remain my own.

So I agreed on one condition: The first time any of those children threatened me in any way -- physically or emotionally -- I was outta there. I refused to put myself in any kind of risky situation that might harm my baby. Mr. Mooney agreed to have a distinct talk with the students about what could happen to them if I received any trouble, and the deal was sealed. I was to send any troublemakers or potential trouble makers to the office immediately.

When the day arrived, I made my way confidently but reluctantly to the band room for the choir class. I had never had an opportunity to teach a high school choral class and loved the idea. But as I neared the room five minutes after the class had arrived, remembering that in my pregnant state I was walking into a large high school class of reputedly wild students, I had doubts. I was totally unprepared for what happened next.

As I opened the door, there arose a loud cheer that went on for about a full three minutes or so. I was completely dumbfounded. The African American students had erupted with joy. And their enthusiasm was so contagious, the others were smiling and clapping, too, even though they didn't even know me. I didn't know what had been said by the superintendent or the students before I arrived, but it was obvious that the students were in complete agreement with this arrangement, even if it was to be temporary.

I knew that day I could never be received as enthusiastically by any other group. It was my finest moment with students.

They walked me to my desk, showed me where the roll was kept, offered to take the absentee slip to the office, run any needed errand. And I didn't even know what to ask of them, let alone need to lay down any school laws. I managed to regain enough composure to find out what they had been doing in class, to give them a challenging lesson. I assured them that they would be treated as kindly as I had, and that they would leave with a little more knowledge than they came in with each day if they continued to cooperate.

I ended by asking them to leave the band room so tidy that the band students would be ashamed of their own messes. The choir was all the more glad that I recognized that they had been blamed for some things they did not do, and I was sort of adopted by them that day. They picked up every scrap of paper; put dropped music folders away; straightened up the instruments, impressed that I knew where they all should go (the choir director had no earthly idea, I was told). They even shined some of them up.

The office staff sent me their personal thanks by note and word of mouth. Constant detentions and other disciplinary actions and communication with other teachers and parents had worn them out. The principal was grinning, and the band director was ecstatic, with generous praise and offers to do anything for me.

Such was our integration experience in Hitchcock. Some was dreadful, and some was very heartwarming to say the least. There may still be scars borne by those who were emotionally injured, but it could have been worse. Galveston ISD could have taken lessons from those of us who really tried in Hitchcock. But Galveston County should be complimented: Physical violence never occurred, and the emotional damage was minimized.

Where there was more excellence in the Black community than in the White community, they know it. Where there has been more spiritual maturity, we all know it. There are and always will be heroes of both races -- acknowledged but mostly unacknowledged. There certainly have been demons of both races, although African Americans have certainly been more victimized and borne more indignities. The Almighty knows who should get rewarded and who should get punished.

CHAPTER SEVENTEEN
CIVIL RIGHTS MOVEMENT

I received my first real dose of segregation not here at home, but in Illinois, on the other side of the Mason-Dixon Line.

To attend graduate school at Northwestern University in Evanston, a suburb of Chicago, I rode the train, the Texas Chief, from Galveston all the way to Chicago. When I left home, I had to ride in a coach car. We were not allowed to ride in the sleeper car, the Pullman accommodation in 1949. The train was relatively modern, but the cars were still unequal in comfort and accessibility.

I'd leave home early in the day, and by the time I was hungry for dinner, we would have arrived in Kansas or somewhere across the imaginary Mason-Dixon Line, and the Negro porters would invite me most courteously to come into the dining car. At the tender age of 19, I felt so proud to be on my own, and riding in such fine style, that the segregation didn't really bother me. It was the return trip that jolted me into reality.

Although it was a 24-hour trip, when I first left home I had been too young and too excited to care about the inconvenience of riding straight up at night in the coach car. But after spending time on the campus of Northwestern and elsewhere in the Chicago area, where I was treated with the proper respect I deserved, the ride home was humiliating.

I would start out for home in whatever seat I desired, because there was no reserved coach seating. But when we crossed that line to go South again, the train conductor, always a white man in those days, would come to me and any other Negro passenger and tell us to transfer up to the car that was next to the baggage car. It was the least comfortable because of its location and because of its furnishings.

Funny -- we all would dryly laugh, in private conversation -- about how our mode of travel differed according to the conveyance. If we rode on the bus, we had to sit in the back, next to the obnoxious fumes, and where it was bumpier. On the train, we had to ride in the front, where the same conditions prevailed. On a ship, the quarters were in the bottom, where the ship had more seasick motion, and there was less to see. In movie houses or places of gathering, we had to sit up top, where it was difficult to see or hear.

So, I rode home, fuming about the way I had to travel, and supposing I could do nothing about it -- except leave home. And I wasn't about to leave all I really loved.

Now, I was aware that as we left Chicago, I could start out riding in the car next to the baggage car. I could spare myself the humiliation of having to move when we crossed into the South, to a car often carrying poor, rural people who knew I was forced to sit there, and who rather enjoyed my plight. I didn't care to do that. Part of the allure of going up that way to school was preserving the illusion that things would be first-class for me all the way -- one of these days.

But that first trip was not yet my first dose of disillusionment. That came when I actually arrived on the Evanston campus, in the summer of 1949.

Naive child that I was, and my mother not knowing what I would face, I actually took a steamer trunk and a suitcase for the six weeks' stay of the summer session, thinking I needed all that clothing and supplies. After all, I had traveled that way to Prairie View every semester – at the town's one small store, you could find very few things that you needed, and most of us had had neither transportation nor the college's permission to leave town.

I had applied for housing when I applied for admission to Northwestern's graduate school. When they received my application and noticed that I was an African American, they replied that I could stay in their "I" House, the International House for all foreign students. I later learned that openings at the house were filled at least a year ahead of time.

Northwestern's letter had also stated that I could live in the community, in any of the available private homes -- that meant Negro-owned homes, of course. But I didn't know all of this meant I had to find one on my own. That is, until I arrived at the dean's office with my trunk and suitcases. There, I learned the evils of segregation firsthand.

So sweetly, this "kind" lady told me that I would have to call around town from a list that she gave me, to locate some resident willing to take me in at the last moment. In disbelief and real fear, I summoned the best that my mother and father had taught me, and from somewhere got the courage to call these strangers. It was a nightmare then, for I had no experience to deal with this.

My first big example of divine intervention was when I located someone who said, "Come right on, honey."

It was the home where my coworker from Bay City, who had convinced me that Northwestern was a good choice for my graduate education, was already living. We compared notes on our landlady, a lady who loved hats and made her own. She had been unaware of my plight, and was glad she could advise me this first trip. I seldom saw her that summer, for our academic and social schedules were different. But I felt a lot safer knowing she was around.

Even though this was an unfair situation, some things do work out for the best. The next summer, I stayed with another family, who just happened to be across the street from a young lady I had just met up there. We had the exact same birthday, we were both in the music graduate school, and we had plenty in common. We have had a lifelong friendship, as a result of this segregation situation.

It was my very last summer there, in 1953, when we students of color were finally allowed to share the dormitories with the other students. I started to ignore the whole thing, but my spirit of adventure won out over my pride. Besides, for the sake of those students who fought for the right, I knew we should take advantage of it. Also, I needed to be closer to the school of music, to put in many practice hours on the piano and the violin; staying off-campus would have caused me big transportation problems. So the last session I attended was the only one in which I had residence on the campus.

I did meet some wonderful people whom I hope to see again one day. But I also encountered a lot of indifference, from those who preferred to ignore me. I didn't have time for idle chit-chat anyway, since I was writing a concert band arrangement as my master's thesis, and practicing up to 10 hours every day for my final piano exam.

As my background for the civil rights movement, I recall those days. I also remember when the Prairie View Coeds were touring in the South and we would be told at some pitiful filling station, by the local joker who ran the pumps for the day, that we couldn't use the restrooms. I remember the very personal experiences with outhouses we young ladies had to use in the rural areas.

I recall also how the Bay City band was not invited to participate in any all-city activities until my band had more people bragging on them than the white high school band did. Then we were invited to perform in the annual Rice Festival parade, which was formerly an all-white community affair, and I was asked to do a couple of early radio shows about our music program. It was a boost to morale in the colored community.

Contrary to the suppositions made by the next generation, no one of color had been content with being segregated and humiliated. Slavery time was over, and while the feelings of our people were no longer going to be kept secret from those oppressing them, most of us simply did not see what could be done. All the power seemed to still be with the majority of the population of these United States. No military force was in the power of the underrepresented and uninformed. No real decision-making power was with us, because only token numbers of our people were in any decision-making body.

To be sure, various places were bubbling with the discontent of the downtrodden minorities. When no justice was evident in civil situations, some individuals and some small groups of protesters found a voice. Newspapers written by our own race recorded indignities and incidents ignored by the white press.

And well-meaning persons of the white race were beginning to see the wisdom of giving some reason to the men and women of color to feel proud of themselves. They recognized the potential for danger from trained military men, even though they retained no weapons of their own;

outnumbering the minority would keep uprisings down only so long, and then ... .

Besides, those who worked alongside the tougher, smarter members of the formerly enslaved race during wartime had learned to appreciate their worth, and even made friends with them at times. Seeing these wartime workers in civilian life as equals was a new experience. They finally realized that these people of color had ambition, love of family, and desire for self-improvement and a better life, the same as they did.

And so, there occasionally were sympathetic ears for accounts of injustice. Even those who were not Negroes no longer accepted a lynching as "just one of those things." Accounts of people, because of color, cheated out of a home after paying for it, or travelers refused lodging at a motel when there were no others within miles, were no longer laughing matters to the average citizen.

Then, one day, it happened. Rosa Parks decided she wasn't going to give up her seat, and the resulting meetings and boycotts are well documented. Every youth who didn't understand this two-faced system became ignited with new hope. Every fatigued adult, bowed by the ignominious lifestyle assumed for so long, took courage and stood taller with purpose. The nation took notice and the meek began to feel that they would actually have a chance to inherit a small patch of the earth, someday.

In 1954, the lives of African Americans in Galveston as well as in the rest of the nation were changed beyond our imagination. Thanks to the genius of Thurgood Marshall and those with his vision, the cry of the men and women in the military was not to be ignored. African Americans of the decade after the Great War, World War II, knew that the old order

Civil Rights Movement

of second-class citizenship was not going to be tolerated. The education community certainly was surprised by the 1954 civil rights decision to integrate the schools of America -- at least, to desegregate them.

In Galveston, that decision met with quite a bit of covert opposition. Lights burned a long time in some of the homes of Galveston while strategy was discussed, thrown out, reviewed and dissected, then trimmed, polished and decorated to look good.

Some of the school district decision makers were in favor of the new order of things, and were simply shy to say it publicly, since they liked staying elected. But then, if they simply kept repeating, "It's the law of the land" over and over again, surely most people would finally believe it. As they have always been prone to do, Galveston ISD officials decided that waiting to see what happened to other districts might be a more prudent idea than rushing to do the right thing without voters' approval.

As stated, Hitchcock decided to integrate the high schools one grade at a time in the early '60s. Galveston watched other districts, did several studies, then decided on a two-step process. Galveston ISD would slowly integrate a whole grade in two elementary schools, as test cases. Later, high school students at Central would get the choice of going to Ball High or remaining at Central. The students at Ball were given no such choice. It was always a one-way street for Southern whites, even if they knew the Negro high school to be superior, in many areas, to the other school.

My niece, Diane Henderson, a student at Central, decided on her own to attend Ball High. She was the first in our family to graduate from Ball. Her brother, Theodore, graduated from Central in 1966, the last in our family to do so, and became the first African-American man to graduate from Rice University in 1970.

My first child, June Viola Collins, born in September of that fateful year of 1954, was of age to start school in first grade when Galveston finally got its plans together. Her school's location in the East End of Galveston later factored into our decision to move back to the neighborhood where my husband and I had both grown up.

We knew that the old ways of race relations were changing. We just didn't know how suddenly our lifestyles were changing also.

Therefore, when the sit-ins started in Galveston, in 1960 when my husband, children and I were still living in the west end, we were only joyful that something was about to force change. We were slightly nervous about the events, but not really afraid. Our time had finally come. Students were setting the example of courage for those of us who had already been in their shoes.

Only a few blocks from our home was the Weingarten's food supermarket at 59th Street and Broadway, where other stores are now. We were living at 5601 Ave. L, and I did most of my shopping there at the time. We were treated with respect and courtesy by most of the employees.

Downtown, the sit-ins started at McCrory's and Walgreen's, where the students were refused service at first, in deference to the perceived wishes of the regular white customers. The newspapers had been filled with how the whole South was active with this procedure, and how some cities had been turned into virtual war zones. The people of Galveston were watching events nervously, and could not believe it the day when the movement came directly to us.

Civil Rights Movement

When the protests begam, I was shocked to visit the store and see that the stools, which patrons had used to drink beverages at a snack counter, had been removed. The proprietors had unscrewed them from the floor, leaving holes where there had been fixtures. All that time, trouble and money just to keep us from sitting next to some white person. It was in my face now, and it was ludicrous to me.

The civil rights effort was recalled on Feb. 24, 2000, when Sue Simpson Johnson's Nia Cultural Center presented a panel discussion in honor of Black History Month at the recently renovated Old Central Cultural Center. As a member of Old Central's board of directors, I am very proud of what its officers earlier members have done in restoring this building to a decent appearance, and to renewed interest and use by the community.

This discussion was even more interesting than I had expected, for the panel consisted of men and women who were actually on the front lines of the movement in 1960 and 1961. Their comments gave me a new appreciation and a new perspective for that historical time. Speakers were Bobby Stevens Johnson, Connie Waddell, Ethel Martin, Shirley Adams and Raymond Simmons, the father of the center's director. Audience members also contributed to the presentation with comments and short accounts of their own experiences.

Ms. Johnson led off with her explanation of what went on in those days. She said that the students met regularly, in the home of Mr. John Clouser, now deceased, with other adults in attendance that included his son, Gerald, and Mr. Thomas D. Armstrong. They also sometimes met at Kelton Sam's house. Most of the students were in the Class of 1961; David

Scurry was among those mentioned. All over the nation, protesters were staging demonstrations, demanding to be treated as equals.

As they recounted, and as I remember, African Americans who wanted to eat or drink at the lunch counters downtown had to wait at the end of the counter until a server, always white, took the time to come and take their orders. Then, we had to stand up to wait for the order. We would stand next to the stools, not allowed to sit on them to eat or drink what we had purchased. Although we paid the same amount of money as other people, or more, we had to take ours "to go."

As Johnson related, Central's Class of '61 had plans. Some sat down at McCrory's; then, before the management had time to contact others, more sat down at other stores downtown. Walgreen's was involved early also. Each time, the students were refused service, and they just moved on. Eventually, Weingarten's got the word, way out in the west end of Galveston. I don't think the students had been there; I believe word got to the management, and they took action to keep the same thing from happening to their store.

Galveston merchants were really nervous. They knew the protest could escalate into something awful. Fortunately, level heads avoided real trouble. However, at the Dairy Queen on 27th Street and Broadway, students who tried to be served were arrested, although they had caused no trouble. For the longest, most of us refused to patronize the establishment. Even years later, with integration of most public facilities completed, and new ownership in place at Dairy Queen, I still didn't care to spend my money there. As time went by, pressured by my own children's pleadings, I eased back into buying there. It takes a while to erase unhappy memories.

Civil Rights Movement

The panel discussion also brought to light other things I had not known in depth or had forgotten. The class that started this protest idea at Central was a social studies class taught by Mr. Willard Dickerson. He also had a jazz trio that was popular in the Galveston area, the Dick Dickerson Trio. Dick, a quiet man, played the piano; Ed Jones played the bass violin; and Roy Merchant played the drums and sang the vocals. Their beautiful music was heard at all the best white and colored affairs. Yet Dick knew discrimination as well.

The Problem Solvers, as the students called themselves, said that their scariest incident at that time was as they tried to integrate Stewart Beach. This facility belonged to the city even then, and should have been available to the African American taxpaying public. We were not allowed down there at all. Central High students went there to mingle and try to ride the rides and buy from the concessions.

When they did, some white youths began to look at them in an ugly way, then started shouting obscenities at them. As they drew closer, the students became very frightened. However, their elders were watching; they said Mr. Armstrong drove up quickly in a Cadillac, and whisked them away before harm could come to them. Bobby said she would never forget how shocked she was, before he drove up, when a Negro employee of Stewart Beach came up to the students and urged them to leave -- walked right up to them and called them names too. And that she still did not understand it.

Others in the audience, including Mr. Simmons, told her they understood that this man was afraid for his job, even his well-being, if the crowd turned ugly. People like that, afraid of change, will take abuse and indignities just to be sure they and their own will not be harmed.

Island of Color

They also recalled a group of white youths that called themselves "The Chain Gang" and tried to retaliate against them.

A headline in the March 12, 1960, edition of *Galveston Daily News* that Bobby kept as a souvenir reads "Negro Sit-Downs Close Counters." Bobby said the NAACP did not participate, but did support them. "They tried to ignore us at first," she related. Students from Texas Southern University in Houston joined the Central students after they started the protests.

Other integration efforts by Galveston students included the University of Texas at Austin dormitories. Panel members said Whiting Hall was the only dormitory used for Negroes, well after Heman Sweatt gained admission as the first Negro student via a lawsuit. Kinsolving Dorm, luxurious and huge compared to Whiting, was only for whites.

Mr. Simmons was brave enough to close the evening's discussion by revealing what he called "the conspiracy." What he said was known but seldom discussed in public: that drugs were placed into the Black community by people outside of it. Although the Black community had been aware of marijuana, "goof balls," and some heroin, a wide range of narcotics all at once became available through several sources. In the area of town where they were most concentrated, when residents wanted to slow down this influx of drugs and the problems they brought, they were accused of initiating the problems. Mr. Simmons declared, "We couldn't afford to bring all those drugs in here. We don't have no ships. We couldn't [even] name all these drugs, they came in so fast!"

The panel also discussed how we found out in these times that Green Power is better than Black Power. The lesson needs to be taught thoroughly all over again; oppression might return one day yet. Unfortunately, too

Civil Rights Movement

many of our people have grown too accustomed to living paycheck to paycheck. The fat of the land has made us indolent.

CIVIL RIGHTS TIMELINE

Following is a timeline of civil rights landmarks from 1944 (the year I graduated from Central High School) to the year 1966 (the year my youngest child was born). Is there any wonder that my children grew up hearing many statements on patriotism and civil rights? How could they avoid being participants in the new order for Galveston's African Americans? Surely we had come to the time to actively seek our long-awaited rights.

1944 Texas white primary declared unconstitutional by U.S. Supreme Court

1948 President Truman's order requires fair employment practices for all federal service

1950 Herman Sweatt -- the brother of Jack Sweatt, a Galveston principal -- won the right to higher education for all Negroes, after his application to the University of Texas was denied strictly because of his race.

1954 Texas adopts a constitutional amendment allowing Negro women to serve on juries.

1954 Despite efforts in Galveston to stall integration, the U.S. Supreme Court ruled that "separate but equal" public schools were unconstitutional

1964 Poll tax as a voting requirement is outlawed by the 24th Amendment

1964 Civil Rights Act prohibits racial discrimination in most public places

1965 Voting Rights Act changes election systems to allow for more participation by minorities

1966 Ban on poll tax upheld by the U.S. Supreme Court

CHAPTER EIGHTEEN
MODERN TIMES

'Ladies' auxiliary of the National Association of Postal Employees.

Where We Are Now

Although the economics of our nation, even our whole world, have changed so drastically that no race can really keep ahead of the game, the successful entrepreneur still keeps a bit ahead. Our organizations have long stressed that we need to be independent owners of property, and financially sound. Our people have long been urged to work together and support each other's businesses now that integration has split up the wealth of the African-American community.

This advice is wiser still as the economy becomes dominated by corporations of a size that defy past description. Larger corporations are constantly playing Pac Man with each other, gobbling each other up, and if you don't have a huge partner in the game, you risk being either gobbled up or ignored completely, with many of our jobs transferred to cheaper work forces in Third World countries.

So where is Galveston and its citizens of color in this economic maze? Major hiring entities in Galveston -- such as the University of Texas Medical Branch, American National Insurance Company, the Galveston Independent School District, Texas A. and M. University Galveston campus, or Galveston College – are few. Other businesses depend on tourism. The entrepreneur has a role to play here in creation of economic opportunities.

Politically speaking, in the effort to further opportunities, the Galveston African American community would also do well to bond more solidly with the community of minorities expected soon to become majorities in this countries. Harold Hodgkins' "The New South" indicates an influx of people to the Southern part of the United States, and more people are expected to come to the United States from Spanish-speaking nations. In Galveston, as well as in other cities in the South, Spanish-speaking people will come to make up most of the population, with the potential to gain much power from this increase depending on their education, political activism and ability to consolidate resources. African-Americans have much in common with Hispanics and other minorities,

Modern Times

with friendships already cherished and nurtured between the communities. To allow any entity to create disharmony between us would be a tragedy.

Although outnumbered and outvoted in city issues, African Americans in Galveston have maintained a sense of strength and purpose for the most part in the years after integration. Our presence began to be felt in so many places where it had not been before. Steadily, with the rest of the nation, Galveston became used to having movers and shakers among people of color. Those prepared well and long ago in times of segregation just stood up and took charge. Changes in the law of the land helped.

Cornelia Harris Banks -
Galveston City Councilwoman

CORNELIA HARRIS BANKS is the first African American woman to be a member of the Galveston City Council. She is serving her second elected term on the Council at this writing. She is a part of this history in that she represents the second generation of Galveston African Americans who have been leaders. She also is one of many who have returned to Galveston to live, after living away from home for quite a while.

Daughter of Cornelius Harris, first principal of Booker T. Washington Elementary School, and Sarah Harris, English teacher at Central and Ball High Schools, Cornelia was also a member of Reedy Chapel A.M.E. Church. Her mother was a member of this church, so she was "raised " as a Galvestonian, graduating from Central High School in the Class of 1966.

Cornelia continued her education at Pepperdine University in California, receiving both her Bachelor of Arts Degree in Psychology, and her Master of Science Degree in School management and Administration there. Additional training was received in the University of Wisconsin and in Los Angeles.

After 20 years in the educational field, including quite of bit of experience as an administrator, Ms. Banks returned to Galveston.

Here in Galveston, she has been the executive director of Community in Schools for two years, and is now the Director of Academics Seaborne Challenge Corps, a part of Texas A&M University. Among the many organizations to which she belongs, she is a former Far Western regional director of Alpha Kappa Alpha Sorority, Inc, has served as president of the local chapter, is a board member of Old Central Cultural Center, and Champions for Children. Membership in Links, Inc. ,Top Ladies of Distinction, the educational sorority of Phi Delta Kappa, and the NAACP all give her foundation for the City Council of Galveston.

Anthony Griffin

Anthony Griffin, a quiet, modest man, worked obscurely in his law office for a while after arriving in Galveston. He later came to command the attention of the city, then the state, and now the nation. Winning several cases without fanfare, he helped to design the plan for single-member districts in Galveston. The NAACP and others sought to change the at-large election system. I was vice president of the school board when Mr. Griffin came before the board with his single-member district proposal. We were given a choice to either declare the districts valid, with their opportunities for voting strength among the city's minorities, or be faced with a lawsuit that could cost the taxpayers a kingly sum to fight the inevitable. Needless to say, the school board voted unanimously to use the well-planned districts that were presented that evening. The City Council had a similar meeting with Mr. Griffin, and decided to convert to single-member voting districts similar to those used by the school district.

Anthony Griffin made his biggest headlines yet when he recently decided to represent the Ku Klux Klan in Texas, in their refusal to turn over membership lists to the courts. Outraged, Texas NAACP officials dismissed Griffin as NAACP legal counsel. Mr. Griffin explained in this fashion: The Ku Klux Klan member pressing the suit originally did not realize that Mr. Griffin was African-American. Griffin accepted the case with the rationale that being forced to turn over one's private membership lists is unconstitutional, and that such a ruling could hurt those most whom the law was supposed to protect, because all private groups, including the NAACP, would be subject to the same law. A man ahead of his time, Mr. Griffin now has a staff of quite a few capable lawyers, and his potential is great for a man in a little city like ours. He speaks softly and carries a big stick. Known also for his culinary genius, I have sampled his dishes every year at his annual holiday parties, which last all day and into the night with wonderful food and beverages, great jazz music, and plenty of friendly security to keep his guests safe and sound.

From the resume Mr. Griffin provided: His firm, Anthony P. Griffin, Inc., 1115 Moody, was established Nov. 15, 1978 as a litigation practice in areas of civil litigation, constitutional/civil rights/statutory challenges and criminal law. He received a degree in political science from the University of Houston, and was licensed by Texas Bar in 1978. Mr. Griffin is also licensed to practice in the 5th, 8th and 11th Circuits of the U.S. Court of Appeals and is a member of the Supreme Court of the United States bar. He has served as an adjunct professor at the University of Houston Law

Center in both the civil and criminal trial advocacy programs. He is a former General Counsel for the Texas Civil Liberties Union (American Civil Liberties Union of Texas) and the former General Counsel for the State Chapter of the National Association for the Advancement of Colored People (NAACP). Currently, Mr. Griffin serves on the advisory board for The Texas Forum on Civil Liberties & Civil Rights (A Journal of the University of Texas School of Law and Individual Rights and Responsibilities Section of the State Bar of Texas). Mr. Griffin is also a cooperating lawyer for both the NAACP Legal Defense and Educational Fund and American Civil Liberties Union in criminal cases, redistricting litigation, school admission policies/affirmative action and cases involving First Amendment privileges (membership lists/prayer litigation).

Mr. Griffin is also listed in the publication <u>Contemporary Authors</u> and is a member of the American Society of Composers, Authors, and Publishers (ASCAP). He has received a long list of honors from widespread sources, and written many presentations, papers, articles and books, which include an unpublished work: <u>No Wizard! No Oz! No Apology! My Representation of The Klan and Other Unlikely Tales.</u>

Dr. Elicia Elaine Williams-King

Elicia Elaine Williams-King, M.D. is the daughter of Maggie and Ennis Williams. Born and raised in Galveston, she has had an outstanding record of accomplishments. Coming through the Galveston ISD, she received much commendation, was a member of many organization s in

Ball High School, served as one of the head drum majors in the Ball High School marching band, where she was an accomplished flute player.

She has the distinction still as the only African American student to be named Valedictorian of Ball High School, class of 1989. From Ball High she enrolled in Texas A.&M. University, College Station, Texas, where she received her Bachelor of Science degree in Biochemistry. She then became a student in the University of Texas Medical Branch here in Galveston, where she received her M.D, degree This was followed by a residency at Christus St. Joseph Hospital in Houston, Texas in Obstetrics and Gynecology

Elicia is now married to Richard King, M.D., Ph.D. . She currently is in Internal Medicine at Cambridge Hospital/ Cambridge Health Alliance, Cambridge, Massachusetts, which is affiliated with Harvard Medical School.

Elicia is a member of several professional societies, as an associate, and as a resident member of the American Medical Association. She has a long list of awards , honors and distinctions from Galveston and Texas A.&M. University. These include the honor of being valedictorian of the Ball High School Class of 1989, Dean's List in 1997 at the University of Texas Medical Branch at Galveston, Phi Theta Kappa National Honorary Fraternity, Old Central Cultural Center, Inc. Presidential Award in 2002, NAACP Peace and Role Model Award, Academic Excellence Booster Club Award, and the Bausch and Lamb Science Award.She has done quite a bit of Public Service from 1996 to the present.

Dr. Elicia Williams-King has a full record of public speaking engagements as well. Her hobbies and other interests include being a flautist , pianist or organist for the Choir at her church in Galveston -

Avenue L Baptist Church, and playing her flute for the First Baptist Church of Cambridge Massachusetts.

Personally speaking, I count most important her personality and character, from my perspective as a school board member while she was in high school, or just friend of the family. Whether she was on the football field, leading the band, playing in her church, or just talking to a group of people in soft conversational tones, it was obvious that Elicia was a role model of excellence for the youth. She always has a warm and genuine smile for everyone, and has a sweet disposition to go with her brilliant mind. She makes Galveston look toward a healthy future in all ways.

A Proposed Agenda for Our Age

Agenda items for Galveston's African Americans in this post-integration age should include reclaiming our heritage, and claiming our share of Galveston's cultural life. To both ends, effort should be made to solve the mysterious fate of the Rosewood Cemetery.

Located between the Luby's Cafeteria strip and the Nations Bank drive-in, by the Seawall near 61st Street, is an area of discarded waste on forgotten property. This area was the location of a cemetery for colored citizens, owned by an organization called the Rosewood Association that included morticians of the period. Mr. Hebert, Mr. T.D. Armstrong were two of the owners. The property has since been sold to someone else, but not developed. On this ground are some tombstones, some small gravestones, and not much other identification. No records seem to be available of who was buried there, but it is believed that the last burials took place there in the 1940s.

As a member of the Strand Theatre's board of directors, I have tried to get the Ensemble Theatre, an African American theatrical organization, to visit to perform a play called Distant Voices, about a similar situation in Houston's Fourth Ward, where an African American cemetery was almost covered over with downtown development and its occupants forgotten. I hope such a performance would achieve three purposes: arousing interest throughout Galveston in our mysterious cemetery, and what can be done to preserve it and any other property of historical significance to the African American community that has fallen into neglect or been torn down; allowing our people in Galveston the seldom-seen sight of a really professional, well-trained African American actors troupe; and encouraging more African Americans to regularly attend and perform in our theaters, as well as participate in other cultural events of the city.

As we seek a better quality of life for African Americans in Galveston, and set our agenda to achieve it, we remember that it has been education that has defined our transition into integration, and education still that will determine how we fare beyond that point. As noted, our people here in Galveston entered a new world in the 1960s, finding ourselves treated as equals for the first time in some areas. The foundation for that new world was formed in the changes made in our school district.

In the changes that were made, we find some that serve as a case study to illustrate what remains to be done to improve education in Galveston's African American community. Plans calling for gradual integration of every elementary school in Galveston, condensed what had been the two elementary schools for Negro children -- Booker T. Washington at 27th Street and Avenue M, and George W. Carver at 35th Street and Avenue M -- into one school for Negro students at Carver's site.

That school was later renamed for Leon A. Morgan, who had served in the highest office in the school district. The honor was conferred while he was alive; the precedent for honoring a living person came when Island Elementary School was renamed for Mrs. Gladnie-O Parker.

But Leon A. Morgan School was never meant to be truly integrated. After Washington was torn down -- integration having progressed to the point that this school was no longer needed and cost too much money to maintain -- that left only one school in a predominantly African American area: Morgan. Zoning laws determined the school membership, and only minority students, many from the housing projects, were enrolled at this new school.

A new building could not make up for the lowered expectations for these students. My dear friend, Mrs. Jewell Earles Banks, became principal of the school when it opened, and fought to get equal facilities and supplies -- equal opportunities for those she always called "my little Black babies." She had a fervent pride in their development that has yet to be equaled by any succeeding administrator.

I was dismayed as a school board member to read the goals set for the schools one year: The other schools were expected to work toward at least 85% mastery of subject matter on achievement tests, but the goal listed for Morgan was only 70% mastery. When I called this exception into question, the superintendent, who like Pilate wanted to wash his hands of the whole thing, called upon an African American administrator who had been principal of the school to explain. The answer was very nauseating: I was told that these poor children had so little previous exposure to learning, coming from such poor circumstances, that it would be too much to expect them to reach the goal set for the other students. I was to give them more time to reach 85% mastery, although those students would soon be sharing classrooms with all the other students, and labeled inferior learners.

Having spent 38 years teaching all kinds of children, using whatever means I could draw upon to get the best results from them, I was thoroughly insulted. Before there ever was any such thing as special education, or any fancy name given to efforts to teach poor children who have been handicapped in some fashion in their learning experiences or readiness to learn, there was automatic "mainstreaming." I taught every kind of child in my regular classes, bands and choirs, and they were all expected to learn whatever was given to them to learn, up to the highest goal set at the time. And I am certainly not the only African American teacher who knows that children of almost no exposure to previous education will rise to the occasion and learn. That is, if enough effort and enthusiasm is put into the learning process, enough love is received in response to whatever success they have daily, and enough planning goes on to ensure continued progress. This lesson bears repeating.

In these last four decades since school integration, Galvestonians of all ages have continued to also learn how to maintain the cooperation that allows us to continue to advance. As we have struggled to survive together, we have needed as many leaders that our community can produce, beginning as always in education.

Many of our children in the African American community have excelled in Galveston's schools. My firstborn, June Viola, was the first of her hue to hold several student offices and positions, and my other two children, Roy and Cheryl, were among the African American students who excelled academically and in extracurricular activities in the post-integration years.

Mrs. June Viola Collins Pulliam

"As stated in the chapter on Education, June Viola was in the first integrated first grade in Galveston. Her teacher was named Mrs. Alice Guest. I knew from that first day of Registration that my child's experience would be calm, even though I did not know what outcomes would occur. I did not know that June's work would make such an impression on her teacher that Mrs. Guest would keep some of the child's writing until long after she had retired and moved to the state of Washington. June wrote an essay in the second grade on the life of Ludwig Van Beethoven. I do not

Island of Color

remember what the assignment was, but even I was shocked to learn that she was so attached to my love for Music, until she wrote about Beethoven, spelling his name corrrectly, and every word she wrote, while only seven years old.

Mrs. Guest also kept a note that June had written, telling her brother Roy about her teacher, and about her life there at school. My son had scribbled something back, himself. Mrs. Guest mailed her copies to me after she moved into an assisted living establishment, not having much space to keep this kind of thing, and wanting us to have these treasures.

Going from Rosenberg Elementary School to Stephen F. Austin Junior High School, June went through many pioneer experiences, becoming finally the president of the Student Council at Auatin School. Making friends with the other top academic students of the school, she honed her skills and talents into a winning combination of band member, majorette, young athlete, and student council executive.

June continued her leadership skills in Ball High School. In a high school which was ranked as 5A, because of its huge enrollment, she was a member of the symphonic band, was the marching band's first African American of the four drum majors used then, a member of the National Honor Society, the French Honor Society, the Key Club, and was the Student Council vice president in her senior year. In her graduating class of about six hundred and fifty students in 1973, she was ranked fourth.

June then went on to Texas Women's University in Denton, Texas, where she majored in Music Therapy. She wanted to reflect the interest of both of her parents. She told adults that she wanted to major in something that would be worthy in Music, and yet have a scientific bend, since her father had been a "Pre-Med" major in college. In talking with my "twin", who chaired a college music department in Texas at the time, Dr. Florence Crim Robinson advised June to become a Music Therapy major, and she took this advice, realizing her dream of becoming of value to so many patients.

In this field she soon obtained a scholarship at TWU, and became the first African American to serve as student president of the Music Therapy Regional Association. Some ten years later, she became the first African American president to serve on a professional level in the same organization. In her Senior year at Texas Women's University, June was elected president of her music fraternity, Sigma Alpha Iota, as well as Redbud princess. She also earned the Pauline Bishop Leman Memorial Award, a very prestigious award at Texas Women's University, given for outstanding artistic contribution to the university.

After working as a Music Therapist, Board Certified, in psychiatric settings, for nine years, she became the first Music Therapist in the Houston area to open up a private practice, settling in the Bellaire area. During this time she received her Master's degree in Behavioral Sciences from the University of Houston, at Clear Lake. She also received her certification in Psychodrama after four years of post-graduate work.

In more recent years, she had been the owner of "Kindermusik on the Island", an early childhood music education program, and gives private instrumental music instruction. Working with a musical organization of parents and children who are home-schooled, including her own two daughters, she is the Band Director. Called the "Co-Op", this organization also has a string ensemble and two grade level choirs. June accompanies the choirs as well. June has served as a church musician in many churches, and was accompanist for a recent compact disc release by the New Galveston

Heritage Choir. Yet Galveston's children often cannot make an affordable living here, or advance professionally. The average wage earner has had a tough time staying on the isle and remaining afloat financially.

Roy Lester Collins, III, my son, is an example of a person of his age who has received an exemplary education here, then in college, worked close to home, and eventually had to go far away to make a living in his field. Family ties kept him interested in coming back as close to home as he could get, and still make some sort of decent wage.

Roy III showed unusual ability in elementary school. His paternal grandmother, while he was in the first and second grades, sent him to take piano lessons from Margaret Bess, who passed away that second year. In the second grade, he became interested in my trumpet, so I casually taught him how to play it, not believing he would stick with it that young. He played well enough to perform with my high school band members in Hitchcock at football games, and in parades here in Galveston, although he was only seven and eight years old.

Later, in the fourth grade, his teacher called me to get permission to put him into what was called a "Major Works" program. This program, conceived by the Galveston ISD, can be compared with what is called "Gifted and Talented" in this day and time. Eventually, this group of students became the secondary school leaders. These students became goal-setters, and attained adult aims.

As his sister did, Roy won awards in full school, and community Spelling Bees, participated in Student Council, representing his classmates in junior and senior high school years. He was a highly skilled band member in junior and senior high, a leader of the bass section in symphonic and marching band, writing his own arrangement for the marching band in his senior year to play during halftime shows He was always very interested in sports and kept aware of all the statistics of the players, although his own participation was limited to junior high football and basketball.

Roy ranked well, academically, in Ball High School, earning a National Achievement Scholarship his senior year. His skills were high in Mathematics and Science, so his father persuaded him to major in Mechanical Engineering, when he enrolled in the University of Houston after graduating from Ball High School. He was also a student intern at the Johnson Space Center. Transferring later to Southern University, he received his Bachelor of Science in Engineering there.

His first position was with General Dynamics in Fort Worth, but Roy recognized other career interests beyond designing airplanes.

Consulting with both parents about taking an examination which was given to potential law students, he remarked that he would be in his latter twenties before he finished his course, inferring that he would be older than most law students by that time. I never forgot how his father replied. "So, how old will you be if you DON'T take the exam, and keep doing what you are now/" My husband had a unique way of getting the point over without a lot of discussion. Our son got the point, decided to take the exam.

Passing it, he enrolled in the University of Houston again, this time in Law School, and graduated with his Doctor of Jurisprudence. In due time, he passed the bar. Although his father passed away before he received his law degree, he was "present" for the admission to the Bar ceremony in Austin, Texas. After a period of time as a practicing attorney, he matriculated in the John Marshall Law School in Chicago, Illinois. From there he received his Master of Laws degree in Intellectual Property. Other than the times of private practice, Roy found it necessary to travel to other places as a part of his quest for a livelihood. This included positions in College Station with Texas A&M University, and in Michigan with the Legal Department of Chrysler Corporation. His technology awareness also took him on trips to explain invention commercialization and negotiation techniques to different entities.

Presently, Roy is a staff lawyer for Texas Southern University in Houston, Texas. He is also an ordained minister, into his second decade of service.

Modern Times

Mrs. Cheryl L.M. Collins Crayton

Along with biographical narratives about her siblings, I must include the Vita of the young lady who made this book come together. She has the professional expertise not only to tell me what I needed to do, or not to do, she has the heart to keep me encouraged, and never let me give up this effort She is the editor of my work, the rewriter, the title creator. SHE is the professional journalist, having her degree in Journalism from the University of Texas at Austin, interned here in Galveston with the Galveston Daily News (now the Galveston County Daily News), and spent twelve years as a copy editor with the Fort Worth Star-Telegram, before she changed her career path to educating the youth. Now how about her name? **Cheryl Lynette Marguerite Collins Crayton.**

All that name is in a petite body, but she has a mighty big heart. Cheryl won't allow my journalistic tendencies to wander on about her in a fanciful vein, but you should know that she too was an honor student, coming along like an only child years nine years after her brother, and eleven years after her sister. She was always gifted with a special way of phrasing whatever she said. She seemed destined to be a doctor, since she was chosen to participate with a few classmates during her senior year in a project at the University of Texas Medical Branch here in Galveston. I still have the newspaper coverage of this time, complete with pictures.

However, Cheryl, who graduated with highest honors from Ball High School also, as ninth in her large class, chose another direction. After being in my Choir at Austin Middle School, earning awards there, she was a cheerleader in Central Eighth Grade School. While at Central, she also represented the whole school in a Galveston ISD Honors program which recognized the top two students from each school. At her Commencement exercise, she wore chords from the National Honor Society, Spanish Honor Society, and had been active in the Student Council of Ball High.

Cheryl was a National Merit finalist, and National Achievement Scholar. Because of her high SAT scores, Cheryl was also invited to join Mensa International, an organization of people whose "IQ"s are at the top 2% of the population.

When she was invited up to the University of Texas for their Honors Colloquium, I had a hard decision to make. The same day I was to take her there, my husband was to be admitted to the hospital for his newly discovered heart problem. He urged me to take her on to Austin, insisting he could admit himself. Remaining in the hospital for treatment, he was allowed out on a pass to see her graduate a few days later. Believing he would do well at home, recovering, he stated, I took her on a planned reward trip to Europe with a Youth Choir touring there. Just as we were about to conclude the tour, we received word that her father, my husband, had passed away. Her schooling was affected, but she grew spiritually. Like her siblings, I am most proud of her spiritual attainments.

Thank goodness, then, for those who have returned, remained or settled here despite the financial challenge, and also ridden out the city's social storms – to take their stands here when dissension and manipulation arise, when the plight of the have-nots is disregarded, when people and their individual achievements are compartmentalized. Thank goodness for those caring persons who love our heritage and culture, and are willing to sacrifice their time, money and physical and mental strength to perpetuate them.

"In this regard, I have to continue with a real Galveston heroine of our time. I have the utmost respect for a young lady who is about the same age as my oldest child- June. Her name is **Monica Banks Netherly**.

Her father's name is very prominent in this book, because of his many contributions to this history - Joseph Banks. Monica will give full credit to both of her parents for her good upbringing. Her mother, Mrs. Doris Banks certainly has been devoted to the best for all four of their children. Bernadette, a brilliant young lady in school, just back home from most of her time in New York City, represents those who have come back home to try again to live here, as has her resourceful and talented brother Gregory Banks. Basil Banks, after a stint in the nationally famous Oklahoma football team, has been back home for a period of

Island of Color

time. But I want to outline Monica's life, since she represents the stamina and survival instincts of Galveston itself. We who live here have gone through generations of what would have diminished or FINISHED many other communities. Monica just never gives up, never quits, and comes up smiling, and optimistic about whatever she can do improve life for everyone else around her.

As I write this, we have had another fatal explosion in Texas City, where the worst industrial disaster has struck years ago, and minor explosions have shaken the community since then. How do the people keep living in that Galveston County city, after tragedy keeps threatening, and struck again today? You might ask Monica that question. She is a fine looking lady with a handsome husband. They live in Houston. But her son used to love to visit with his grandparents here in Galveston. His name was Marcus. Marcus was a strong and handsome fourteen year old when he ran into some awful folk here. Gangs were taking over teenage activities, and there seemed to be little that the adults could do about it, about ten years ago.

He was advised by one of his uncles, his mother's brother, to leave when things were getting out of hand, but he was a little stubborn, and wanted to correct the wrong in his own way. He was killed in a drive-by shooting. Dealing with this death was hard on even us neighbors. It was a scary time, and we could not believe our quiet neighborhood had experienced such a tragic, immediate cost.

Monica's reaction, after a period of deep grieving over the loss of her son, was to set up a system of seeing to it that no other boy, or girl could be left with no hope, or future, if she had anything to say about it. With strong support of her family, she established a fund to be used to give out scholarships to worthy youngsters of color who graduated from high school here in Galveston. She wanted to encourage them to stand for good things, set standards for themselves, and follow through, go to college, have a climate of hope for those to follow them. Since I expressed interest in her lofty goals, Monica asked me to be on her Board. I have seen this project grow over the last ten years. Instead of just a family enterprise, we have compiled a list of persons who annually donate to this cause, and the annual scholarship awards program has drawn interest from many sources, with great speakers, music, and local talent involved. The recent scholarship winners have hope to get a decent amount of money to help them in their scholastic dreams. But is this the end of Monica's story? NO!

After this tragic loss, she became pregnant with another child. This time her child was a little girl, born about eleven years ago, just after Marcus was killed. We were so happy for her, starting over, becoming a mother again. Alas! Her little girl was born with a physical challenge. Certainly, she has met with a lot of family love, but she has needs that other children do not have, and demands more attention, and care than is usual. Along with this ever-present fact is the reality that Monica works at M.D.Anderson hospital, a place of constant need for great spiritual strength - a prominent treatment center for cancer patients.

Recently, her husband had serious surgery, but is recovering. Then she herself had a bout with influenza, respiratory problems. She is trying to organize this year's award program, anyway. Does she cry or look downtrodden? NO! She smiles, asks how you are doing, apologizes for disturbing you, thanks you for every assistance, attendance, feeds us board members at every meeting we attend, "because we appreciate your giving us your time" she and her mother still say, Her father, Joe, used to cook special food for us. I told him he was sure spoiling us. We looked forward to the food just as we did the meetings to decide for some children's future. But we have seen a serious purpose perpetuated. And I call Monica my No.1 Hero (ine) because she never gives up. God Bless!

To mention a few other returning persons whose parents were well known in the community of Galveston, but have passed on:

Dr. Geraldine Lyons, Galveston native who attended college and remained in the Atlanta, Georgia area until both of her parents passed away. She has settled in her parents' home at present Her mother, Ida Lyons, was a member of the famous Wings Over Jordan vocal ensemble, sang soprano in the choirs of church as well as school, and was a frequent soloist here in Galveston. She was a teacher in the Galveston ISD system. Dr. Lyons' father, Jesse Lyons, continued to live here after his wife's death, retired from the Longshoreman's ILA, and served GISD as well, until his own passing.

Dr. Rufus H. "Billy" Stanton, mentioned earlier in this book, was the last of the Stantons to practice in the medical field. As a dentist, he was successful in the community, which has changed so much. Because of changes in the delivery of Healthcare, it has become difficult for any and all physicians and dentists to maintain independent practices.

Dr. Stanton's wife, Janice, has been very active in community life, herself. In addition to working with the SER-Jobs for Progress (a federal job training program), she served for 21 years on the Board of Regents of Galveston College, and has received several awards for these times of service, from church and community organizations. The most significant award was probably the "Steel Oleander" award for community service given to an outstanding woman of any race by the Galveston Historical Foundation. Now that Dr. Stanton has passed away, and Janice Stanton has retired from The Galveston College Board, their children stay in closer touch.

Their three children - Rufus H. "Skip" Stanton, Deborah Stanton Burke, and Robert Stanton II, have all enjoyed successful careers away from Galveston, but return as often as they can. Deborah Stanton Burke, an outstanding attorney, has a maturing family of her own, but is close enough (San Antonio) to visit when convenient. Robert "Bobby" Stanton, an experienced journalist, now with the Houston Chronicle is closer, so visits more often. The eldest, "Skip" Stanton lives farther away in Reston, Virginia. He has already retired from the position of Director, Biotechnology Sales for the U.S., Perkin-Elmer Life Sciences

These are but examples of the intellectual prominence of our people being passed down to other generations already, spread all over the world. In our church, Mrs. Earnestine Staton was interviewed after her retirement from the teaching profession, and her children, now retired from teaching, as well, at the time of the interview. Her children, Mrs. Joyce Lacy, and Mrs. Rosalie Tottenham have children who are well into their own careers. Some of their children live close, in the Greater Houston area, following professional positions and jobs with industrial firms. Others, farther away- such as Donna Lacy Marshall, well known as Anchor News person in the broadcast media of the East Coast - represent those who went to wherever their interests could be served. But they took their traditions and culture with them.

The far reaching effects of our culture are beginning to come full circle as our local economy is having a rebirth, presently. The cruise ship popularity all over the world has been particularly advantageous to Galveston. Our Wharves Board and Port Authority have managed to negotiate contracts with three cruise lines, so far. Their ships coming to, and leaving from Galveston regularly, have obtained a popularity with countries of close proximity. These ports of call are enjoying the boom of this kind of travel for luxury not experienced any other way, and yet for a price that is affordable to many. Therefore, people who were not interested in our quiet lifestyle are beginning to realize its potential. People all over Texas are especially interested in the reduction of time and money for cruises, not having to travel all the way to Florida or California to get a short cruise. Recently, I had a twelve day cruise to the Panama Canal area, with stops and tours of several popular points in between. The ability to leave from my home and arrive right back here was most enjoyable after having traveled to Florida and Hawaii for other cruises over a thirty year span of time.

With more time and interest to spend in Galveston, shopping and vacationing in a historic port is becoming more attractive to passengers from all over the world. Construction is booming in Galveston in 2005. Condominiums, hotels, restaurants, other retail shops are going up all over town; some stores are expanding their facilities, and homes are being improved in many locations. Beautification projects are taking on new life and meaning.

At the least, our adult children of African-American roots have more reason to visit their birthplace, and review their own history. Should this period of reconstruction become more lasting, with wise city, county and state leadership, Galveston can rise again to its former status of importance.

Modern Times

As a luminous model for our youth to emulate, we now have in Galveston an African American young woman who is a NASA ASTRONAUT. Her name is STEPHANIE D. WILSON Although her home is Boston, Massachusetts, she comes to Galveston regularly for spiritual affiliation, because of our dynamic pastor, Reverend Brenda Beckford Payne. She joined the church which Rev. Payne pastored previously in Clear Lake, near NASA. When Rev. Payne was sent to Reedy Chapel A.M.E. Church in 2000, she and several others came also, wanting to keep a spiritual relationship. Therefore, we claim her as our own, since she is a very active participant in the church, with a very sweet personality.

Stephanie Wilson graduated from Taconic High School in Pittsfield, Massachusetts in 1984. Ms. Wilson received a Bachelor of Science degree in engineering science from Harvard University in 1988, and a Master of Science degree in aerospace engineering from the University of Texas in 1992. She is a member of the American Institute of Aeronautics and Astronautics.

After graduating from Harvard in 1988, Wilson worked for 2 years for the former Martin Marietta Astronautics Group in Denver, Colorado. As a Loads and Dynamics engineer for Titan IV, Wilson was responsible for performing coupled loads analyses for the launch vehicle and payloads during flight events. Wilson left Martin Marietta in 1990 to attend graduate school at the University of Texas. her research focused on the control and modeling of large, flexible space structures. Following the completion of her graduate work, she began working for the Jet Propulsion Laboratory in Pasadena, California, in 1992. As a member of the Attitude and Articulation Control Subsystem for the Galileo spacecraft, Wilson was responsible for assessing attitude controller performance, science platform pointing accuracy, antenna pointing accuracy and spin rate accuracy. She worked in the areas of sequence development and testing as well. While at the Jet Propulsion Laboratory, Wilson also supported the Interferometery Technology program as a member of the Integrated Modeling Team, which was responsible for finite element modeling, controller design, and software development.

Selected by NASA in April 1996, Wilson reported to the Johnson Space Center in August 1996. Having completed two years of training and evaluation, she is qualified for flight assignment as a mission specialist. She was initially assigned technical duties in the Astronaut Office Space Station Operations Branch to work with Space Station payload displays and procedures. She then served in the Astronaut Office CAPCOM Branch, working in Mission Control as a prime communicator with on-orbit crews. Following her work in Mission Control, Wilson was assigned technical duties in the Astronaut Office Shuttle Operations Branch involving the Space Shuttle Mai Engines, External Tank and Solid Rocket Boosters. Wilson is assigned to the crew of STS-121.

At this writing, Stephanie Wilson is supposed to make her first flight in September of this year, 2005. Stephanie is a member of the Reedy Senior Choir and the New Galveston Heritage Chorale. We who can, from Reedy Chapel African Methodist Episcopal Church in Galveston, intend to journey to Cape Canaveral, Florida to see our family member's flight into space.

ROBERTA "Cookie" TAYLOR

We all knew her as "Cookie" when she was growing up. Her whole family is quite talented. Born to and raised here in Galveston by Robert and Miriam Taylor, two wonderful and educated parents, Cookie went to private and public schools, graduating from Ball High School in 1975. She then attended and graduated from Sam Houston State University with a bachelor's degree in speech and drama and her teacher's certification, in 1979.

Realizing the real world of acting rejection, away from here, she came home and taught with me at Stephen F. Austin Middle School Like me, she prefers the age of the seventh and eighth graders, who are too old to be babied, and too young to be sophisticated. She wanted to follow in her brother's footsteps, and become an actress. Known for several major roles on TV, on stage, and in movies, her brother Ron was nominated for a "Tony Award" for one of his Broadway performances. He died suddenly of a heart attack in 2002

Turning to teaching in the Washington D.C. area, she soon became principal of St. Thomas Moore Catholic School. In this environment, which was fraught with problems, including drug abuse and gang violence, she learned to work with the police department, and the parents of the troubled students. She returned to Galveston and started teaching in the most successful school in the county-the Mainland Preparatory Academy, which goes from Pre-K to 8th grade. In a day and time when African American teachers are very scarce, especially because they are paid so poorly and treated with disrespect and lack of support, Ms. Taylor is so very needed. To quote her statement in the paper -

"I teach a wide range of students, from the gifted and talented to those who are academically challenged, but my philosophy is that children will perform however you expect them to perform.... I try to empower my students..." She has spent 26 years in education, and says she finally understands what it means to be a teacher. As she has said, "...honesty, compassion, and patience are the most important characteristics a teacher can have. You have to be honest with children because they can spot a fake very fast....whatever I am doing, it will involve children and education." I can say a loud "A-MEN," and pray for her continued success with the persons who will one day affect our lives directly. I have had the pleasure of being invited to speak to the 8th grade graduating class of Mainland Preparatory a couple of years ago, and to discuss this book with the older students there this past Fall. They are extremely intelligent, well-mannered, and well behaved in this era of wild behavior in the schools. What a pleasurable experience!! I told my family members that I was inspired to go beyond my usual presentation, and was challenged to use my brain with these potential leaders. Hats off and much praise to Diane Merchant and her staff, and especially to Roberta Taylor!!

I have every confidence that a united Galveston will build upon the possibilities that we have here in our diverse culture. I believe that enough persons of the darker hues will stand up and be counted with those who want to be accountable for their own successes, and will train their children to see past their immediate needs to a brighter tomorrow. I believe our children of Galveston will take hold and lead us into a wider circle of opportunity for all. I see Galveston becoming a cultural center of great magnitude, with a path of education from the secondary level to the university level and well beyond, partially due to the plan of Universal Access, put into place by the Board of Regents and President "Bix" Rathburn at Galveston College.

After a National School Boards Association convention in New Orleans in the late '80s, I proposed to the Galveston ISD Board of Trustees that we start a Galveston Education Foundation to give every student a chance at a better life. In the model outlined at a convention workshop, students who did not have a high scholastic average but had shown good citizenship and solid work habits were guaranteed a college education if they did their best. A guaranteed education will make any serious student work harder, believing in his or her future; students were approached in sixth grade and told of the opportunity. With teachers' recommendations, these students were sent to college on a trial basis. If they maintained B averages or above, their scholarships continued. Where before no more than 10 minority students each year had received scholarships, now 30 received aid under this new plan.

Crucial to Galveston's plan was the foundation's financing: Officials devised a payroll deduction plan that did not compete with the United Way, or Community Chest as it used to be called, and allowed people from all walks of life to contribute. The Galveston Education Foundation floundered after a great start, but turned its money over to the Galveston College Universal Access Fund; two organizations with the same purpose could not both survive in a small city like ours. And additional money started rolling in. The surviving organization has shown great courage and purpose. It is my fervent hope and prayer that Galveston's future can be made secure by these next few years of graduates.

Leadership from many grassroots sources is now possible. Only when all of the people who share this island life have a say in how it will proceed, will peace, tranquility, and the optimum development of its citizens emerge. It is not an impossible goal.

In one small California town featured recently on TV, the mayor of the town is Asian and the leading townspeople are of all major races. The students all get along. There are mixed-race couples of all sorts. They experienced no "white flight" when other races came into their town, and communication between the races is quite good.

The most important thing the newscaster said were these words: "The education level of these residents is very high." He went on to say that most of them were college graduates, and had been trained in several professional fields. The reason for their success is clear: They are not stupid, they are not prejudiced, because they have been exposed to truth. They don't judge people on outside appearance, and they know how to appreciate their differences and use their similarities to the advantage of all.

My first thought was, "Oh, I would love to visit their town." My second thought was a prayer: "God, please don't let some evil-minded or some pinhead person go there, now that we know about them." But I also hoped that most of the persons who saw this documentary would be encouraged by it, and receive the same encouragement for noble ideals.

Let us give voice to those ideals together, all across this island. Let us give rise to leadership in building an economy here that will sustain this community. Leadership in ensuring representation within this community that is diverse and disallows disenfranchisement. Leadership that can help us to maintain a heritage that informs our future.

The Negro National Anthem offers the words for our chorused effort:

>"Lift ev'ry voice and sing, till earth and heaven ring --
>Ring with the harmonies of liberty,
>Let our rejoicing rise, high as the list'ning skies,
>LET IT RESOUND LOUD AS THE ROLLING SEAS..."

BIBLIOGRAPHICAL ESSAY

Material for this book came from diverse sources. The Introduction uses facts from my family's written records, the Ralph Scull papers "Black Galveston: A Personal View of Community History in Many Categories of Life," The Clayton Library in Houston, Alex Haley's *Roots*, and Lerone Bennett's *A History of Black America,* subtitled "Before the Mayflower."

In Chapter One I am reliving the beginning of my family's residence on this Island, as I journey to Port Bolivar's elementary school on a visit as President of the GISD Board.

In Chapter Two, I am happy to give full credit to Bill Cherry, author of a regular column in the *Galveston County Daily News* called "Tales of Galveston." He augments my own observations. Charles Hayes' two volume book *Galveston* gives foundation to more of Chapter Two's revelations.

In Chapter Three, I continue to pull facts from Hayes' *Galveston,* and Alice Wygant's oral report to the Advisory Board of The Galveston Historical Foundation, based on her research while she was executive director of the Galveston County Museum.

In Chapters Two and Three, the source of the exact text of the Emancipation Proclamation and the reasons for the decision to implement this document by President Abraham Lincoln is the World Book Encyclopedia, Vol.6, 1999, World Book, Inc. Publisher, Chicago, Ill. My own commentary on the situation surrounding the freedom of my people, and the way in which it is celebrated today round out the reason for the chapters.

The first Interlude, so-called because it has no direct relation to the flow of material before or after it, is a conversation I had on a Galveston KGBC-AM radio program with Charles McCullough, then staff member with KGBC .

The next most difficult chapter for source material was the following chapter-Chapter Four, on Education. The problem was quite the opposite. I was fortunate to have at my disposal almost too much material. My own grandfather has recorded much about the churches, used in the preceeding chapter, but much more about Education, since this was his life's work. I am humbled by the fact that he wrote the details that were not recorded in any other source. His comments on the education of all children came before the Minutes of the Board of Education in this city. Since my grandfather's writings start with 1865, and the Galveston School Board Minutes start with 1882, they can rely on his word. can receive information from him, concerning the education of African-Americans.

For Chapter Five, several resources were utlilized. Starting with the school district's information of 1882, all of the material which my grandfather wrote, including names of teachers, dates they were hired, other pertinent facts are all borne out in the official Minutes of that governing body. I should mention that the School Board Minutes of those days were very detailed, and very elaborate, since there was none of the technology used today. There were no recording devices, so the details that were recorded are amazingly complete.

Also, I had access to the information contained in Rosenberg Library, coming from Dr. Leon A. Morgan, Mr. Bert Armstead, and others who left pictures, and papers, including my sister and myself. The Centennial of Central High School, advertised in a section of the Galveston

Daily News, dated August 18,1985, was a valid and helpful source. Dr. Barry Crouch's material on the Freedman's Bureau is used in this chapter, further proving that Galveston was the site of the first planned education of African-Americans in Texas.

Comments from the many people I interviewed is certainly a large source, since the older people in Galveston have always valued our education opportunities, and loved to tell about them. Also, pertinent information came from William Preston Vaughn's book, titled "Schools for All" , "The Blacks and Public Education in the South", 1865-1877, University of Kentucky Press. The seventh section of Chapter Six is based on a research paper of Leon A. Morgan and Ernest S.Barrett entitled "The Impact of Desegregation on the Black Child", which included the school years of 1967-68, and 1969-70.

Chapter Six was probably the most difficult to document, because I went from church to church, and from person to person, in order to get the needed histories, and waited for some material, which I never obtained. On the other hand, one of the former leaders of the congregation of Saint Augustine Episcopal Church sent so much material to me, that I had to work industriously to condense it for this purpose, without leaving out the many solid pieces of information. I actually wanted to include the many comments made about their churches from the persons interviewed. Another book could be written just on the subject of African-American churches, alone. Since the church was often the focal point of the lives of most of our people, this influence has received the lion share of attention. On the downside, I must use this opportunity to request of our churches that they concentrate on compiling histories that contain more than the names of the pastors of the church, and what material improvements were made to the church property over the years. Knowing what was accomplished in spiritual welfare, and in the community by some of these churches, I was rather disappointed in the reports received by some. Another book on churches, only, should be one of interviews of the core personnel of these churches, and a discussion of what was most important about them to the persons interviewed.

It is obvious to me that everything that happened to my people could not be covered in any one book. It is my hope that this book will be a springboard from which to launch interest in many related topics about Galveston's quite unique and colorful African-American population. Individual credits go to Dr. Barry Crouch, Professor of History at Gallaudet University, speaker on the Freedman's Bureau for the Texas A&M University Lecture Series, here in Galveston; to United Methodist

Methodist Historian, Mrs. Bernice McBeth, of Houston, Texas, who came down to my home, and talked leisurely with me about the bond between Reedy Chapel African Methodist Episcopal Church, and the

United Methodist connection, which she had researched so thoroughly. She also gave me material from "Methodism in Texas", with its Chapter 5 on Civil War and Reconstruction, p.110 quotation, and the details about how Reedy Chapel was started by the (white) Methodist South people.

On page 84, Ryland Chapel is pictured, the Methodist Excitement in Texas, and the chapter on "Statehood to Secession" is found here. Ryland Chapel was partly financed by a gift from William Ryland of Baltimore. From this same source came the information that Reverend David Elias Dibble, born in 1811, died in 1885, was the first "ordained• African-American Methodist minister in Texas. Biographical information came either from the subjects themselves, or from immediate family members of the subjects.

Biographical sketches came from my own knowledge of the persons described, their relatives, and from Rosenberg Library.

Other sources for the proceeding Chapters are Dr. Barry Crouch, Texas A&M Lecture Series, 1999, Reverend Ralph Albert Scull Memoirs, Ellen Beasley's "Back Alleys of Galveston", "Women, Culture, and Community", Chapter 8, by Dr. Elizabeth Turner, "Black Texas Women" by Ruthe Winegarten. Biographical Sketches of Norris Wright Cuney, by his daughter, Maud Cuney Hare; William H. Noble and George T. Ruby, and Doc Hamilton and the Lone Star Cotton Jammers from Rosenberg Library.

Chapters Seven and Eight were my personal interest chapters, and I had to be careful not to put everything and everybody I knew best into this chapter. Since this chapter dealt with my own profession, I knew each person well, and wanted to tell about any and everything they could supply to me. I have selected the persons and descriptions which I feel mean the most to Galveston, and to the world outside of Galveston, who know us through their creativity.

Here I wish to start with a mention of a lady who spoke to me just a few days ago, in a local restaurant. She is Mrs. Stinson, and she has a whole family of singers, whose names represent the word Music to so many Galvestonians. I feel honored that she came over to me to say a few kind words of remembrance. She has just lost her oldest son, and she still exuberates warmth, and care for others. The Stinson family has greatly enriched Galveston with its religious and spiritual songs of quality over the years. Rev. Ralph A.Scull, my grandfather, has recorded in his community memoirs names of musicians who were actively playing music in the earliest years of the middle nineteenth century. African-Americans who played symphonic instruments, as well as the folk instruments of the period, are named here.

Listed here are sources including the obituary of Mrs. Theresa Mae Lewis, lifetime musician, primarily at Live Oak Baptist Church. Her funeral music was arranged and organized by her lifelong friend, Mrs. Bernice Hightower. Mrs. Hightower has a well known history of teaching excellence, herself, in the field of music. She has taught in the public schools of Galveston for more than three generations, but has made a larger mark with her private piano students. Each of her private students has a reputation for musical excellence, but the ones who played for Mrs. Theresa Lewis' funeral were probably her best of all times [a] Mrs. Sharon Barron on piano, and Reverend Nathan Johnson on organ. Their music was individually, and jointly, indescribably beautiful, tasteful, and professionally superior to anything heard before, at this kind of service. Dr. Elizabeth Turner's "Women, Culture, and Community" is utilized here, again.

Oral interviews from many persons supported this section of the book. These persons were Mrs. Lois Davis Tyus, Rev. Handley Hickey, Mrs. Earnestine Staton, Mr. Thomas Green, Dr. Rufus and Janice Stanton, Dr. Leroy and Luella Sterling, Mr. Thomas Green, Mrs. Della Sims, Mr. John Clouser, Mrs. Gwendolyn Bridge Heard, the Thomas family (Mrs. Ruth Thomas Hall, Rev. James Thomas, Carrie B. Clay), Mrs. Ada S. Butler.

Biographies of John W. Coleman and his wife, Elizabeth Coleman, came from the reserved section of Rosenberg Library. The biography of

Fleming Smizer Huff came from Mrs. Florence C. Henderson, and myself, from family records. Mrs. Amelia Curtis, and her son, Bernard Curtis, gave me the life story of Eddie "King" Curtis, son and brother.

Taped conversation with Clifford Duvall and Phillip "Buddy" Williams gave me most valuable information on the earliest great jazz musicians and the styles which set the tone for the nation's rich jazz heritage. Autobiographies of three outstanding musicians concluded these chapters. They are Patrick Williams, jazz trumpeter extraordinaire," Clyde Owen Jackson, and "Dr. Frederick Tillis.

Chapter Nine are my grandfather's memoirs, family records of Dr. Ralph Horace Scull, his son, the interview with Joseph Banks; "From Africa to America: African Contributions to America's Healthcare System - A Celebration in Memory of Herman A. Barnett III, M.D." by Melvin Williams, Director of Affirmative Action, UTMB at Galveston, a printed program of "The Hospital Aid Society" by Miss Annie L. Williams, and my own observations.

Then there is my second Interlude. This was a very sweet and heartwarming memory of mine, of a time I was inspired to do something impulsive, that led to a very happy time for the recipients of my gesture, but more for myself, as time went on. I decided to have my older women friends over for a lunch time dinner here in my home. I knew that they seldom got around to seeing each other, were lonely, and needed to have a relaxed time together, since they talked about each other when I had a chance to visit them.

This was in the Summer of 1993, and I titled their casual conversation, recorded on my tape recorder,"Ladies in their 80s". These ladies, all in the eighth decade of their lives, then, were

Mrs. Bernice James, lifetime neighbor and former teacher of mine, Mrs. Alice Hunter, mother of my classmate, and valedictorian of our class, Joselyn Hunter, who was one of the most optimistic and sweet senior citizens I was privileged to know, and who appreciated any attention given to her, and my maternal cousin, whom I knew as Aunt Edna, Mrs. Edna Barrett. All of these ladies lived alone, husbands and family members deceased before their time. Present, also, was my sister, Mrs. Florence Henderson.

Chapter Ten contains the scantiest list of sources, but is probably the most publicized, because of the centennial celebration this year in Galveston. Along with this list goes my fervent prayer that history will not repeat itself in this fashion. The Great 1900 Storm, still standing as the worst natural disaster in the nation's history is documented in Rev. Ralph A. Scull's "...Personal View of Community History..."

Primary source is the actual recorded voice of the matriarch of my family, as I grew up, my great aunt, Mrs. Annie Smizer McCullough.

I have her voice on tape, telling of her personal experiences, as a young wife, going through the horror of the storm, and how they survived. Thank goodness, my cousin Corrinne Scull Williams was visiting us from her home in Chicago, and wanted Aunt Annie to tell us all about the Great Storm, and I decided to tape it. Aunt Annie passed away soon after this taping.

I have my memories of my own mother, then twelve years old, telling me her version of the storm. Finally, I have the taped interview with lifelong family friend, Mr. Joseph A. Banks, who remembers vivid details of what his grandfather, Mr. Shelton Banks, Sr., told him. I am very grateful for the thoughtfulness of Mr. Shelton Banks, who was a church role model for me, as a child. And I am grateful for the wonderful memory of his grandson, known to me as Joe.

Sources for Chapter Eleven on Economic and Social Recovery depend almost completely on the oral interviews I have taken. This is one of the sad facts of African-American history. Little, if any, records were kept of what skills, professions, and occupations were achieved by the recently freed and needy people of color. Again, I am grateful for the tireless and detailed writings of my grandfather, who spelled out exactly who the persons were who built, who were the founding fathers of any enterprise, what businesses there were, who ran them, and so on. He gave names of persons in every field of endeavor, and on these names I was able to complete a foundation of information, and go from there to sources that confirmed the original facts.

Some sources of confirmation of occupation were the City Directory at Rosenberg Library (I found my great grandfather's name, Horace Scull, listed there as a cabinet maker), the census information at the Clayton Library in Houston, County of Galveston records, Galveston Independent School District Board Minutes, Galveston Seaport Museum information, Galveston County Museum pictures and reports, and developing information from UTMB Minority Affairs, and Affirmative Action departments.

Persons who were interviewed, giving this information, were Dr. and Mrs. Leroy Sterling (Luella), Mrs. Elizabeth Harrell, Dr. and Mrs. Rufus H. Stanton (Janice), Mrs. Ina S. Garner, and her daughter, Wilina Gatson, Mr. Thomas J. Green, Mrs. Della R. Sims, Mrs. Evelyn S. Jones, Reverend and Mrs. Handley Hickey, Ms. Gertrude Siverand, Mrs. Melinda Price, Mr. John Clouser, Mr. Courtney Murray, Mr. Joseph A. Banks, Mr.

John Leltz, and Mr.and Mrs. Warren Butler (Ada). The newspaper known as the "City Times•, by William H. Noble was a written source, as well.

Concerning Chapter Twelve the prosperity that evolved in this period of time is largely written on my own personal experience, family records, but refers to the chapter entitled "Women Organizing for the Vote" of Dr. Elizabeth Turner's "Women, Culture, and Community". Her information came from The Galveston Daily News in 1912.

Chapter Thirteen details the Depression of the nation and the way it affected African-Americans in Galveston.

Chapter Fourteen discusses the roles played by African-Americans from Galveston in World War II, the Social Change which resulted, and Greek Societies which formed during this period of time. Most of this information came from my taped interview with Andrew"Brother" Bess, who went overseas to Europe with the U. S. Armed Forces, then. I also was helped in my research by the information in "One Woman's Army - A Black Officer Remembers the WAC" by Charity Adams Earley. This served as a reference for others to remember the experiences of persons from Galveston.

Chapter Fifteen continues with biographical sketches of persons whose lives were important to the community during the time of Recovery. As stated for previous chapters, these sketches came from the individual's families, or from the Rosenberg Library, or Galveston Historical Foundation, augmented by what I knew, personally.

Chapter Sixteen is really more of a discussion of other communities and their African-American people in the County of Galveston. So many of these County residents came from the City of Galveston, originally, or lived in these other communities, but had to come to the island to go to school, and to do most of their business, and shopping.

Chapter Seventeen deals with the Civil Rights Movement and Integration. Sources for this extensive and ongoing situation are a panel of ex-Central High School students, who called themselves "The Problem Solvers". They spoke in February - 2000, for the Nia Cultural Center's efforts to inform, Mrs. Sue Simpson Johnson, Director.

Also used was the lecture of Harold Hodgkins, with slide presentation - "The New South". This lecture was presented by Galveston College Lecture Series in the 1894 Grand Opera House a couple of years ago. I had also heard this presentation by Mr. Hodgkins in Washington, D.C. several years ago, in the early 90s, as a part of the Danforth Foundation's presentation to the various state school boards, in preparation to having these school boards initiate their own programs to develop better achievement in the schools of the nation. His research was outstanding, insightful, and served as a real wake-up call to me as to what motivation was really out there to have our disadvantaged children learn, and achieve.

One source, other than those already discussed, is "No Color is My Kind: The Life of Eldrewey Stearns and The Integration of Houston" by Thomas R. Cole. Stearns is one of the leaders of the "Sit-Ins" that helped to end segregation of public facilities here in Galveston. He is a native Galvestonian.

Closing out these discussions are biographical sketches of the lives of several Galvestonians who have made, or are still making a huge difference in the lives of African-Americans. They include Mr. Anthony Griffin, Esquire, the internationally famous Jack Johnson, heavyweight boxing champion of the world, Leroy "Buster" Landrum, George Prader,

Mrs. Albertine Yeager, Mr. Ray Sheppard, Kelton Sams, and Mr. Thomas D. Armstrong.

Along with my own projections into the future, Chapter Eighteen deals with a vision of the future of Galveston. I do not pretend to have covered every worthwhile purpose or endeavor, and certainly not every worthwhile Galveston African-American. I am already dismayed at not having information on certain individuals. This is just a beginning. Sources will open up to others who can continue the efforts already begun.

INDEX

Symbols

1900 Storm. *See* Storm

A

Abolition 9
Adams, A. D. 209, 211
Alderman 24
Anderson, Loleta 89
Antone, Alice 83, 340, 356
Arceneaux, Valencia Huff 395, 397, 399
Architects 53
Armstrong, Thomas D 244, 380, 383, 384, 385, 386, 387, 414, 416, 428, 463
Ashton Villa 10, 362
Avenue L Baptist Church 118, 125, 131, 135, 136, 194, 386

B

Back alley houses 19
Banks, Cornelia Harris 422
Banks, Jewell Earles 60, 104, 105, 106, 143, 430
Banks, Joseph Arnold 87, 88, 270, 272, 274, 301, 376, 458, 459, 460
Barnes Institute 39, 51, 59
Barnett, Dr. Herman 244, 245, 246, 247, 248, 249, 250, 251, 252, 253, 254, 259, 262, 458
Bathhouse 16, 17, 103, 171, 359
Bess, Andrew "Brother" 84, 85, 86, 342, 344, 345, 348, 349, 461
Blues ix, 208, 212, 224, 228, 299
Bolden, Robert "Rip" 209, 210
Booker T. Washington School 42, 59, 86, 104, 105, 110, 112, 319, 388, 429
Boxing ix, 65, 290, 301, 302, 363, 462
Brady State Training School for Negro Girls 33
Bridge, Addison 81, 83, 185, 194
Brown, Charles 211, 219
Brown, Gertrude 89, 171, 172
Businesses ix, xiii, 8, 17, 19, 103, 289, 290, 293, 296, 298, 304, 352, 357, 361, 386, 393, 421, 460
Butler, Fannie 90, 143
Butler, Robert and Ada (Simmons) 89, 90, 185, 457

C

Cadet Band 167, 168
Carpetbaggers 20
Celebrations 169, 183, 304, 338
Central High School 42, 43, 52, 53, 55, 56, 57, 60, 62, 63, 83, 84, 93, 101, 104, 107, 110, 140, 184, 197, 198, 201, 205, 238, 242, 244, 252, 256, 294, 322, 324, 330, 379, 382, 383, 418, 453, 462
Central High School, accredited 55
Central High School Band 184, 197, 231
Central High School Glee Club 58
Charles McCullough Conversation 66
Churches ix, 10, 15, 21, 34, 117, 118, 119, 121, 130, 131, 135, 140, 142, 155, 163, 171, 173, 174, 181, 190, 191, 271, 304, 306, 453, 454, 455
Cistern 48, 96
Civil War ix, xv, 2, 6, 9, 10, 14, 15, 23, 26, 88, 95, 120, 135, 167, 168, 260, 264, 330, 379, 455
Clouser, John Henry 58, 94, 99, 100, 101, 102, 183, 184, 291, 292, 414, 457, 460
Coleman, Elizabeth Onzella Miller 192, 193, 195, 196, 457
Coleman, John W. 123, 125, 176, 187, 188, 189, 190, 191, 193, 194, 195, 213, 225, 457
Collins, Roy L. III 371
Collins, Roy Lester Jr. 113, 183, 366, 368, 369
Confederate 10, 11
Crayton, Cheryl Collins 87, 183, 239, 323, 373, 431, 438, 439, 473
Cummings, W. N. 40, 44, 49, 59, 81, 94, 101, 123
Cuney, Norris Wright 23, 24, 25, 28, 43, 44, 101, 123, 137, 191, 198, 211, 386, 456
Curtis, King 211, 212, 458

D

Dansby, Hall 55, 330, 331, 332, 333, 334, 356
Davis, Lillian 83
Delta Sigma Theta Sorority, Inc. 32, 102, 105, 110, 355, 387
Dent, Jessie McGuire v, 17, 32, 55, 79, 81, 92, 98, 102, 110, 175, 355
Depression 31, 201, 304, 305, 309, 339, 461
Desegregation 52, 63, 76, 87, 206, 454
Dickerson, Willard "Dick" 212, 214, 223, 416
Disaster. *See* Storm
Doctor. *See* Medicine
Duvall, Clifford 209, 213, 224, 458

E

East District School 38, 41, 45, 88, 112, 271, 276, 301, 376
East End 37, 43, 91, 177, 183, 272, 303, 306, 342, 413
Economic Recovery xvi, 286
Emancipation Proclamation 10, 28, 169, 452
Employment 90, 103, 112, 113, 199, 278, 286, 288, 289, 297, 304, 325, 357, 376, 390, 391, 393, 418
Entrepreneurs. *See* Businesses
Equal Pay 103

F

Fatha, Emile 123, 186, 187
Fedford, Brister Marshall 95, 123, 305, 306, 376, 377
Fedford, Viola Cornelia Scull 13, 33, 88, 89, 92, 95, 184, 265, 266, 267, 268
Foreman, Emma N. 89, 91
Freedman's Bureau 37, 40, 454, 455
Freedom 2, 4, 5, 10, 11, 12, 15, 22, 23, 34, 57, 69, 101, 117, 118, 120, 169, 232, 452
Fry, Annie 315
Funeral Homes 159, 180, 293, 294, 361, 384, 385, 386, 387

G

Galveston, incorporation 27
Gardner, Bernice 130, 230
Garner, Ina Ivory Sibley 292, 293, 460
General Granger 10
George W. Carver School 42, 59, 86, 99, 193, 429
Gibson, John R. 40, 43, 44, 45, 49, 53, 59, 78, 81, 101, 176, 189, 256, 271
Grade-raising xv, 16, 31, 54, 269, 270, 272, 287, 288
Greek Societies 356, 461
Green, Thomas James 174, 360, 361, 457, 460
Griffin, Anthony 423, 424, 425, 462

H

Hamilton, Doc 27, 28, 456
Hare, Maud Cuney 178
Harrell, Elizabeth Bess 172, 173, 342, 363, 460
Heard, Gwendolyn Bridge 184, 240, 457
Henderson, Florence Carlotta Fedford 95, 109, 110, 233, 458, 459
Henderson, Theasel 5, 58, 101, 107, 108, 111, 115
Hickey, Rev. Hanley 77, 79, 80, 175, 176, 177, 178, 188, 191, 357, 358, 457, 460
Hightower, Bernice 86, 233, 388, 457

Holy Rosary Roman Catholic Church 98, 100, 119, 146, 147, 148, 150, 229
Hospital Aid Society 95, 264–269, 356, 458
Houston, Alfreda 160, 162
Huff, Fleming Smizer 83, 86, 92, 185, 186, 188, 194, 196, 197, 198, 199, 231, 355, 395, 458
Hurricane. *See* Storms

I

Integration 50, 51, 52, 57, 58, 59, 62, 63, 64, 65, 71, 75, 110, 113, 154, 268, 291, 356, 386, 388, 399, 400, 404, 415, 417, 418, 421, 422, 428, 429, 430, 431, 462

J

Jackson, Clyde Owen 200, 201, 202, 203, 204, 205, 206, 207, 458
Jackson, Rev. Perry Joy 140, 141
James, Bernice 90, 92, 233
James, Costello 92
Jazz ix, 136, 167, 199, 205, 208, 209, 210, 211, 212, 214, 222, 226, 228, 229, 231, 232, 233, 299, 327, 328, 338, 353, 416, 424, 458
Johnson, Carrie 90, 91
Johnson, Charles L. 79, 358
Johnson, Conrad 216
Johnson, Jack 290, 300, 301, 302, 303, 363, 379, 380, 462
Jones, Evelyn Sanders 80, 172, 303, 304, 460
Jones, Mable Boone 89
July Fourth 11
Juneteenth 117, 135, 169, 183

L

Landrum, Leroy C. "Buster" 289, 379, 380, 462
Lee, Audrey 83
Leltz, John 304, 314, 461
Lewis, Theresa Mae Roberts 180, 457
Lincoln, Abraham 4, 10, 452
Little Susie Railroad xiii, 170, 272
Lone Star Cotton Jammers 27, 28, 456
Lyons, Dr. Geraldine 443

M

Mainland Growth 390, 399
Martin, Lois Davis Tyus 90, 91
Mason, W.J. 101, 189
McBeth, Bernice Watkins 121, 455

McCullough, Annie Smizer 186, 278, 459
McCullough, Nettie 89
McDonald, A.W. 58, 89
McGuire, Robert "Bob" 16, 17, 103, 168, 174, 362
Military. *See* World War I, II
Ministers. *See* Churches
Morgan, Leon A. 50, 58, 59, 252, 430, 453, 454
Municipal Band 198
Murray, Courtney 358, 359, 360, 460

N

National Association of Negro Musicians 193, 194
Netherly, Monica Banks 440
Noble, William H. 25, 26, 28, 456, 461

O

Organizations 22, 27, 92, 95, 99, 109, 110, 111, 204, 243, 264, 265, 328, 355, 356, 386, 420, 450

P

Parades 11, 48, 167, 168, 184, 198
Patriotism 32, 418
Payne, Brenda Rev. 128
Perkins, Elisha "Lish" 186, 187
Pipe organ 92, 123, 125, 132, 188, 233
Playground 18, 112
Politics 9, 14, 15, 20, 21, 22, 23, 26, 28, 35, 36, 39, 365
PollTax 29, 30, 34, 418, 419
Pope, Buster 209, 214, 223, 239
Prader, George 380, 381, 462
Prairie View College Coeds Orchestra 209, 328, 338, 360
Price, Melinda 83, 290, 395, 460
Principals, Schools 59, 61
Property Ownership 13, 15, 19, 20, 291
Public Schools, African-American 40
Pulliam, June Viola Collins 432

R

Reconstruction 9, 14, 23, 26, 37, 101, 386, 455
Reedy Chapel African Methodist Episcopal Church xv, 10, 25, 37, 39, 84, 92, 108, 110, 111, 119, 120, 122, 124, 126, 135, 142, 143, 175, 176, 182, 186, 188, 189, 267, 271, 363, 364, 376, 377, 455

Rosenberg Library Branch 46, 53, 54, 268, 453, 456, 457, 460, 461
Ruby, George T. 26, 27, 28, 456

S

Saint Augustine Episcopal Church 152, 155, 156, 454
Sams, Kelton 383, 463
Sandcrabs baseball team 222
Scull, Clara 40, 41, 49, 81, 90, 189
Scull, Dr. Ralph Horace 242, 243, 458
Scull, Rev. Ralph Albert xi, 2, 3, 39, 45, 46, 49, 59, 122, 123, 242, 243, 267, 271, 456, 459
Scull family xiv, xv, 283
Seawall xv, 17, 168, 174, 177, 279, 287, 311, 312, 428
Segregation xvi, 17, 20, 34, 35, 50, 52, 71, 75, 84, 89, 146, 155, 201, 220, 249, 251, 288, 289, 309, 325, 326, 338, 342, 358, 383, 399, 406, 408, 409, 422, 462
Shelton, Odelia 81, 89, 91
Sheppard, Ray 110, 382, 463
Shiro, Charlie 217
Sims, Della Rivers 170, 172, 294, 295, 296, 457, 460
Siverand, Gertrude Elizabeth 81, 82, 288, 289, 301, 460
St. Paul Methodist Church 142, 143, 144
Stanton, Dr. Rufus and Janice 175, 244, 364, 457, 460
Staton, Earnestine Poston 182, 457
Sterling, Dr. and Mrs. Leroy 77, 173, 244, 362, 457, 460
Storm, 1900 xiii, xv, 41, 45, 81, 100, 101, 123, 132, 140, 143, 155, 156, 255, 269, 270, 271, 272, 274, 278, 286, 287, 288, 297, 360, 459
Suffrage 28
Sweatt, Jack 114, 418
Sweatt, Mary Lee Canada 86, 294, 353

T

Tarver, John "Bubba" 211, 363
Teacher salaries 47, 49
Texas City explosion 356, 390
Texas Federation of Colored Women's Clubs 29, 30, 32, 33, 95
Thomas family 135, 136
Thompson, Lola 83
Thurgood Marshall 20, 411
Tillis, Dr. Frederick C. 130, 223, 230, 231, 232, 233, 458

U

U.S. Supreme Court 33, 63, 103, 418, 419, 424
Unions 27, 28, 220, 292

Urquhart, Alecia Victor 90, 97, 98, 99
USO 32, 334, 337

V

Voluntary integration 75
Voting Rights 29, 30, 31, 34, 419

W

Ward, Irma McCullough 94, 301
Ward, Jeannette 94
Wesley Tabernacle United Methodist Church 139, 140, 141, 164, 172, 385, 386, 388
West, school 38, 39, 40
West District School 41, 42, 44, 45, 47, 50
Williams, Annie 83, 175, 458
Williams, Patrick Michael 227, 228, 229, 458
Williams, Phillip "Buddy" 209, 213, 224, 458
Williams-King, Dr. Elicia E. 426, 427
Wilson, Marendy "Aunt Rendy" 303, 363
Wilson, Stephanie 446, 447
Windom, Frank 61, 93, 98
World War I xv, 31, 32, 193, 242, 243, 258, 292, 293, 297, 298, 345
World War II xv, 33, 108, 151, 322, 325, 342, 345, 350, 351, 356, 357, 376, 381, 411, 461

X

Xenia, Ohio 77, 188, 189

Y

Yeager, Albertine Hall 381, 382, 463

ABOUT THE AUTHOR

Izola Ethel Fedford Collins was born in the family home in Galveston, Texas on October 26, 1929, educated in the Galveston school system. She received her Bachelor of Arts degree from Prairie View University and the Master of Music degree from Northwestern University in Illinois.

She organized and directed three school bands in Texas - Bay City, Hitchcock, and Galveston Catholic. Retiring from Galveston ISD as an award-winning Choir instructor, she then was elected city-wide to the GISD Board of Trustees and served nine years, the last as president.

Ms. Collins has written articles published in "Southwestern Musician"[Texas Music Educators Association], "Fanfare" [School of Music of Northwestern University], the story of St. Mary's Hospital [Galveston], poems in "The National Library of Poetry", and has her own book of poetry, "Divine Light Never Goes Away". She was married to Roy Lester Collins, Jr., now deceased, and has three children - June, Roy III, and Cheryl, who have given them eight grandchildren.